STO

Republicans and Labor

1919-1929

Robert H. Zieger

University of Kentucky Press

Lexington   *1969*

1533534

To my father

JOHN H. ZIEGER

& to the memory

of my mother

GRACE ZIEGER

Preface

THROUGHOUT THE LATTER half of the nineteenth century and into the twentieth the labor problem was one of the most difficult and divisive issues in American life. Generations of Americans viewed with perplexity an economic and social system that was productive and vigorous, yet at the same time troubled by unemployment and frequently racked with violent strikes. For nearly a century the alleviation of labor strife and the achievement of harmonious relations between labor and capital were basic concerns of American society. The repeated failure of the country to accomplish these ends threw into question the ability of the American economic and political system to absorb masses of urban workers and to deal effectively and justly with their demands and aspirations. Faced with such an explosive and persistent problem, Americans often turned to their elected representatives to cope with it, and for many years labor issues captured and held political and governmental attention.

By 1920 the situation had not basically changed. Indeed, between 1919 and 1922 nationwide strikes, massive unemployment, and bitter political and legislative debates over labor affairs indicated that the problem was even more explosive than before the war. Yet by 1928 the Republican party and its national administrators appeared to have the labor situation under control. Unequaled prosperity and an economy that seemed to be functioning smoothly produced a period of rare tranquillity and apparent harmony in labor relations. Labor militancy and strikes declined sharply, and Herbert Hoover and other Republicans proclaimed the end of discord and hostility between labor and capital. Cooperation and accord, Hoover contended, had been achieved not through socialism or governmental regulation but through persuasion and understanding, encouraged—but not dictated—by the federal government. With outstanding specific issues such as railroad labor legislation, injunctions, unemployment, and labor difficulties in the soft coal industry either resolved or obscured, the Republican party's achievements did indeed seem impressive. Whereas division, dogma, and dissidence had dominated labor affairs in the months immediately after World War I, consensus, compromise, and accommodation characterized most discussion regarding labor matters in the Coolidge era.

The Republican achievement was short-lived and indeed soon proved to have been no achievement at all. The economic breakdown of 1929 revealed that the labor problem was still a basic fact of American life. The 1930s produced labor turbulence, major strikes, extensive organizing drives, and basic modern labor legislation. The peace of the late 1920s had been possible only because significant economic problems had been ignored and because organized labor had been too weak, complacent, and timid to render effective criticism. In the 1930s it became clear that Republican policies and programs regarding labor, however effectively they had stilled labor's political voice and temporarily removed dramatic issues, had not eliminated or even come to grips with the labor problem.

This study traces the labor policies and politics of the Republican party from the end of World War I to the accession of Herbert Hoover to the presidency. My original intention was to carry the story through the Hoover administration, but work in manuscripts and other materials for the years between 1929 and 1933 convinced me that the postwar decade merited attention in its own right and that the depression altered the nature and impact of the labor problem to such an extent that I would have had to write a general history of the domestic affairs of the Hoover administration to treat it effectively.

Since there are several competent books on this subject and since I wanted to focus attention upon the relatively neglected labor policies and politics of the 1920s, I decided to stop with the transition from Coolidge to Hoover.

I owe more than I can acknowledge to Professor Horace Samuel Merrill of the University of Maryland, whose guidance was always kindly, whose encouragement was unfailingly timely, and whose criticisms were invariably on the mark. That his indispensable scholarly counsel was accompanied by his and Mrs. Merrill's hospitality and personal interest increases my appreciation. I am indebted to Darrell Le Roy Ashby of the University of Bridgeport who read and criticized much of the manuscript and who shared with me useful information from the Peter Norbeck, Frank B. Kellogg, and Herman Hagedorn Papers, none of which I saw personally. William E. Akin of the State University of New York, Binghamton, Paul W. Glad of the University of Wisconsin, and Elwin W. Sigmund of Wisconsin State University, Stevens Point, also deserve my deep thanks for their reading of and suggestions regarding particular topics. Others who read parts of the manuscript and who saved me from stylistic blunders, errors of fact, and misinterpretations include Gene M. Brack of New Mexico State University, Frank O. Gatell of the University of California, Los Angeles, Ruth Dorgan Rondy, and though he has probably forgotten, Gordon Russell. K. Austin Kerr of Ohio State University provided both scholarly and mundane help at key moments. Lawrence E. Gelfand of the University of Iowa suggested the topic and generously gave both advice and encouragement while I worked on it. Professor Richard L. Watson, Jr., of Duke University very kindly helped my completed manuscript to find its publisher.

I am also grateful to the many librarians and archivists who helped me. My greatest debts are to the staffs of the Library of Congress (especially the Manuscript Division); the National Archives (especially the Legislative and Social and Economic

Branches); and the Library of Wisconsin State University, Stevens Point. Other libraries that provided aid and made materials available are: AFL-CIO Library (Washington); Alderman Library (University of Virginia); Butler Library (Columbia University); Deering Library (Northwestern University); Herbert Hoover Presidential Library (West Branch, Iowa); McKeldin Library (University of Maryland); New York Public Library; Ohio Historical Society (Ohio State Museum, Columbus); Rutgers University Library; State Historical Society of Wisconsin; Van Pelt Library (University of Pennsylvania); and Yale University Library. I did not visit the Minnesota Historical Society (St. Paul), but its staff graciously reproduced and secured permission for me to quote from several letters in the Frank B. Kellogg Papers housed there.

The Department of History, Wisconsin State University, Stevens Point, made available typing and clerical help. A grant from the Wisconsin State University, Stevens Point, local research committee provided funds that expedited the completion of the manuscript. Esther Lepak typed the manuscript with great skill and speed. For permission to draw upon materials originally published in the *Journal of American History* and *Labor History*, I thank the editors of those journals.

Finally, I thank my wife, Gay Pitman Zieger. She helped with research and typing. She proofread and edited. She offered highly useful criticism and even more necessary encouragement. She created a happy home that eased the pressures of scholarship. How she did all these things while raising a family and pursuing her own career I shall never fully understand. And Robert, thank you, too.

Contents

1 The Labor Problem

IN THE CENTURY between the 1830s and the 1930s America underwent industrialization and acquired a labor problem,[1] but produced no consistent and unified national labor policy. Although the industrialization and urbanization of American life alarmed many Americans, and although strikes, unemployment, and industrial violence aroused protest and dismay, it was not until the 1930s that most of the country's basic national labor laws were written. Throughout this period Americans sought continually to resolve the labor problem. Scores of court cases, the efforts and proclamations of governors and presidents, many state enactments, and voluminous congressional hearings and a few federal statutes attested to the nation's concern and its desire to achieve a proper relationship among its workers, capitalists, and governments. The early years of the twentieth century and particularly the involvement of the United States in World War I quickened this search for an answer to the labor question. Yet with all the theoretical discussion and the practical experimentation of these years, the events immediately after the war made it clear that the country's quest was still unfulfilled.

One of the most pressing tasks of the Republican party in the 1920s was to renew this search. The occurrence during the decade of bitter labor controversies and knotty industrial problems put Republican politicians, policymakers, and legislators to a hard test. But by the election of 1928, Republican candidates and orators claimed success, and Americans, sharply aware of the past conflict and untroubled as yet by the impending tribulations of the 1930s, endorsed their claims.

2 Republicans and Labor

The railroad and the factory initiated sweeping changes in American life, transforming rural villages into busy cities, disrupting traditional values and communities, and establishing new and often disturbing modes and customs. Americans reacted ambivalently to the rising order, seeking advantage in an expanding society, but often recoiling in shock and revulsion at the rapid pace of economic and social change. The aspect of the new America that most frequently, dramatically, and explosively gave expression to these changes and intruded into the public consciousness was "the greatest social problem of the age," the labor problem.[2]

It was the factory worker who most vividly manifested the interdependence and turmoil that characterized the new order. He manned the new machinery and crowded into the expanding urban centers. He stood in the soup lines and slept in the doorways when the industrial machine slowed and halted. And it was the industrial worker who marched in the sprawling, angry, and embattled armies of labor, whose skirmishes and campaigns for over half a century frightened and troubled an America unused to militant, collective action by wage earners.[3]

Although the rise of the industrial system, and hence the origin of the labor problem, happened at the time the country was absorbed in the debates over slavery and the Union, the rapidly emerging labor problem even then compelled attention. In 1826 one social critic had warned of an impending class war, while reformers in the 1840s voiced restless concern over the horrors of the factory and the life it spawned. In 1840 Orestes

---

[1] For a definition of the labor problem, see p. 279. See also, in addition to works cited elsewhere in this chapter, James Leiby, *Carroll Wright and Labor Reform: The Origin of Labor Statistics* (Cambridge, Mass., 1960), 4, 40, 57-58, 67-68, 74-75, and 90-91.

[2] Albert Sidney Bolles, *The Conflict Between Labor and Capital* (Philadelphia, 1876), 17.

[3] Useful summaries of the early development of labor controversies and organizations are contained in Selig Perlman, *A History of Trade Unionism in the United States* (New York, 1922), 3-41, and Gerald Grob, *Workers and Utopia: A Study of Ideological Conflict in the American Labor Movement, 1865-1900* (Evanston. Ill., 1961), 3-10.

Brownson, after watching young New England girls maimed and enfeebled in the textile factories, declared that "a crisis as to the relation of wealth and labor is approaching. . . . We or our children," the passionate reformer asserted, "will have to meet this crisis."[4]

But throughout the 1800s the labor problem remained unsettled. Violent, bitter, and bloody labor battles erupted during the last quarter of the century. It was a struggle that "darkens all countries," declared one commentator in the nation's centennial year. In the middle of the troubled eighties, another writer asserted, "The laborer and the capitalist throughout the civilized world stand face to face this day in grim antagonism." The depression of the 1890s created new labor antagonisms and revived old ones. Such problems, wrote a concerned author, were especially difficult and frustrating in the United States. "One would suppose," he continued, "that they should be simpler, less frequent and less bitter in a country where freedom abounds, intelligence is so widely diffused and industrial opportunity is so inviting . . . ," but, he concluded, "labor issues were never sharper, more numerous or more involved than at present and right here in this goodly land."[5]

[4] Louis Adamic, *Dynamite: The Story of Class Violence in America* (New York, 1931), 3, quotes Frances Wright's prediction. Brownson's essay "The Laboring Classes," *The Boston Quarterly Review*, III (July 1840), 366, contains his bitter comments. See also Arthur M. Schlesinger, Jr., *Orestes A. Brownson: A Pilgrim's Progress* (Boston, 1939), 89-100, and Norman J. Ware, *The Industrial Worker, 1840-1860: The Reaction of American Industrial Society to the Advance of the Industrial Revolution* (Boston, 1924), esp. 18-25.

[5] Bolles, *The Conflict Between Labor and Capital*, 17; James A. Waterworth, "The Conflict Historically Considered," in *The Labor Question: Plain Questions and Practical Answers*, ed. William E. Barns (New York, 1886), 17; James P. Boyd, *Vital Questions of the Day, or Historic and Economic Reviews of the Issues of Labor, . . .* (n.p., 1894), 21. For secondary comment on the phases of industrial unrest in the 1870s, 1880s, and 1890s, see respectively, Robert V. Bruce, *1877: Year of Violence* (Indianapolis, Ind., 1959); Henry David, *The History of the Haymarket Affair: A Study in the American Social-Revolutionary and Labor Movements*, 2d ed. (New York, 1958), esp. chaps. 1 and 2; and Almont Lindsey, *The Pullman Strike: The Story of a Unique Experiment and of a Great Labor Upheaval* (Chicago, 1942), esp. chapt. 1.

Nor did the new century bring relief or resolution. While the level of violence and discord receded somewhat from the high-water marks of the 1880s and 1890s, unrest continued, and the activities and occasional success of militant, revolutionary labor groups and parties added to the fears of an apprehensive nation. "Of course," wrote Theodore Roosevelt in 1903, "the two great fundamental internal problems with which we have to deal . . . are the negro problem in the South, and the relations of capital and labor. . . . The last is the greatest . . . and is the one which, in some of its phases, most immediately demands a solution." Seven years later, the conviction of two young unionists for blowing up the Los Angeles *Times* building in protest over the newspaper's antiunion views triggered renewed debate over the labor problem. Journalist Lincoln Steffens challenged the country to face conditions that led the McNamara brothers to use dynamite, while economist E. R. A. Seligman felt that this incident illustrated "a type of mind that has begun in this country to despair of equality and economic opportunity, and is being driven into violence because of the conviction that no other kind of action is possible." Strikes, socialism, and syndicalism troubled America and revealed the "spirit of unrest and discontent now sweeping over the world," declared a journalist, "which is the most significant characteristic of the twentieth century."[6]

Despite three-quarters of a century of intense concern, America in the second decade of the twentieth century seemed as far from resolving the labor problem as it had been in the

[6] Roosevelt to Carl Schurz, Dec. 24, 1902, in *The Letters of Theodore Roosevelt*, ed. Elting E. Morison and John M. Blum, 8 vols. (Cambridge, Mass., 1951-1954), III: *The Square Deal, 1901-1903*, 679. Steffens and Seligman are quoted in Graham Adams, Jr., *Age of Industrial Violence, 1910-1915: The Activities and Findings of the United States Commission on Industrial Relations* (New York, 1966), 23 and 28, respectively. The journalist quoted is James Boyle, *The Minimum Wage and Syndicalism: An Independent Survey of the Two Labor Movements Affecting American Labor* (Cincinnati, 1913), 4.

middle of the nineteenth century. But if the nation had not eliminated its industrial difficulties, it was not for want of proposals and efforts to implement them. From laissez faire to Marxism, from the cooperative commonwealth to class conflict, and from suppression to socialism, the country had proposed, debated, experimented with, and discarded a myriad of solutions, panaceas, programs, and formulas. Some of these solutions were fanciful, some simple, and some both. Thus, in the 1880s "A Friend of Mankind," after a study of the "Science of Equivalents," asserted that "reformation can be brought about by simply joining a trades-union . . . with an expense that need not exceed fifty cents." Equally confident and utopian was the declaration of a railroad official who said, "The rights of the laboring man will be protected and cared for, not by labor agitation, but by the Christian men to whom God in His infinite wisdom has given control of the property interests of the country."[7]

More realistically, the American people had enlisted the aid of their governments. In 1886 economist Richard T. Ely argued that "reformation of our State must precede any solution of the labor problem," but unreformed governments had not deterred legislators, executives, and judges from positing at least partial solutions. From the early nineteenth century the courts had attempted to describe and define the rights of labor and property and to square new conditions with the common law. In the post-Civil War years the eastern industrial states had led in efforts to find legislative answers to questions of wages, hours, conditions, and general rights of labor organization.[8]

[7] Amicus Humani Generis [pseud.], *The Labor Question, or an Exact Science of Equivalents* . . . (Chicago, 1881), 186. George Baer's famous remark is contained in a letter to William F. Clark, July 17, 1902, which is reproduced in Robert L. Reynolds, "The Coal Kings Come to Judgment," *American Heritage*, XI (April, 1960), 61.

[8] Richard T. Ely, introduction to Barns, *The Labor Problem*, 9. There is a brief and useful survey of major state legislative efforts in Joshua Bernhardt, *The Railroad Labor Board: Its History, Activities and*

6   Republicans and Labor

In the late nineteenth century the federal government was drawn into labor controversy. The immense importance and interstate nature of the railroads impelled federal concern, at first through presidential and judicial processes usually in behalf of embattled managers, and later through legislation. These early executive actions, injunctions, and railroad labor enactments helped to forge the beginnings of federal strike policy, but gropings toward a more comprehensive and fundamental labor policy were limited to periodic legislative proposals, isolated instances of presidential leadership, and a series of industrial and labor inquiries that were conducted during the late nineteenth and early twentieth centuries.[9]

Still, despite decades of activity and scores of proposals, the plea that Albert Bolles made in 1876 remained unfulfilled in the twentieth century. Exploring the conflict between labor and capital, the economist-businessman-historian declared that the crucial test of modern society was its ability "to make a peace between the working-man and his employer grounded in justice and stamped with perpetuity." Bolles predicted for "whoever succeeds in doing this . . . a title of perpetual remembrance . . . [beyond that of] any victor of battles."[10]

Even so, with the new century came the progressive movement and a sense of experimentation and urgency. Progressives focused attention upon the social ills connected with the rush

---

Organization (Baltimore, 1923), 1-7. See also U.S., Bureau of Labor, *Special Report: Labor Laws of the Various States, Territories, and the District of Columbia* (Washington, D.C., 1892).

[9] An excellent recent statement on the origins of federal policy concerning labor disputes is Gerald G. Eggert, *Railroad Labor Disputes: The Beginnings of Federal Strike Policy* (Ann Arbor, Mich., 1967), 1-23. The major federal inquiries regarding labor are *Report of the Committee of the Senate upon the Relations Between Labor and Capital, and Testimony Taken by the Committee,* 4 vols. (Washington, D.C., 1885); *United States Strike Commission Report* (Washington, D.C., 1895); *Report of the Industrial Commission,* 19 vols. (Washington, D.C., 1900-1902); and *Industrial Relations: Final Report and Testimony Submitted to Congress by the Commission on Industrial Relations Created by the Act of August 23, 1912,* 11 vols. (Washington, D.C., 1916). Many other investigations concerning particular strikes and circumstances were also held.

[10] Bolles, *The Conflict Between Labor and Capital,* 17.

toward urbanization and industrialization, and many progressives sought answers to the labor problem. While the main thrust of progressivism was in the direction of general reform and away from class-oriented programs, events led reformers to recognize that wage earners were uniquely affected by the social and economic forces that they attempted to control and mitigate. To some progressives, labor organizations seemed potentially as dangerous to American society as did corporate monopolies. To others, the worker most fully embodied the aspirations of the new industrial man, unencumbered by the anachronistic values of the rural, agricultural past. Although the many-faceted progressive movement arrived at no general solution to the labor problem on the national level, progressives in the states and local areas introduced and supported a wide variety of programs related to labor's problems, especially in the eastern cities.[11]

Regardless of the efforts of reformers, the entrance in 1917 of the United States into the World War made resolution of some labor problems imperative. The national interest demanded the harnessing of labor to the war effort and imposed a partial truce in the conflict between workers and employers. The needs of wartime production stimulated important innovations in federal labor policy. The government for the first time encouraged producers to deal with unions and even became involved in forming a labor organization in the lumber industry. Federal operation of the railroads resulted in gains for railroad workers, while the War Labor Board and the President's Mediation Committee sought new approaches to the amelioration of industrial disputes. While not all these

[11] For discussions of the variety of progressive thought regarding labor, see George E. Mowry, *The Era of Theodore Roosevelt and the Birth of Modern America, 1900-1912* (New York, 1958), 101-103; David W. Noble, *The Paradox of Progressive Thought* (Minneapolis, 1958), 152-56, 170-73; Irwin Yellowitz, *Labor and the Progressive Movement in New York State, 1897-1916* (Ithaca, N.Y., 1965), chaps. 5-6; and Allen F. Davis, "The Social Workers and the Progressive Party, 1912-1916," *American Historical Review,* LXIX (April 1964), 671-88.

wartime experiments succeeded, many laborites, reformers, and concerned citizens felt hopeful that breakthroughs had been achieved and that the necessities of the war had ushered in a new era of accord and stability. Perhaps, after years of difficulty and disharmony, the labor problem was on the road to settlement.[12]

Events quickly destroyed these hopes. Postwar readjustments soon revealed that the conflict had merely been suspended for the duration, not permanently quelled. Labor unions sought to extend their gains, while businessmen instituted an aggressive antiunion campaign. "The greatest of all wars between organized labor and capital seems to have begun," declared a journalist. "Unless this is to be a war of extermination . . . Capital and Labor *must be brought together*," proclaimed William Jennings Bryan in 1919. In that year of strikes, an enterprising reporter posed as an ordinary workman in an effort to discover what was on the worker's mind. He concluded, " 'Worse than at any time in history'—that seems to be the only way to describe the present [industrial] relations."[13]

The conflict and turmoil which followed the war indicated that Americans once again would confront essentially the same labor problems that the country experienced in the past. Thus it remained for the triumphant Republicans, whether they looked backward to "normalcy" or forward to the New Era, not only to find specific answers to specific labor questions

[12] For a summary of the labor measures of the war months, see John S. Smith, "Organized Labor and Government in the Wilson Era, 1913-1921: Some Conclusions," *Labor History*, III (Fall 1962), 265-86. Robert L. Tyler, "The United States Government as Union Organizer: The Loyal Legion of Loggers and Lumbermen," *Mississippi Valley Historical Review*, XLVII (Dec. 1960), 434-51, discusses a unique wartime experiment, while valuable information can be found in Louis B. Wehle, *Hidden Threads of History: Wilson Through Roosevelt* (New York, 1953), 10-63.

[13] "A Battle of Titans," *Current Opinion*, LXX (March 1921), 295; Bryan's remarks are quoted in Lawrence W. Levine, *Defender of the Faith, William Jennings Bryan: The Last Decade, 1915-1925* (New York, 1965), 251; Whiting Williams, *What's on the Worker's Mind, By One Who Put on Overalls To Find Out* (New York, 1920), v.

but also to forge a general attitude, program, and political stance with regard to labor. The task that had challenged Americans for a hundred years remained with them, made harder by the increasing tempo of American life and made more imperative by the worldwide convulsions that followed the war.

While the war did not resolve the labor problem, the spirit of experimentalism did linger. Businessmen, laborites, reformers, engineers, and politicians supported a number of innovations in the field of labor relations. Kansas created a Court of Industrial Relations, an attempt to make operative the oft-stated analogy between labor disputes and legal controversies. In 1920 Congress established the Railroad Labor Board, whose nine members sat as a tribunal of adjustment in labor disputes, representing a sharp departure from previous federal efforts in this area of federal presence. Some unionists, dissatisfied with the "pure and simple" approach of the craft unions, urged various plans of nationalization of resources, to be accompanied by reforms in labor matters. In 1920 the American Federation of Labor (AFL) convention endorsed the Plumb plan, which provided for continued federal operation of the railroads through a joint carrier-worker-government body, and the railroad unions worked vigorously for it. During this period also the "industrial democracy" and "progressive union" movements attracted much attention, the former with its emphasis upon the mutuality of interest between labor and capital, and the latter with its advocacy of worker participation in industrial decisionmaking through vigorous local unions. The postwar years also witnessed the rise of professional industrial relations specialists and the continuing interest of engineering and efficiency experts in labor relations. Indeed, in 1920 one professional consultant on industrial relations declared that despite the strikes and unrest, "A most encouraging fact in the present situation . . . is the large and growing number of industrial executives, and students of labor questions who have definitely turned their backs on panaceas and are approaching all industrial questions with what might be called the engineering sense." Careful gathering and scrutiny of data, "close acquaintance with the success and failures that have attended various experiments," and a dispassionate and scientific approach, he added, would enable labor relations consultants and engineers to go beyond old controversies and settle labor problems on an impartial and equitable basis while eliminating the waste and inefficiency that sprang from industrial discord.[14]

Of course, not all these approaches survived. The Kansas Court and the Railroad Labor Board quickly fell victim to employer-labor antagonism and unfavorable Supreme Court decisions. Industrial democracy often became a euphemism for the open shop, union-smashing of the "American Plan," while the nationalization and progressive union movements soon declined. Industrial consultants, engineers, and efficiency experts frequently proved to be agents of the speedup and the empty promise. Even so, the Republican administrations of the 1920s found themselves not only heirs to a basic unresolved problem but also beneficiaries of much useful experimentation

[14] There is a good description of the progressive union movement in John Howard Keiser, "John Fitzpatrick and Progressive Unionism, 1915-1925" (unpublished Ph.D. dissertation, Northwestern University, 1965), iii-v and 187-201. The case for "industrial democracy" is made by a leading proponent, Edward A. Filene, in a speech "Why Men Strike," in *America Speaks*, ed. Basil Gordon Byron and Frederic René Coudert (New York, 1928), 151-64, while Milton Derber discusses the movement in "The Idea of Industrial Democracy in America, 1915-1933," *Labor History*, VIII (Winter 1967), 3-29. For the efficiency and engineering activities in the labor field and the unions' reaction, see Robert Franklin Hoxie, *Scientific Management and Labor* (New York, 1915; 1966 reprint), 7-19; Milton J. Nadworny, *Scientific Management and the Unions, 1900-1932: A Historical Analysis* (Cambridge, Mass., 1955), 148; and Samuel Haber, *Efficiency and Uplift: Scientific Management in the Progressive Era, 1890-1920* (Chicago, 1964), chapts. 7-8. The words quoted are those of Meyer Bloomfield in *Selected Articles on Problems of Labor*, comp. and ed. Daniel Bloomfield (New York, 1920), 2. The Bloomfields were consultants in employment management and industrial relations in Boston.

and innovation born of the war and the progressive movement. The Grand Old Party needed this background of experience and information, for in the 1920s the overall labor problem and specific labor issues were acute. Labor issues filled the postwar decade and compelled the federal government and political parties to pay careful attention to the status of the worker and the words and actions of union leaders. Despite the downward trend of union membership and the apparent calm of the late 1920s, these years were rich in upheaval, legislation, controversy, and political involvement. In 1922, for example, the country experienced its greatest industrial crisis since the 1890s, when nearly a million coal and rail unionists struck. Strikes, economic conditions, and federal policies forced basic readjustments in the labor patterns in the soft coal industry. Controversies flared over the labor injunction, the role of the courts in labor matters, unemployment, immigration, the open shop, and the twelve-hour day. This decade also produced two major pieces of railway labor legislation as well as the only instance of union-led major independent political action in American history.

Republicans responded to these labor situations in a variety of ways. In the 1920s, the GOP included many groups and individuals interested in labor affairs: businessmen, agriculturists, progressives, members of patriotic societies, professional people and academicians, and some unionists. All these interests sought to influence the party's and government's attitudes and policies. While the clash of sections, groups, individuals, and interests in this loose-knit and locally influenced party caused wide divergence of labor matters, certain general views eventually emerged. The Republicans finally concentrated their discussion on four broad approaches to labor problems: the progressive approach, the open shop approach, the efficiency-engineering approach, and the political approach. None of these was an absolute position; all bore relationships to the others. But when labor issues affected party affairs—as they often did—and when they provoked controversy and division, it was usually along these lines.

In the 1920s, as before World War I, progressives viewed the labor problem ambivalently. Some prewar progressives drifted away from reform and made their peace with the status quo, with a few emerging from the war in the forefront of those eager to hamstring organized labor. Many progressives, however, retained their desire for reform and sought to build a liberal coalition that could cure the nation of its economic and social ills. It was in these efforts that they had to consider the industrial worker and his organizations, for many laborites shared the progressives' unhappiness with the postwar order and were willing to function politically. In the years 1922-1925 independent political action reached a peak, and reform-minded Republicans (as well as Democrats and Independents) tried mightily to come to terms with organized labor's potentially enormous political power.

Most progressive activity occurred outside the main councils of the GOP, for progressives played little part in the Harding and Coolidge administrations. Within the party structure and the government, the debate over labor policy developed between those who saw the worker and his organizations as threats and those who sought to calm antagonism and to establish new concepts of industrial relations, as well as to employ the federal government in new capacities of labor relations.

Antilabor extremism enjoyed much support within the GOP, echoing as it did the open shop campaign of some of the nation's most powerful corporations. Opposition to organized labor remained strong in the party throughout the 1920s, but it reached its peak in the immediate postwar period and during the Harding administration. Angered by labor's aggressive pursuit of its interests during the Wilson administration and shocked by postwar radicalism and militancy, businessmen, "patriots," and politicians resolved to end labor arrogance.

Most expressions of this attitude took the form of employer opposition to labor unions, but the open shop crusade also found considerable support from politicians, many of whom were Republicans and some of whom were in the inner circle during Harding's brief term. Thus, the foe of unions found vocal allies in GOP Senators Miles Poindexter of Washington, Joseph Frelinghuysen of New Jersey, and Frank B. Kellogg of Minnesota, former Senators Albert J. Beveridge and Jonathan Bourne, Jr., and banker-politician Charles G. Dawes. Within the Harding administration the most outspoken and powerful antilaborite was Attorney General Harry M. Daugherty, who used his position and his close relationship to President Harding to attack labor organizations.

The uncompromisingly antilabor point of view, however popular with some businessmen and party figures, was usually diluted by political and administrative realities. Moreover, some powerful Republicans deplored assaults upon labor unions and sought to forge new methods of handling the labor problem. Chief among these was Herbert C. Hoover, the secretary of commerce. With his strong (though at times submerged) sense of sympathy for the unfortunate, his close ties to the efficiency-minded and socially conscious engineering movement, his shrewd commonsense, and his abhorrence of controversy and confrontation, Hoover worked constantly to mute labor-management antagonism and to reduce the waste and disruption that both caused and grew from labor troubles. Throughout the decade Hoover sought to implement his views on labor, attracting the interest and support of many businessmen, reformers, politicians, and unionists who wished to join the effort to dissipate traditional antagonisms, use the federal government in a more judicious manner than previously, and create a whole new pattern of labor relations based on concepts of efficiency and cooperation.

Progressives, proponents of the open shop, and efficiency advocates sought throughout the 1920s to influence the labor policies of the Republican party. At times supporters of the various views quarreled openly. Progressives denounced the open shop movement and criticized particularly the resort to judicial fiat that often accompanied antilabor policies. Open shop enthusiasts deemed progressives to be demagogic agents of class rule and attacked Hoover for his unwillingness to join in labor-baiting. The secretary of commerce in turn had little patience with either progressive rhetoric or intransigent anti-unionism. Indeed, Daugherty and Hoover clashed directly in the fall of 1922 when the attorney general promoted and the secretary of commerce denounced a sweeping injunction aimed at striking railroad workers.

Running through these approaches to the labor problem lay the factor of politics. No politician in the 1920s could entirely ignore either the political weight of workers or the public antagonism that greeted some of their activities. Because the national Republican party embraced men of a variety of viewpoints, time and again it mangled and hammered labor issues that appeared to many Americans to be clear-cut and unambiguous into bland, harmless generalities. Over and over again, for example, open shop enthusiasts sought to commit the party to an aggressively antiunion program, only to be put off with rhetoric and blandishments. In all the national elections of the 1920s Republicans made serious efforts to attract worker and union support and to mute expressions of hostility toward organized labor. Continually, all but a handful of professional Republican politicians attempted to smooth the ragged edges of labor controversies and to steer clear of confrontations with aroused unionists. The master of the political approach to labor was Calvin Coolidge, but party officials, senators, congressmen, and members of the executive branch also followed it, as did the often-beleaguered Warren G. Harding.

At times some Republican policies appeared to be antilabor,

at times prolabor. Usually they were aimed at avoiding or softening labor issues. In whatever manner, though, from the antiunion rhetoric of 1919 through the various elections and controversies of the decade until Hoover's triumph in 1928, politics played a vital role in GOP labor attitudes and policies. During the Harding administration labor controversies were frequent and raw, but the ascension of Calvin Coolidge to the presidency and the growing awareness of GOP leaders to the dangers of antagonizing organized labor dulled the labor issue somewhat. Even during the 1921-1923 period, when Daugherty was at the height of his influence, Hoover, as secretary of commerce, proved to be an effective architect of labor policy. With Daugherty gone and Republicans apprehensive over organized labor's political activities, Hoover emerged in the 1923-1928 period as by far the most important source of labor programs and policies. Not only did he help to arrange the carrier-union conferences that led to the Railway Labor Act of 1926, but he also made efforts to cure the labor sickness of the soft coal industry and to establish a general program of accord and moderation. His efforts were not always successful, but by 1928 most controversies were dormant and Hoover enjoyed the reputation of being the country's "foremost industrial statesman,"[15] as he received the Republican nomination and won election to the presidency.

The following decade would reveal vividly that the labor problem had not been solved in the 1920s. Hardly had Hoover taken office when the depression struck, exposing the injustices and imbalances in the American economy, creating massive unemployment, and paving the way for the basic labor legislation of the 1930s and for the formation of the industrial unions. Whatever the eventual inadequacies of the policies of the 1920s, however, the labor problem by the latter part

15 The words are those of John L. Lewis (New York *Times*, Sept. 18, 1928).

of the decade seemed to have disappeared in most industries. Given the turbulence of 1919 and 1920 and the decades of unrest and violence prior to that, many Americans had reason to believe that the New Era of Republican prosperity had indeed given the country the labor peace for which it had been searching.

2 Labor and the Election of 1920

LABOR PROBLEMS LOOMED large in 1919 and 1920 as the Republican party struggled to recapture control of the federal government. The American Federation of Labor had participated in the Wilsonian coalition, and labor's advances under the Democrats had antagonized many Americans. Moreover, the industrial unrest and violence of the postwar years discredited even nonsocialist and nonrevolutionary labor organizations in the public eye. Hence, Republicans attacked the Democratic party through its connection with the AFL and other unions, especially at the beginning of ·the campaign. As the contest progressed, however, the GOP softened these attacks òn organized labor, and by election day its candidates were courting workers' support. This shift was due to the party's unfamiliarity with labor as a major political force and to the Democrats' partial repudiation of their party's former alliance with labor unions. During the campaign and the election the Republican party retreated from its antilabor position, successfully neutralizing a potentially massive anti-Republican labor vote that seemed likely early in the campaign.

In 1919 and 1920, many Republicans considered the place of organized labor in American life to be the major domestic question of the presidential campaign. Because unprecedented labor legislation had been passed during the Wilson administration there was widespread feeling that labor unions had duped and dominated the Democratic party. Politicians, journalists, businessmen, and many other citizens thought that the AFL, the railroad brotherhoods, and other unions menaced America. Declared New Jersey Republican Senator Joseph Frelinghuysen, the Wilson "administration has . . . completely played into the hands of the nation's agitators, with socialistic tendencies." To him, even the League of Nations, "which threatens the overthrow of our national independence, [is] of lesser moment . . . than the labor question." The *Wall Street Journal* asserted that labor autocracy "may provide an issue for the American people . . . greater than all the others put together."[1]

Controversies over labor legislation and the government's relationship to labor unions had dotted the Wilson years. Labor's representatives had achieved status with the federal government for the first time and had finally realized some of their legislative goals. The Wilson administration had supported in 1914 the labor provisions of the Clayton Act, in 1915 the La Follette Seamen's Act, and in 1916 a child labor law, and the Adamson Act, which provided for an eight-hour day for operating railroad workers. These gains had aroused intense opposition. Critics charged that President Wilson had sponsored class legislation and had bowed to organized labor's sinister ambitions. In 1916, business and political attacks upon the Democratic-labor connection had reached a peak, for shortly before the election a Democratic Congress passed the Adamson Act in an obvious bid for the support of the railway unions, thereby antagonizing conservative opinion.

The war tended to dampen antilabor fervor, for all the major trade unions were loyal and cooperative during the conflict. Antagonism toward labor remained, however, and it exploded once again after the armistice when labor's and Wilson's opponents resumed attacks on their alliance.

Even so, the renewed assault on the labor-Democratic alliance might have remained merely a hollow discussion of

[1] Joseph Frelinghuysen to DeWitt C. Reynolds, July 21, 1919, Joseph Frelinghuysen Papers (Rutgers University Library), File Cabinets; hereafter cited as Frelinghuysen Papers; *Wall Street Journal*, June 14, 1920. Throughout 1919 and 1920, newspapers and magazines were filled with concern about the labor situation. See, for example, the *Literary Digest*, Jan.–March 1919.

past policies had not economic dislocation staggered the nation after the war. The country was grossly unprepared for the transition from war to peace, with an ailing president and a budget-obsessed Congress making the change even more difficult. Returning veterans, hastily mustered out of the armed forces, faced bleak prospects with little governmental assistance. Joblessness multiplied but Congress slashed the appropriations of the United States Employment Service, the federal government's only tool with which to fight unemployment.[2]

Labor unrest also characterized the postwar period. The Industrial Workers of the World (IWW) showed signs of life along the West Coast. The long-dormant Amalgamated Association of Iron, Steel, and Tin Workers of America revived and struck the steel industry. Conservative unions advanced radical-sounding programs. The railroad brotherhoods joined together in support of the Plumb plan, which called for continued federal operation of the railroads. And when Glen Plumb, the movement's chief spokesman, presented the case for nationalization at the 1919 convention of the United Mine Workers of America (UMW) he was warmly applauded for, like the railroad men, the miners did not want to return to unregulated private operation. The AFL sought to maintain high wartime levels of membership and to raise wage ceilings. Organized as never before, hopeful of continued governmental support, and buoyed up by the successes of the 1914-1918 period, American labor embarked upon a militant course in the postwar years.[3]

[2] James R. Mock and Evangeline Thurber, *Report on Demobilization* (Norman, Okla., 1944), 208-209; John D. Hicks, *Rehearsal for Disaster: The Boom and Collapse of 1919-1920* (Gainesville, Fla., 1961). Actually, the postwar depression did not start until late 1919. See George Soule, *Prosperity Decade: From War to Depression, 1917-1929*, Economic History of the United States, Vol. IX (New York, 1947), 83.

[3] Philip A. Taft, *Organized Labor in American History* (New York, 1964), 320-21; Robert K. Murray, *Red Scare: A Study in National Hysteria, 1919-1920* (Minneapolis, 1955), 111-19; David Brody, *Labor in*

Labor was not alone in its aggressiveness. Business groups such as the National Association of Manufacturers (NAM), the United States Chamber of Commerce, and the American Iron and Steel Association had reacted apprehensively to the rise of labor. William Barr, president of the National Founders' Association, spoke for many businessmen when he asserted that radicalism had been gaining ground, in part because of "the tenderness with which our governmental officials have handled anarchists and agitators." The war had hindered blatant antiunion activity, but when soldiers began to return to America and unemployed laborers began to gather on the sidewalks, businessmen perceived an opportunity to check the presumptuous laborites. Employers' organizations and business groups commenced a vigorous campaign for the open shop. Armed with the then-legal yellow-dog contract, by which an employer could require a prospective employee to agree not to join or support a union, America's industrialists launched a well-financed general attack on the very concept of collective bargaining.[4]

Crisis: The Steel Strike of 1919 (Philadelphia, 1965); Robert L. Friedheim, *The Seattle General Strike* (Seattle, 1964). The mood of the railroad workers is described in Edward Keating, *The Gentleman from Colorado: A Memoir* (Denver, 1964), 477-79, and that of the United Mine Workers' convention in John Brophy, *A Miner's Life*, ed. John O. P. Hall (Madison, Wis., 1964), 152. In 1920, over the objections of Samuel Gompers, the rail unions and the UMW secured overwhelming endorsement of the Plumb plan at the AFL convention (New York *Times*, June 18, 1920).

[4] To many people outside the business world, the term *open shop* was an innocuous one, meaning merely that workers should not have to join a union to gain employment, but to businessmen it signified an all-out attack on labor unions. Political figures tended to be vague and unrealistic, in their utterances at least, regarding the open shop. Except for those who were rabidly antilabor, most men in public life equated it with a benign defense of individual freedom and industrial cooperation between worker and employer. See Herbert Hoover, *The Memoirs of Herbert Hoover*. II: *The Cabinet and the Presidency, 1921-1933* (New York, 1952), 101, and letter from George Sutherland to Warren G. Harding, June 26, 1920, George Sutherland Papers (Manuscript Division, Library of Congress), Box 3; hereafter cited as Sutherland Papers. The term *open shop* herein carries the business connotation, not the political connotation. For a discussion of the open shop issue, see Allen M. Wakstein, "The Origins of the Open

Business and labor became embroiled in a series of damaging strikes in vital industries. Continuing industrial crisis focused public attention on labor. Over four million workers participated in strikes during 1919. Seattle underwent a general strike in February, and the tempo of unrest increased in the fall. In September, 300,000 steelworkers struck. In November, with the steel strike still in progress, the soft coal miners defied both the government and their own leaders, and walked out of the mines. It took the threat of a federal injunction to prevent the railroad workers from striking. Indeed, it seemed that the very fabric of society was ripping apart, especially when the police in Boston left their jobs in protest against low wages and arbitrary restrictions.[5]

Public fear of radicalism complicated these labor problems. In 1917, the Bolsheviks had seized power in Russia, the most orthodox of nations. Apprehensive Americans feared that the United States might be vulnerable. Stories of communism, anarchism, and socialism filled the newspapers. Self-seeking politicians and sensationalistic journalists inflated the few cases of genuine radical activity. It was easy for Americans to see in the dramatic strikes justification for their fears. After all, some labor agitators were radicals and some anarchist bombs did explode. The country seemed to ignore the staunch conservatism and the complete wartime loyalty of the orthodox unions and focused exclusively upon the unrest, radicalism, and conflict of the postwar months.

The atmosphere was troubled and explosive. "Both sides," wrote Ray Stannard Baker, "are trying quack remedies: the employers a sure-cure labeled: 'Deportation-Suppression': and the workers a bottle with a red label: 'Bolshevism.' " Union militancy, business intransigence, unemployment, fear of

Shop Movement, 1919-1920," *Journal of American History*, LI (Dec. 1964), 460-75. For Barr's remarks, see National Founders' Association, *Weekly Letter Number 89*, Oct. 9, 1919.
    [5] Murray, *Red Scare*, 119-65; Brody, *Labor in Crisis*; Friedheim, *The Seattle General Strike*.

radicalism, and a nation unwilling or unable to see the effects of rapid demobilization on the economy, and hence on labor, joined in a nexus of fear, hysteria, and invasions of civil liberties.[6]

Organized labor, conservative and radical, quickly became a target of public antagonism. Republicans immediately sensed this and were eager to use the labor issue as a means of assaulting the Democrats. Some Republicans regarded labor purely in a political context; others felt that the party should undertake the patriotic duty of preserving American institutions from the machinations of the Democratic-labor coalition. Whatever their motivation, Republicans struck out at labor and the Democrats with invective and denunciation. The most consistently outspoken GOP critic of labor was Senator Miles Poindexter of Washington, who campaigned actively, if ineffectively, for the 1920 presidential nomination. Repeatedly throughout 1919 and into 1920 Poindexter blasted organized labor, lumping the AFL indiscriminately with the IWW. His attacks were personal and vicious as, for example, when he accused James Duncan, the controversial AFL leader from Seattle, and others within the organization of "attempting to organize an armed revolution." The senator claimed that Secretary of Labor William B. Wilson, whom many businessmen accused of favoritism toward labor, "is no better than a professional criminal . . . [and] is known . . . as a good anarchist." Poindexter launched his campaign for the presidency in 1919 with this shrill cry and consistently denounced

6 Ray Stannard Baker, *The New Industrial Unrest: Reasons and Remedies* (Garden City, N.Y., 1920), 57. The best accounts of the antiradical hysteria are Murray, *Red Scare*, and William Preston, *Aliens and Dissenters: Federal Suppression of Radicals, 1903-1933* (Cambridge, Mass., 1963), chapts. 4-8. For the economic crisis and unpreparedness following the war, see Soule, *Prosperity Decade*, 81-106, and Hicks, *Rehearsal for Disaster*. For the labor aspects, see Brody, *Labor in Crisis*; Friedheim, *The Seattle General Strike*; Taft, *Organized Labor in American History*, 341-75; and John R. Commons and others, *History of Labor in the United States. IV: Labor Movements*, by Selig Perlman and Philip A. Taft (New York, 1935), 435-514.

organized labor in letters, speeches, and magazine articles throughout 1919 and into 1920.[7]

Poindexter commanded little support within the GOP, but his labor utterances were indicative of the general mood of the party. More influential Republicans saw the problem in a similar light, and invariably sought to connect labor unrest to the policies of Wilson. Former Senator Albert J. Beveridge, for example, warned late in 1919 that "the crowning domestic issue . . . is whether labor unions shall run the American government"; William Howard Taft, traveling in the Middle West, found public sentiment almost unanimous in its opposition to both Wilson and the machinations of unionists and radicals.[8]

The major effort of Republicans who sought to identify the Wilson administration with the industrial crisis was to trace labor arrogance to the Adamson Act of 1916. The Democratic Congress had passed this measure on the eve of the presidential election, and Republicans accused their opponents of having surrendered to assure labor's political support. Even more important than the Democrats' passage of one unjust bill were the general repercussions of the "surrender." Thus, said Beveridge, the labor law's "method of enactment . . . was as violently lawless as that of robbery at the mouth of a gun." Other prominent Republicans echoed this charge. Nicholas Murray Butler called the law "un-American and unpatriotic,"

[7] Miles Poindexter to H. D. Moore, Jan. 17, 1919, Miles Poindexter Papers (University of Virginia Library), Series VI, File 15; hereafter cited as Poindexter Papers. Poindexter to Joseph M. Brown, Feb. 24, 1920, Poindexter Papers, Series IV, Box 56; "Announcement by U.S. Senator Miles Poindexter of his Candidacy for the Republican Nomination . . . ," ca. Oct. 1919, in Albert J. Beveridge Papers (Manuscript Division, Library of Congress), Box 223; hereafter cited as Beveridge Papers; Miles Poindexter, "Labor and the Open Shop," *The Outlook*, CXXV (May 5, 1920), 17-18. See also Howard Allen, "Miles Poindexter: A Political Biography" (unpublished Ph.D. dissertation, University of Washington, 1959), 489-97.

[8] Beveridge speech in *The North American* (Philadelphia), Dec. 23, 1919; William Howard Taft to Clarence Kelsey, May 27, 1920, William Howard Taft Papers (Manuscript Division, Library of Congress), Letterbooks, Series 8, Vol. 96; hereafter cited as Taft Letterbooks.

while Ogden L. Mills, a New York City congressional candidate and a member of the Republican National Committee, linked the postwar unrest directly to the 1916 measure. Said Mills, "Mr. Wilson has quailed and temporized before the threat of Organized Labor, until that threat has grown into a menace." When the rail unions demanded the Adamson Act and "the President surrendered, the foundation for the existing crisis was laid."[9]

In the immediate postwar years, the railroad unions remained at the center of controversy. In a rare show of unity, all the major brotherhoods—operating and nonoperating alike—joined to form the Plumb Plan League through which they sought to continue government operation of the railroads. The unions had fared well during the war and their leaders felt that return of the roads to private ownership would jeopardize their gains. Many progressives, such as Frederic C. Howe and Amos R. E. Pinchot, who joined them regarded the League as a step toward efficiency, but railroad operators and other critics regarded the Plumb plan as naked socialism and waged a vigorous, and eventually successful, campaign against it. As their hopes for continued government operation diminished, and as conservative attacks mounted, the railroad workers felt isolated and resentful. In November 1919 the editor of the rail unions' newspaper, *Labor*, warned his readers, "Labor . . . was never more alone than it is at the present time. . . . Congress and the administrative agencies of the government have joined with capitalism in a war upon labor."[10]

[9] Beveridge speech in *The North American*, Dec. 23, 1919; speech by Governor [of Indiana] James P. Goodrich, "The Menace of Class Control," Oct. 14, 1919, pamphlet in Samuel McCune Lindsay Papers (Butler Library, Columbia University), Box 123; hereafter cited as Lindsay Papers; Nicholas Murray Butler, *The Faith of a Liberal: Essays and Addresses on Political Principles and Public Policies* (New York, 1924), 75; Mills address, Feb. 1, 1920, Ogden L. Mills Papers (Manuscript Division, Library of Congress), Speech Book, Vol. 2; hereafter cited as Mills Papers.
[10] Keating, *Gentleman from Colorado*, 477-79; K. Austin Kerr, "American Railroad Politics, 1914-1920" (unpublished Ph.D. dissertation, University of Pittsburgh, 1965), 206-15; *Labor*, Nov. 8, 1919.

This foreboding proved justified when Congress confronted the railroad issue. In late 1919 and early 1920, it became clear that the Plumb plan had no chance of adoption. Even Senator Robert M. La Follette's proposal for a two-year extension of federal operation was easily defeated. Indeed, as the Esch-Cummins Transportation bill took shape, it grew apparent that Congress, far from granting the unions' wishes, was in a mood to chastise the railroad labor organizations. The Senate version contained an antistrike provision that gained bipartisan support in both houses. It passed the Senate on two occasions, although the House rejected it, favoring a milder but still restrictive labor statement. Finally, House and Senate conferees agreed to drop the antistrike proposal, but only after the AFL and the brotherhoods had lobbied intensively against it. Even so, the bill's labor provisions created a nine-member Railroad Labor Board with quasi-judicial powers. This innovation departed sharply from the traditional means of governmental involvement in railway labor questions, which had always relied upon mediation rather than adjudication. Though relieved at the failure of the antistrike provisions, labor leaders regarded the Transportation Act's Railroad Labor Board as a harbinger of compulsory arbitration and industrial tribunals. Gompers called it an outstanding example of Bourbon success. Yet even with this drastic innovation in labor relations Cummins and others were disappointed: "I confess," the Iowa Republican mourned, "that I yielded upon these [antistrike] provisions of the Senate bill with extreme reluctance, [for] the principle is everlastingly right."[11]

[11] For the legislative history of the Esch-Cummins Act, see Rogers MacVeagh, *The Transportation Act of 1920* (New York, 1923). For Gompers' comment, see Report of the AFL Executive Council, in *Proceedings of the 40th Annual Convention of the American Federation of Labor* (1920), 211. For Cummins' comment, see U.S., Congress, Senate, *Congressional Record*, 66th Cong., 2d sess., 1920, 59:3328. See also Ralph Mills Sayre, "Albert Baird Cummins and the Progressive Movement in Iowa" (unpublished Ph.D. dissertation, Columbia University, 1958), 497-99; 508-509.

Many businessmen welcomed the growth of antilabor feeling within the party, for they were determined that labor would lose its "privileged" position. With both businessmen and Republicans critical of labor and eager to discredit Wilson there were excellent possibilities for a joint attack upon the Democrats through the labor issue. When Judge Elbert Gary of United States Steel stood staunchly for the open shop in the 1919 steel strike, business groups appealed to their congressmen to support the steel magnate's stand with antilabor legislation. "Every business interest [in] this country expects you to use your influence favoring American ideas [and] institutions [such as the] open shop," telegraphed one industrialist to a Republican congressman, and many echoed this appeal. In questionnaires that the GOP platform advisory committee circulated, virtually all businessmen urged explicit Republican support of the open shop.[12]

Business organizations were particularly eager to demonstrate, or at least to publicize, a close connection between organized labor and the Bolshevik menace, for it was an opportunity to gain public support for the employers in their battles against strikers. Thus, in the steel strike, the companies effectively courted public opinion, which probably supported the strikers' original demands, by exposing "radicalism," real or imagined, in the steelworkers' ranks. Antiradicalism would be a potent weapon in their campaign for the open shop, as well as in connection with these specific strike situations.[13]

Seemingly the theme of radicalism reinforced the case of the GOP and business; hence, it appeared to strengthen their antilabor alliance. However, while Republicans could accuse

[12] Telegram of a representative of the John A. Granger Company to Congressman Richard Yates, Oct. 9, 1919, House of Representatives Records (Record Group 233, National Archives), Petitions and Memorials to House Committee on Labor, 66th Cong., 1st sess.; Charles S. Bird to Ogden L. Mills, May 5, 1920, and memorandum by Harry A. Wheeler of the Union Trust Company, May 10, 1920, Lindsay Papers, Box 123.

[13] Murray, *Red Scare*, 150-52; David Brody, *Steelworkers in America: The Nonunion Era* (Cambridge, Mass., 1960), 244-50.

the Democrats of pampering labor and catering to a special interest group, they could not charge that the Democrats were unaware of the radical "threat." In 1919 Attorney General A. Mitchell Palmer began his amazing assault on civil liberties, attacking and arresting alleged radicals of every stripe. In the fall the Department of Justice made nationwide arrests of radicals and agitators. Palmer followed these with other forays; on January 2, 1920, Department of Justice agents conducted raids in 33 cities and took 2,700 persons into custody. These incursions and their attendant deportations continued until May 1920.[14]

Although Palmer had been a friend of organized labor in Congress, he turned upon the AFL, the UMW, and the brotherhoods. When the coal miners struck, he secured an injunction against them under the wartime Lever Act, from which labor leaders claimed exemption. He threatened the brotherhoods with similar action when they prepared to strike. The former progressive was beginning to launch his campaign for the Democratic presidential nomination on this antiradical and antilabor stand.[15]

Palmer's injection of Democratic antiradicalism into the labor question complicated matters for Republicans. The attorney general's callous disregard for civil liberties provided the party with still another antiadministration issue; Republicans quickly seized upon and generalized it into an assault on "one man," arbitrary rule, thus taking a slap at the "autocratic" President Wilson as well as his attorney general. Paradoxically, though, the attorney general's dramatic and apparently popular raids and legal assaults threatened to steal the labor issue from the GOP. He had, in effect, repudiated the Wilson administration's connection with labor, and he had done it with a vengeance. Thus, in terming the steel, coal, and threatened railroad strikes of 1919 "three signal failures

[14] Stanley Coben, A. Mitchell Palmer: Politician (New York, 1963), chapt. 12.
[15] Ibid., 171-88.

to promote economic and social revolution," he echoed many Republican orators.[16]

Palmer's attack upon labor gratified the militant open shop groups, for his analysis of the industrial crisis coincided with their own. But as a major contender for the Democratic nomination, Palmer proved perplexing to the Republican party. Most Republicans criticized labor on a different and less emotional basis than did Poindexter, the NAM, and the Democratic attorney general. Mills, for example, blasted the presumption and arrogance of the standard labor organizations, not their allegedly revolutionary aims. Hence, as Palmer became increasingly rabid, the GOP faced a dilemma: if it supported Palmer's attack, as its antilabor utterances seemed to require, the party in effect would endorse the position of a leading Democratic contender; if it repudiated Palmerism, it would open the door for him to capture an important issue. The party might forfeit support of patriotic societies, some of the business groups, and a public that was hypersensitive to the Bolshevik menace.

The sudden appearance of vigorous antilabor, antiradical activity in the Democracy revealed a split within the GOP on the labor-radical issue. Liberals such as William Allen White, Senator William E. Borah, Senator Robert M. La Follette, and others deplored the red raids and spoke forthrightly against Palmer's activities. But many in the party endorsed the attorney general's assaults, turning their criticism upon those in the administration such as Assistant Secretary of Labor Louis Post who tried to thwart Palmer.[17]

[16] Quoted in *ibid.*, 188.

[17] For example, John Callan O'Laughlin, secretary of the executive committee of the Republican Committee on Policies and Platform, supported Palmer (Washington *Post*, April 18, 1920). The anti-Palmer Republicans' stand is revealed in "What We Will Prove Concerning the Attack upon Honorable Louis F. Post," mimeographed booklet, May 5, 1920, in Lindsay Papers, Box 123. "I am against Palmer and for Post," declared William Allen White in a letter to Homer Hoch, May 25, 1920, William Allen White Papers (Manuscript Division, Library of Congress), Box 20; hereafter cited as White Papers. Of course, the Palmer-Post affair

Poindexter and the extremist but unofficial Republican Publicity Association kept up their violent abuse of the AFL "radicals," tacitly endorsing the attorney general's stand. Republicans closer to the party machinery were more circumspect. Former Senator Albert J. Beveridge, a key GOP spokesman during the election, tried to separate the related issues of labor and bolshevism. The Hoosier charged that, in response to a bogus threat of radicalism, the Wilson administration had trampled upon civil liberties. "Obviously," he charged, "this spurt of reactionary activity was nothing more than an effort to allay the wrath of that conservative public opinion which had been grievously outraged by the Administration's pandering to law-defying force in labor disputes." Later in the same month, Beveridge told a Republican rally in Atlantic City that among the five key issues in the coming campaign were the Democrats' protection of labor and the party's vile attacks on free speech. Thus, Beveridge sought to separate the issue of labor, which his party could attack, from the issue of radicalism, which Palmer had usurped and perhaps rendered a liability.[18]

Meanwhile labor affairs became steadily less prominent. In January of 1920 the last of the major strikes ended when the steelworkers admitted defeat and returned to the mills. Politics seized the headlines, as several major contenders fought for the nomination in both parties. With the last of the big strikes, with labor in full retreat on all fronts, and with the attorney general ferreting out the "Reds," the public could face the spring primaries with reassurance.

The contest for the Republican nomination in the spring reflected the decline of the labor issue. None of the three major candidates publicly followed the pattern which Mills,

also split the Democratic party. See E. David Cronon, ed., *The Cabinet Diaries of Josephus Daniels* (Lincoln, Nebr., 1963), entry for April 14, 1920, p. 518.

[18] Beveridge quotation from his own unfinished article contained in Beveridge to Will Hays, chairman of the Republican National Committee, April 3, 1920, Beveridge Papers, Box 221; New York *Times*, April 25, 1920.

Beveridge, and others had established, that of attacking the Wilson administration through its friendship with labor. Still less did they rally to the flag that Poindexter flaunted; on the contrary, the candidates emphasized their friendly relations with labor. California Senator Hiram Johnson built his campaign on opposition to the League of Nations to the virtual exclusion of other issues, but labor knew him as sympathetic to its interests. Another leading contender, Governor Frank O. Lowden of Illinois, had enjoyed cordial relations with labor groups in his state which even the 1919 coal strike failed to destroy. Certainly the governor had no desire to emphasize the labor issue, for he sought repeatedly to convince Illinois labor leaders that his marriage to George Pullman's daughter was not incompatible with friendliness toward labor. Even General Leonard Wood, the darling of many of Theodore Roosevelt's former supporters, mitigated his early attacks against labor-inspired radicalism. In 1919 his main issue had been law and order and, said William Allen White in the midst of the labor unrest of that year, if the "issue persists until June, 1920, I think he may be nominated." Wood soon dropped the issue, calling only for a Rooseveltian square deal for labor and capital. The general continued to attack radical influences in organized labor, but these, he assured the public, amounted to only 1 percent.[19]

Labor affairs gained little attention in discussion about two secondary candidates, Senator Warren Harding of Ohio and Herbert Hoover. Although Harding, whom many people considered the best dark horse possibility, had voted in favor

[19] New York *Times*, April 3 and 25, 1920; William T. Hutchinson, *Lowden of Illinois: The Life of Frank O. Lowden*. II: *Nation and Country-side* (Chicago, 1957), 416-19; William Allen White to Hiram Johnson, Dec. 2, 1919, White Papers, Box 19; Evan J. David, "Leonard J. Wood on Labor Problems," *The Outlook*, CXXIV (Feb. 25, 1920), 326-28. Perhaps Wood took White's advice, for the Kansas editor enjoined him to stop "this crazy notion to hunt 'em down and shoot 'em, and see red, and all that sort of thing." White to Wood, Dec. 26, 1919, White Papers, Box 19. There is hardly a mention of the labor issue in Wood's diary during the spring of 1920.

of the antistrike provision of the Esch-Cummins bill, his friends
gave no outward indication in their quiet campaign in his
behalf that he would use labor as a scapegoat. Indeed, so
eager was the Ohio senator to demonstrate his moderation that
he advised one supporter to "ask those [laborites] who oppose
me what they are to expect at the hands of General Wood
and the administration of this government through military
force." Hoover emerged from his wartime duties with much
popular acclaim but with little support from professional
politicians. Even his party affiliation was not clear, and labor
leaders paid little attention to the low-keyed campaign that
a few ardent supporters urged in his behalf.[20]

In June, as Republicans gathered in Chicago to nominate
a president, the labor issue reappeared. Although the debate
over the League of Nations had dominated the primaries, many
Republicans felt that domestic concerns—chief among them
labor—would quickly reemerge. It was a basic issue, temporarily
quiescent, but still dangerous. For the GOP to capitalize on
the nation's anti-Wilson mood, one veteran Republican felt,
it would have to be clear and assertive on the two crucial issues
of the day—the League of Nations and labor.[21]

The debate among the members of the GOP platform committee revealed deep splits within the party on these two
crucial issues. A conservative, antilabor, and antiprogressive
atmosphere pervaded the convention. Republicans were
determined to smash Wilson and all his works. Business
interests were strong, and delegates, from powerful Senate
leaders to ordinary party members, wanted a vigorous stand on
the labor issue. This, most observers felt, would come in the

[20] Harding to John J. Buckley, April 5, 1920, Warren G. Harding
Papers (The Ohio Historical Society), Box 684; hereafter cited as Harding
Papers; Oscar Straus to Watson Washburn, May 12, 1920, Oscar Straus
Papers (Manuscript Division, Library of Congress), Box 15; hereafter cited
as Straus Papers.
[21] Chicago Tribune, June 3, 1920; Oscar Straus, "Republican Convention and Subsequent Interview with Senator Harding . . . June 8-22, 1920,"
in Diary Material, 1919-1923, Straus Papers, Box 24.

form of a proposal to endorse the rejected antistrike provision of the Esch-Cummins legislation.[22] Some Republicans, led by Kansas Governor Henry J. Allen, urged the party to support the principle of the Kansas Court of Industrial Relations, which limited strikes in that state and stipulated that judicial decisions would settle industrial disputes.[23]

Although the convention favored a strong stand on labor, the party was by no means united. Prior to the convention the GOP committee on platform and policies had sent out a questionnaire regarding labor to a number of leading Republicans in business, labor, civic affairs, women's groups, and the professions. The replies to this survey demonstrated that party members held sharply divergent views. One question dealt with the Kansas Industrial Court. A large majority of the 374 replies favored its use in public employment, but the tally on its application to general private industry was almost evenly split. The industrial relations subcommittee made no recommendation on the party's labor planks, commenting only that the issue found the rank and file of the party deeply divided.[24]

At the convention antilabor sentiment was prevalent, but

[22] Washington *Post*, June 8, 1920.

[23] Chicago *Tribune*, June 7, 1920. The concept of the Kansas Court of Industrial Relations was to render judicial decisions that would settle industrial disputes just as court decisions settled civil and criminal cases. Implied, of course, was a fundamental restriction on the right to strike if the state followed the parallel between regular court cases and industrial disputes. The Kansas Court attracted much attention and support in the early 1920s, but a United States Supreme Court decision (*Wolff Packing Company v. Court of Industrial Relations of Kansas*, 262 U.S. 522 [1923]) soon stripped it of most of its power. Labor opposed it on principle because it appeared to be a step in the direction of compulsory arbitration. Labor leaders also feared—with reason, as it turned out—that antilabor officials would usually control the machinery. See Julia E. Johnsen, comp., *Kansas Court of Industrial Relations*, The Reference Shelf, Vol. I, No. 4 (New York, 1922); *Debate Between Samuel Gompers and Henry J. Allen*, May 28, 1920 (New York, 1920); William Allen White to Gov. Henry Allen, June 11, 1925, White Papers, Box 84; and Dominico Gagliardo, *The Kansas Industrial Court: An Experiment in Compulsory Arbitration* (Lawrence, Kans., 1941).

[24] "Analysis of 374 Questionnaires on Industrial Relations . . . ," ca. spring 1920, Lindsay Papers, Box 120.

a small articulate and influential group of moderates opposed the majority on the labor question. New York congressional candidate Ogden L. Mills, Kansas progressive editor William Allen White, and Idaho's aggressive and magnetic Senator William E. Borah led the dissident elements both in the convention and on the platform committee.[25]

Governor Allen, urging his Kansas Court of Industrial Relations, appeared before the platform committee, as did Gompers and Matthew Woll of the AFL. Allen and the AFL president engaged in a sharp newspaper controversy on the right to strike; when the question reached the committee itself, the debate became heated and "revived [among Republicans] many old animosities and brought into focus several of the issues raised by recent strikes and unrest."[26]

Conservatives defeated an attempt by the moderates to elect Mills as chairman of the platform committee, choosing instead the orthodox Senator James E. Watson of Indiana. Moreover, they inserted an antistrike plank into the preliminary draft of the platform. But the moderates refused to be stampeded. Senator Borah, perhaps the most powerful force at the convention outside the inner circle, announced that he would fight the antistrike plank, and the moderates threatened to take controversial platform issues, including labor, to the floor of the convention.[27]

The antilaborites retreated. Victory over the Democrats was their goal, and, although sympathetic to an antistrike plank, they feared nothing more than a split in their own party. The

[25] Mills and others attacked labor, but only when they felt that it aspired to a specially privileged position. They were against class legislation, and antistrike bills were examples of class legislation every bit as much as the Adamson Act. For examples of this position, see letter of William E. Borah to W. A. Heiss, Jan. 9, 1920, William E. Borah Papers (Manuscript Division, Library of Congress), Box 198; hereafter cited as Borah Papers; and Mills' interview in New York *Times*, Oct. 3, 1920.

[26] Washington *Post*, June 7, 1920.

[27] Chicago *Tribune*, June 7; New York *Tribune*, June 8; Baltimore *Sun*, June 10, 1920; William Allen White, *The Autobiography of William Allen White* (New York, 1946), 585.

prospect of a floor fight and the press of business helped the moderates to eliminate the antilabor statement.[28]

In the end, the Republican platform equivocated on the labor issue. It called for impartial tribunals to settle disputes in public utilities, but did not propose that their decisions be legally binding. It said nothing about labor's legislative demands, such as an anti-injunction law and immigration restriction, but it contained no attack on labor. "The labor plank," commented a Democratic newspaper, "is a rather excusable straddle. It represents what the average man is thinking." William Allen White, a key member of the moderate group within the platform committee, agreed that it was a straddle. He added, "We pulled the thing as far to the left as we could, otherwise it would not have been a straddle but would have been a reactionary document."[29]

When the convention turned from the platform to nominating its candidate, none of the three leading contenders mustered a majority on the early votes. On the tenth ballot, the convention, fearful of a deadlock, turned to Senator Warren G. Harding. The genial Ohioan was the ideal choice for a party whose road to the White House could be blocked only by troublesome issues. Handsome, affable, oratorical, Harding had been a regular party man in the Senate, compiling an undistinguished record. He was not an irreconcilable on the League of Nations, but he was a strong reservationist. He had voted for the antistrike provision, but he had few pronounced opinions on labor matters. Harding was a candidate to whom all factions in the party could rally, pinning their diverse hopes on his vague and high-sounding statements.[30]

[28] For a statement favorable to the antistrike position, see William Howard Taft to Clarence Kelsey, June 10, 1920, Taft Letterbooks, Series 8, Vol. 96.

[29] Baltimore *Sun*, June 12, 1920; William Allen White to Rodney Elward, June 15, 1920, White Papers, Box 20; Kirk H. Porter and Donald B. Johnson, comps., *National Party Platforms*, 3d ed. (Urbana, Ill., 1966), 232-33.

[30] For the Republican convention, see Wesley M. Bagby, *The Road*

Harding was the choice of the party wheelhorses, but the delegates picked his runningmate, Governor Calvin Coolidge of Massachusetts. The convention leaders had named a vaguely liberal individual, Senator Irvine L. Lenroot of Wisconsin, as their vice presidential choice, but dissident Oregon delegates put the Massachusetts governor's name in nomination. Amid great hoopla, the delegates rebelled against the attempt to balance the conservative Harding with the liberal Lenroot and chose Coolidge by a 500-vote margin, thus indulging their antilabor feelings. "Gov. Coolidge," proclaimed the patriotic Chicago *Tribune*, "is a red, white and blue American by birth."[31]

The nominees, the platform, and the mood of the convention were ominous to laborites. "The bunch that made the platform and picked the candidates," declared the United Mine Workers *Journal*, "solemnly decided to give labor a good hard licking . . . and turn everything over to the big interests." The AFL convention, which met simultaneously with that of the GOP, denounced the Republican party as "defiant in its defense of the enemies of labor." Some conservatives shared this analysis of the convention's actions. The *Wall Street Journal*, a leading voice of open shop, antilabor opinion, rejoiced at the GOP's refusal to heed Gompers' demands and urged the party to use the opportunity to deal organized labor a chastening blow.[32]

Both sides misinterpreted the results of the convention. The Ohio senator and the Massachusetts governor would conduct

---

to *Normalcy: The Campaign and Election of 1920*, The Johns Hopkins University Studies in Historical and Political Science, LXXX, No. 1 (Baltimore, 1962), chapt. 3; and Andrew Sinclair, *The Available Man: The Life Behind the Masks of Warren Gamaliel Harding* (New York, 1965), chapt. 9.

[31] Bagby, *The Road to Normalcy*, 100-101; Chicago *Tribune*, June 13, 1920. See also Donald R. McCoy, *Calvin Coolidge: The Quiet President* (New York, 1967), 119-21.

[32] "Labor's Disappointment at the Republican Platform," *Literary Digest*, LXV (June 26, 1920), 16-17; AFL, *Proceedings of the 40th Annual Convention*, 329-31; *Wall Street Journal*, June 14, 1920.

their campaign largely without reference to labor problems. Both entered the contest with somewhat antilabor reputations —Harding because of his recent antistrike vote and Coolidge because of his telegram to Gompers in the Boston police strike— but neither emphasized labor. As president, Harding would eventually prove to be confused, prejudiced, and inconsistent, and this perplexity would sometimes lead to antilabor acts and pronouncements. But he was no doctrinaire and during this campaign his few mild utterances regarding labor were designed to mitigate union antagonism and to make him more acceptable to workers. Coolidge had been nominated by a convention that was impressed by his firm opposition to labor in 1919, but the taciturn governor played little part in the campaign. Indeed, as vice president and as president he would demonstrate that, far from desiring to assault labor, he wanted accord and tranquillity in every area of public affairs, and that his outstanding political talent was his ability to submerge issues and placate opponents. In 1920 the candidates and the party wanted to win and were quite unwilling to take firm stands on issues as controversial as labor.

Nonetheless organized labor felt threatened. After the Democratic party's convention the AFL formally endorsed its candidate James M. Cox, and vowed an aggressive campaign in behalf of labor's congressional friends and against its enemies. The AFL kept a record of the labor votes and utterances of all members of Congress and distributed these to local union bodies with recommended endorsements. Frank Morrison, the secretary-treasurer of the AFL, who was in charge of this Nonpartisan Political Campaign, reported that congressmen and senators seeking reelection were eager to claim labor support.[33] By summer the AFL had already demonstrated the political value of its endorsement. In the contest for the Democratic nomination A. Mitchell Palmer had secured the

---

[33] Frank Morrison to Victor Olander, April 30, 1920, Frank Morrison Campaign Book (AFL-CIO Library, Washington), Vol. 2; hereafter cited as Morrison Campaign Book.

support of many important members of the Democratic National Committee, but he placed a poor fourth in the Michigan primary, partly because labor turned massively against him in that state. Democratic national committeeman A. R. Titlow of Washington had worked assiduously for Palmer in his early drive for the nomination, but during the convention, which met late in June, he confessed, "There was no sentiment and no votes in our delegation for Palmer. Labor would not have Palmer and we knew it."[34]

Even without Palmer's example Republicans were aware of the potential strength of the labor vote. The membership of the AFL had declined slightly since the war, but it still hovered around 4,000,000. Combined with the membership of the railway brotherhoods and other labor organizations, and with the votes of union members' families and those actively sympathetic to labor, the labor vote could theoretically approach 10,000,000. Of course, labor had never voted as a bloc in such massive numbers, and political leaders in both parties knew that union leaders could not deliver such a vote.[35] The American labor movement was historically nonproletarian in outlook. Its voting patterns revealed that, to the worker, such considerations as traditional party affiliation, religion, regional issues, and ethnic background were often more important than his union membership. Still, the labor vote, when one party or another presented a specific threat to fundamental labor interests, had been decisive in many congressional races in the past, and it had also played a role in some presidential contests. For example, labor resentment over the Homestead strike of 1892 had helped sway the election of that year to

[34] Quoted in Coben, A. Mitchell Palmer, 261.
[35] New York Times, July 11, 1920. The Harding organization, however, did not take lightly the threat of the labor vote. One staff report warned that "labor is more united this year than at any time in recent years" and pointed out the importance of the labor vote in key states such as Indiana and Ohio. Above all, this memorandum emphasized "the need of avoiding so far as possible the administration entering office with labor in a surly mood." "Memorandum on Labor Relations," summer or fall 1920, Harding Papers, Box 469.

Cleveland. Of more recent importance, the railroad brotherhoods had stood for Wilson and against Hughes in 1916
when the Republican nominee denounced the Adamson Act.
Their support had been crucial in several key states in Wilson's
narrow victory.[36] The campaign of Albert B. Cummins of Iowa for reelection
to the Senate provided another warning. Cummins, seeking
nomination for a fourth term in 1920, was a powerful and
respected political figure. However, in the spring and summer
of 1920, the farm and labor groups in his state rose against
him in the Republican primary in protest over his role in the
Esch-Cummins Act, supporting Smith Wildman Brookhart, a
political unknown. Frank Morrison contacted the railway
brotherhoods and announced labor's intention "to prosecute
a special drive in Iowa." Cummins defeated his rival, but the
challenger received an unprecedented 96,000 votes; "in view
of the hostility of organized labor and of the large number of
farmers," who were opposed to him, Cummins predicted that
he would have a hard fight for reelection. In many congressional districts throughout the Middle West, incumbents
who had supported the Esch-Cummins Act were fearful of
retaliation from labor. All these considerations militated
against a Republican campaign against labor and put a premium
on moderation. The path to the White House was too
dangerous to allow Republican candidates to indulge in overt
labor-baiting.[37]

Harding, too, recognized the political influence of organized

[36] Arthur S. Link, Woodrow Wilson and the Progressive Era: 1910-
1917 (New York, 1954), 249; New York Times, April 25, 1920.
[37] Morrison to W. G. Lee, May 5, 1920, Morrison Campaign Book,
Vol. 2; Cummins to Beveridge, July 23, 1920, Beveridge Papers, Box 219;
Congressman Oscar Ray Luhring to Congressman Everett Sanders, Nov. 4,
1920, Everett Sanders Papers (Manuscript Division, Library of Congress),
Box 1; Jerry A. Neprash, The Brookhart Campaigns in Iowa, 1920-1926: A
Study in the Motivation of Political Attitudes (New York, 1932), 33;
Herbert F. Marguiles, "The Election of 1920 in Wisconsin: The Return
to 'Normalcy' Reappraised," Wisconsin Magazine of History, XLI (Autumn
1957), 15-22.

labor. His Senate voting record was unimpressive to laborites, and at times he appeared to condone labor-baiting, but he worked hard to convince unionists of his friendliness toward them and to avoid identification with extremist elements. Thus, when one supporter recalled to Harding the consequences of Hughes' condemnation of the railroad unions in 1916, he replied in a public letter, "I appreciate all you say about the handling of the labor question. . . . I do not think we shall make some of the mistakes which characterized the campaign of four years ago."[38]

Indeed, far from antagonizing workers, Harding retracted earlier statements that had been critical of labor and began to campaign actively for a share of the labor vote. Shortly after the war, the Ohio senator had attacked labor's alleged influence in the Wilson administration, arguing that "the war will have been waged in vain if we do not go back to the old conditions that prevailed before the war." In another speech, he had contended that postwar economic distress had its cause in unfair taxes on business and that it was time to stop pampering overpaid workers and to show greater concern for businessmen. As the campaign progressed, however, he reconsidered his enchantment with the good old days, assuring one audience that in regard to labor relations "we would never return to prewar conditions." In the same address, he denied that he had ever intimated that wages were too high.[39]

The Republican candidate welcomed labor support. Gompers and the AFL Nonpartisan Political Campaign jumped to

[38] For the AFL's evaluation of Harding's voting record, see New York Times, Aug. 30, 1920. For his flirtation with antilabor elements, see an exchange between Jonathan Bourne, Jr., and Harding, Nov. 14 and 17, 1919, Harding Papers, Box 684. For counterpressures on Harding and his favorable response to them, see an exchange between Raymond Robins and Harding, Aug. 1 and 5, 1920, Raymond Robins Papers (State Historical Society of Wisconsin), Box 16; hereafter cited as Robins Papers. For Harding's statement regarding the mistakes in the 1916 campaign, see New York Times, July 7, 1920.
[39] New York Times, June 13 and Sept. 7, 1920; Chicago Tribune, Sept. 7, 1920.

the side of the Democratic nominee, James M. Cox, as soon as the Democrats revealed their platform, but not all labor leaders approved. Shortly after Harding's nomination, James H. Potts of the International Brotherhood of Carpenters and Joiners sent a telegram of support for the Republicans, and Harding followers advertised it widely as proof that their man could attract labor support. Later, Terence V. O'Connor, president of the International Union of Longshoremen and a longtime Democrat, came out for Harding, for he feared reactionary elements within the Democratic party far more than a possible Republican threat to labor. The postwar repressive measures of the Wilson administration had antagonized many labor organizations, especially in the west; in all, thirty-nine labor leaders publicly denounced Wilson and Cox during the campaign and praised Harding's labor record.[40]

As governor of Ohio, Cox had been mildly friendly toward labor, but the Republicans conducted their campaign largely against Wilson rather than against the lackluster Democratic nominee. Although Palmer's assaults had come late in an administration which had compiled a generally prolabor record, the GOP saw an opportunity to capitalize upon labor's disenchantment. The Palmer injunction under the Lever Act in the fall of 1919 had outraged even the staunch friends of the Democrats within labor's ranks. Samuel Gompers, for example, had protested Palmer's use of the wartime measure, claiming that former Attorney General Thomas W. Gregory had assured labor leaders that the administration would never use the Act's emergency provisions in labor matters. Ominously, for the first time in the twentieth century the Democratic platform contained no anti-injunction plank; however, Gompers sanguinely interpreted this to mean that the party was tacitly repudiating Palmer's action. But to many labor leaders, Gompers' almost uncritical acceptance of a Democratic platform that differed

[40] New York *Times*, June 18, Aug. 4, and Oct. 31, 1920.

little from the Republican document on labor matters indicated
that he had made a prior commitment to the Democratic
party. They felt that the AFL president, by committing the
organization prematurely to the Democratic party, was squand-
ering the bargaining power of the labor vote.[41]

Republicans quickly seized this opportunity to divide labor
politically. While party spokesmen had attacked labor earlier
as an overpowerful and sinister force in the Wilson administration, they soon began to criticize the Democrats for being
unfair to the workingmen. Thus, the Republican National
Committee issued a pamphlet which reminded the laborer of
Palmer's injunction in the coal strike of 1919. This injunction,
asserted the campaign document, betrayed the pious declarations of the Democrats and exposed the meaningless labor
provisions of the 1914 Clayton Act. "This," the pamphlet
scolded, "is how the Democrats have kept their faith with
labor. . . . But don't you be fooled again, workingman."[42]
Earlier, a leading Republican had denounced this strike as a
threat to "organized government itself," but the GOP saw no
need to bind itself to past utterances when the prospect of
capturing labor votes appeared.

Harding continued his policy of refusing to attack labor,
despite the presence of the antilabor extremists within the
party. In his speech of formal acceptance, which he delivered
a month after the nomination, he termed collective bargaining
"an outstanding right" and uttered vague but impressive pleas
for harmony between labor and capital. He included nothing
in this speech to stir labor against him or to appeal to voters
on an antilabor basis. Beveridge, to whom he had sent the
speech for criticism, assured the nominee that the comments

[41] Gompers to A. Mitchell Palmer, Feb. 10, 1920, Samuel Gompers
Letterbooks (AFL-CIO Library, Washington), Vol. 262; hereafter cited as
Gompers Letterbooks; Gompers news release, July 15, *ibid.*, Vol. 268;
"Labor and the Democrats," *Literary Digest*, LXVI (July 31, 1920), 10-11.
[42] "The Story of an Injunction," ca. autumn 1920, Republican Na-
tional Committee pamphlet, in Lindsay Papers, Box 119.

"on labor would gratify all except those whom Mr. Gompers controls; and they will be Democratic in any event."[43]

Actually, the politically conscious workingman had other alternatives. If he rejected the blandishments of Harding and Cox, he could vote for Eugene V. Debs, the hero of the Socialist party, or for Parley Parker Christensen, the candidate of the newly formed Farmer-Labor party. While some of the pioneering industrial unions supported the Socialists, Debs' imprisonment and the party's doctrinal difficulties helped to reduce its vote from the high point of 1912. The Farmer-Labor party, a coalition of dissident farmers, progressive unionists, and reformers, concealed a far-reaching program of nationalization and economic reform behind rather conventional terminology. But, despite describing themselves as "forward looking men and women who perform useful work . . . [and who are] united by a spontaneous and irresistible impulse to do righteous battle," the new party ran behind the Socialist party. Socialist leader Morris Hillquit had predicted that most unionists would vote for the major parties and that only dedicated radicals would support Debs. Few radicals appeared in 1920.[44]

Radical politics, however ineffective at the polls, did stimulate the United States Chamber of Commerce and other business groups in their militant antiunion campaign in the summer of 1920. But Harding, unconcerned about Socialists and Farmer-Laborites, remained silent on the open shop issue. Moreover, he repudiated compulsory arbitration, a stand that labor favored. The AFL had attacked the Republican platform

[43] New York *Times*, July 23, 1920; Beveridge to Harding, July 10, 1920, Beveridge Papers, Box 221.

[44] For the Socialist party and for Hillquit's words, see James Berton Rhoads, "The Campaign of the Socialist Party in the Election of 1920" (unpublished Ph.D. dissertation, American University, 1965), 356-57, 375, 377, and 381. For the Farmer-Labor party, see Nathan Fine, *Labor and Farmer Parties in the United States, 1828-1928* (New York, 1928), 378-93. A copy of the 1920 Farmer-Labor platform is contained in the Mercer Green Johnston Papers (Manuscript Division, Library of Congress), Box 67; hereafter cited as Johnston Papers.

for failure to endorse most of labor's demands, but as the campaign developed Harding spoke for at least one major legislative request. The AFL, ever fearful of job competition, had repeatedly asked for restrictive immigration laws; although the platform committee, which had to appease manufacturing interests that supported continued immigration, made no declaration on the subject, the nominee announced in September that his administration would support changes in the immigration laws which would guarantee the stability of American traditions and standards.[45]

Harding made particular efforts to attract railroad workers. The brotherhoods had opposed him in the Republican primary in Ohio because of his vote favoring the antistrike provisions of the Esch-Cummins measure, and the candidate was mindful of their telling opposition to Hughes in 1916. Harding had voted for the antistrike clause because it dealt with a public service which Congress had authority to regulate and whose financial returns it could and did limit. "I do not know that such a law will prevent railway strikes," he had said, "but I do know that it ought."[46]

He did not retract this statement, even in addresses to railroad workers; he denied, however, that it was an antilabor vote. In addition, he sought to persuade the railroad men that the Railroad Labor Board, which the Esch-Cummins Act had established, was a unique endorsement of labor's right to organize, and that it constituted a recognition of the unusual importance of the railroad worker. On August 27, speaking before 900 supposedly hostile railroad workers near Galion, Ohio, he defended the Esch-Cummins Act. "Some day," he predicted, "you . . . will hail that law as the greatest forward

---

[45] For Harding's labor statements during the campaign, see Sherman Rogers, "Senator Harding on Labor," *The Outlook*, CXXV (Aug. 18, 1920), 668-70. For his comments on immigration, see Chicago *Tribune*, Sept. 15, 1920.
[46] New York *Times*, June 20, 1920.

step in all . . . railway legislation." Mixing affably with the crowd and eating apple pie with his fingers, the Republican candidate faced down would-be hecklers. On September 13, a group of railroad workers in his hometown, Marion, greeted him with signs reading "Harding will not sidetrack us," and cheered when he told them that the Esch-Cummins Act was in labor's interest and that it manifested a degree of recognition and protection to labor that had never before existed; it was, he continued, "the most considerate piece of legislation ever enacted in the protection of any group of workmen in the United States." Far from being antilabor, as Gompers charged, the law recognized the special problems and special attention due railroad employees whom the candidate considered truly "a favored group."[47]

Harding also rejected antiradicalism as an issue. Journalist Stanley Washburn, a prominent New Jersey Republican, tried to arouse the party and its standard bearer to the possibilities of the radicalism-labor connection, but Harding spurned this approach. Writing to New Jersey Republican congressional aspirants, Washburn warned them that the most serious issue in the campaign was the nation's need to stabilize industrial relations. "This," he declared, "we can never do while the country is beset with radical agitators, encouraging strikes, lockouts and industrial unrest." When Washburn learned that Harding, before his nomination, had indicated casually that American recognition of the Soviet Union would probably occur fairly soon, the journalist rushed to the nominee a lengthy analysis of the dangers of bolshevism and advised Harding that there were immense political possibilities in the radicalism issue. Virtually urging Harding to ape Palmer's demagoguery, he counseled the nominee to dwell upon the Red menace. "My own experience in speaking," he advised, "has led me to believe that one always receives the greatest response in America

[47] *Ibid.*, Aug. 28 and Sept. 14, 1920; Chicago *Tribune*, Sept. 14, 1920.

for a moral appeal"; he indicated that the issue of radicalism would be perfect for such an appeal. As election day approached, however, Washburn feared that the Republicans would allow the opposition to steal this issue. The party and nominee had ignored Washburn's call; worse, many Republicans appeared to champion radicalism. Thus, social worker Raymond Robins, who had just returned from Russia, and other progressive Republicans were in the forefront of the campaign to free political prisoners, even leading parades in their behalf. When the Democrats published a letter that Harding had written before the nomination in which he seemed friendly to recognition of the Soviet Union, Gompers followed it with a direct attack on radicalism at home and abroad. Troubled, Washburn feared that if the Republican party remained silent in the face of this Democratic maneuver the nation might think "that the Republican Party is either neutral on the subject or tacitly in favor of it."[48]

Despite admonitions such as these, Harding largely ignored the Red issue. He did withdraw his vague comments on American recognition of the Soviet regime, and he warned the electorate, as a matter of course, against the dangers of radicalism. Nonetheless, he made no effort to identify organized labor with radicalism and he refused to follow the hypersensitive journalist's advice regarding political prisoners and related matters. Indeed, the Republican nominee issued a joint statement with Dean Roscoe Pound of the Harvard

[48] Washburn's intense antiradicalism can be found in various letters. See Washburn to 12 New Jersey congressional candidates, March 3, to Harding, June 20, to Elihu Root, Aug. 16, 25, and Sept. 30, and to Harry M. Daugherty, Sept. 30, 1920, Stanley Washburn Papers (Manuscript Division, Library of Congress), Box 1; hereafter cited as Washburn Papers. So concerned was the journalist on this subject that he felt that the GOP, far from acquiring a reactionary label, might appear to be a champion of radicalism. "I am especially exercised," he informed Root on Aug. 25, "just now as to the possible effect of the connection of these thinly disguised radicals [such as Raymond Robins] in our highest [party] councils are going to have on the election."

Law School condemning the refusal of the New York State
Assembly to seat five duly-elected Socialists. Beveridge, White,
and other Republicans took similar steps. The antiradical
hysteria of 1919 and early 1920 had receded and the amiable
Harding found it advantageous to calm frayed nerves and to
allow the burden of unpopularity to fall upon the Democrats
who had instigated the Red scare. The Republican nominee
assured the populace that there was no radical plot and no
danger of imminent Bolshevik takeover.[49] Washburn's pleas
were obsolete and the candidate ignored them.

Harding did not wage a prolabor campaign. He merely
sought to deaden the labor issue, to render the labor vote
harmless.[50] If he could convince workers and their leaders
that the GOP constituted no threat to collective bargaining and
that the party was not in the hands of the vocal reactionaries
who called loudly for an all-out attack, perhaps the labor vote
per se would not materialize, and workingmen would cast their
votes on the other issues, such as the League of Nations and
the allegedly dictatorial rule of Wilson. Although elements
within the party had wanted to include in the campaign an
attack upon labor in an effort to court antilabor votes, the
party leadership swung toward an increasingly moderate course.

In this, the party was wise and successful. The GOP did not
give Gompers and Morrison a burning issue with which to
lead their forces to the polls, and Republicans captured every
industrial center in the country. As the *Literary Digest* ob-
served, despite the AFL's commitment to Cox, "Harding and
Coolidge were swept into office on a tidal wave of votes, of
which many millions must have been cast by laboring men
and women." Evaluating the labor vote, one radical complained
that the president-elect had been the beneficiary of postwar

[49] Murray, *Red Scare*, 243, 261.

[50] Thus, when a group of Massachusetts AFL members wrote Harding
that they were supporting him because of his position on the League of
Nations, the candidate replied that they were wise, for the issue of foreign
policy transcended class lines. New York *Times*, Sept. 21, 1920.

confusion and disillusionment. "Workers disregarded the
Farmer-Labor party appeal, the Socialist appeal, and the
Gompers-American Federation of Labor appeal," declared an
editorialist in the *New Majority*, "and vented their revenge
on the Wilson administration for its effort to smash labor in
the coal, steel, and railroad strikes by voting for Harding."[51]
With the labor vote split because Harding did not appear
to threaten organized labor, workers voted as millions of other
Americans voted: on the basis of ethnic considerations, traditional party loyalty, or antagonism toward the Democrats.
Harding's campaign was one of mood, not of issues. Obscuring
and even repudiating the extreme antilabor views within the
party, the Republican candidate had, in effect, extended an
invitation to working people to join him on his trek to normalcy. Desiring, as millions of Americans did, a respite from
twenty years of reform and five years of deep and uncomfortable involvment with other nations, many workers accepted
the invitation, seeing few obvious pitfalls along the Harding
path away from Wilsonianism. In the final month of the
campaign the AFL issued a report depicting Harding's hometown as militantly open shop, and Harding, who owned the
town's newspaper, as a leading contributor to antilabor sentiment there, but the country paid scant attention.[52]

Still, labor leaders interpreted Harding's victory as a repudiation of organized labor. John Philip Frey, president of the
International Molders' Union, could virtually "see the gloating
expression upon the countenances of those directing the
activities of every antiunion association of employers in the
country." Gompers and labor's officialdom girded themselves
for an assault upon their organizations. Many unionists

[51] "How Labor Voted," *Literary Digest*, LXVII (Nov. 20, 1920), 9;
quoted in Eugene Staley, *History of the Illinois State Federation of Labor*
(Chicago, 1930), 378.
[52] John Philip Frey and Chester Wright to Samuel Gompers, Oct. 29,
1920, John Philip Frey Papers (Manuscript Division, Library of Congress),
Box 10; hereafter cited as Frey Papers; New York *Times*, Nov. 1, 1920.

expected the Harding administration to commit itself to the open shop movement and to act openly against labor.[53] Harding, however, heard voices of restraint within his party. Former Senator George Sutherland, to whom Harding frequently turned for advice, counseled the president-elect to hold to a moderate position, for organized labor was still a dynamic element in American life.[54] But by far the most remarkable expression of the party's postelection tendency toward moderation came from the vice-president-elect. Catapulted into fame by the Boston police strike and nominated as an antilabor candidate, Coolidge sharply criticized antilabor extremists. Three weeks after the election, he addressed a group of Boston business leaders and did not fail to note that the election provided a much-needed check to the pretensions of organized labor. Gompers and others had tried to use their great power to dictate to the American public, he said, and the electorate had wisely rebuffed this effort. "But now," Coolidge warned his conservative audience, "we do not want to make the same mistake with organized labor that was made with organized capital—to divorce it entirely from the affairs of government." Labor was still powerful and represented the ideals and aspirations of millions of Americans. The American people, Coolidge told his listeners, had a penchant for extremes once they had identified a problem. Hence, in regard to labor, the new administration and its supporters had to be cautious and unprejudiced, for there was grave danger of a reaction against labor.[55]

[53] Frey to Gompers, Nov. 4, 1920, Gompers-AFL Papers (State Historical Society of Wisconsin), Box 41; hereafter cited as Gompers-AFL Papers; Gompers' aide to Hayes Robbins, Nov. 9, 1920, Gompers-AFL Papers, Box 41; Washington *Post*, Nov. 7, 1920.

[54] Sutherland to Harding, Nov. 10, 1920, Sutherland Papers, Box 3. See also the "Memorandum on Labor Relations," ca. summer or fall 1920, Harding Papers, Box 469. This Harding staff analysis of the labor vote urged reassurances to labor regarding the appointment of the new secretary of labor. Gestures toward labor during the campaign would "make for an era of good feeling March 4th and thereafter."

[55] New York *Times*, Nov. 24, 1920.

The words of the hero of the Boston police strike revealed the extent of his party's shift. Fast-moving events and a rapidly changing labor scene prodded the party to abandon the once explosive labor issue and allowed it to enter the White House without a commitment to vigorous union-smashing. While many Republicans still clung to the antilabor position of 1919 and early 1920, the balance of the party had shifted against extremism; indeed, Coolidge's speech and Harding's remarks at first indicated that the new administration might even welcome labor as an active participant in the administration's programs.

Several factors impelled this moderate course. Republicans realized the potential weight of the labor vote. Industrial unrest and labor violence died down suddenly, making it expedient for the GOP to wage the campaign on a vague and relatively issueless basis. In December 1919 William Allen White had foreseen this drift of events. Assigning Leonard Wood's popularity to his strong antiradical stand, the Kansas progressive predicted that if the industrial situation worsened, "Wood's chance will get vastly better. But if it is relieved, the people may forget him." This change had taken place, for, as the AFL executive council later reported, "As the campaign progressed, practically all domestic questions were over-shadowed by questions of an international character."[56] Moreover, Republicans began to realize that by refraining from sharp criticism of labor they might win labor votes, capitalizing upon the disenchantment of many laborites with the Wilson administration. Finally, Palmer's tactics had helped save labor from the worst of Republican antagonism, for, even though he found a responsive chord among some elements within the GOP, the attorney general's Red-baiting and antilabor position had strengthened those Republicans who favored a moderate ap-

[56] White to Frederick Moore, Dec. 1, 1919, White Papers, Box 19; Report of the AFL executive council, in *Proceedings of the 41st Annual Convention of the American Federation of Labor* (1921), 149.

proach to labor problems. As Palmer usurped the extremist position, the party became increasingly aware of civil liberties and increasingly reluctant to identify itself with the attitudes of the "Fighting Quaker."

These convolutions made it difficult for labor to know what to expect from the new president and his triumphant party, but it could take heart that the most rabidly antilabor elements within the party had not triumphed. The leaders of organized labor would have to be extremely cautious and they would have to accustom themselves to a heavy loss of prestige and influence within the government, but at least they did not immediately face a militantly antilabor administration, committed to the open shop and openly hostile to unions.

3 Interim: November 1920 to March 1921

THE GOP WON a resounding victory in 1920, but the campaign had done little to clarify major issues. Among the ambiguities Warren Harding and his party left unresolved during the campaign was the labor problem. While foes of unionism interpreted the election as a repudiation of labor, the attitude of the candidates and the party during the campaign made it impossible to predict with confidence the course that the GOP and its new administration would follow. Harding's cabinet appointments and the pronouncements of Republicans in the months between the election and the inauguration, rather than dispelling the uncertainty, deepened it further.

If the election itself had revealed anything about the Republicans and labor, it was that the party was divided. Sharp differences of opinion had been apparent throughout the postwar period, and the election had done little to settle them. Many businessmen urged party support for the open shop drive. The Republican Publicity Association, an unofficial party organ, continued its vitriolic attacks upon unionists and radicals, often failing to distinguish between the two. At the same time other Republicans rejected antilabor extremism. In Congress, progressive stalwarts such as Senators Borah, La Follette, Johnson, and George W. Norris would join forces in the House with such Republicans as John I. Nolan of California and John G. Cooper of Ohio, both former union officials and friendly to organized labor's aspirations. The ranks of Republican progressives in general, while divided and demoralized, contained many a labor sympathizer.

The president-elect's own position was as unclear after the vote as it had been during the campaign. He seemed to respond to the views of the last person to advise him. On the whole, the advice he received was conservative and critical of labor's political maneuvers, yet generally cautious and undogmatic. Harding responded favorably to the counsel of former Senator George Sutherland of Utah and former President William Howard Taft, both of whom, in 1920 and 1921 at least, were concerned as much about antilabor extremism as about labor's "arrogance." Occasionally the alert listener could even detect the progressive voices of William Allen White and Raymond Robins in the Harding camp, warning against rightwing influences. And of course the vice-president-elect had already sought to dissuade the business community from an assault upon labor.

Still, laborites could not be complacent. If Harding had not endorsed the antiunion drive, neither had he repudiated it. Jonathan Bourne, Jr., president of the Republican Publicity Association, remained Harding's friend and received no rebuke; as late as 1919 Harding's name had appeared on the organization's letterhead. Labor leaders could not fail to be apprehensive about an administration that contained unknown, but obviously purely political, appointees as Harding's crony Harry M. Daugherty, the new attorney general. Harding's tendency to be swayed by the latest and most forceful advice could place his fellow Ohioan in a key position of influence.

Harding received much unsolicited advice about labor affairs. Newspapers such as the *Wall Street Journal* and the Washington *Post* called for the repeal of the labor legislation of the Wilson period. Bourne's Republican Publicity Association urged party endorsement of the open shop as a means of opposing "the cruel autocracy of Mr. Gompers." Business groups, encouraged by the prospects of a friendly administration, pressed their assault upon unionism, and one executive reported that since the election the workers "have lost their

old-time frisky spirit." The collapse of labor's political ambitions had stung the employees, and employers reported that
they were getting much more work out of their men since
the election.[1]

Men closer to the president-elect counseled restraint. Immediately after the election, Sutherland urged Harding to
meet with several labor leaders through an invitation from
Ralph M. Easley and John Hays Hammond of the National
Civic Federation. The unionists, Sutherland declared, had
been chastened by the election, and they would no doubt be
eager to "establish . . . themselves on a friendly footing."
Sutherland, who supported the open shop as a means of
preserving individual freedom, urged Harding to reject the
advice of those who counseled him to lead a crusade against
the unions. "I do not think," he wrote, "it would be wise to
adopt a course of drastic opposition which would incur their
enmity and deprive us of their help in case of trouble." Harding
agreed with Sutherland, pledging himself to a moderate course.
His administration, he vowed, would not seek confrontation
but would attempt to promote harmony and accord.[2]

To Will Hays, chairman of the Republican National Committee and engineer of the 1920 victory, the resounding defeat
of Cox (and hence of Gompers) provided the party with an
opportunity to woo organized labor from the Democrats and
to wed it to the GOP. In December 1920 he sent Harding a
long memorandum prepared by Harry Fidler, a unionist who
was serving as a special representative on labor matters for the
committee. Wrote Hays, "I am so impressed with [Fidler's
views] . . . that I want you to have this letter." Harding, he
was certain, would find it "quite worth while."[3]

Fidler started from the premise that the labor vote was

[1] *Wall Street Journal*, Nov. 4, 1920; Washington *Post*, Nov. 7, 1920;
New York *Times*, Nov. 5 and 7, 1920.

[2] Sutherland to Harding, Nov. 10, 1920, and Jan. 4, 1921, Sutherland
Papers, Boxes 3 and 4; Harding to Sutherland, Jan. 9, 1921, *ibid.*, Box 4.

[3] Will Hays to Harding, Dec. 18, 1920, Harding Papers, Box 655.

crucial for the future of the Republican party. While it had not been harmful in the recent election, it could defeat the GOP in the future unless the party took immediate steps "to use this opportunity to utterly crush Mr. Gompers." The AFL leader, Fidler argued, had been discredited by the election, further weakening his influence in the labor movement. Yet despite his antagonistic attitude toward Harding, and despite his loss of prestige, Gompers would now seek to ingratiate himself with the GOP. He would use the friendly offices of the National Civic Federation and would employ the same idealistic rhetoric that had fooled Woodrow Wilson so often. Fidler advised Harding not to compromise with Gompers, not to "admit him into the councils of the next administration." He predicted, "If we make the right moves and get under Mr. Gompers' guard, we can break forever the alliance between union labor and [the] Democracy . . . , the strongest link in the Democratic Party's chain." Indeed, Fidler went further. By smashing Gompers and by encouraging his opponents within the labor movement, he emphasized, "The Republican party has a chance today to get control of the AF of L."[4]

All Harding's advisers, whether they urged destruction of, control over, or indifference toward organized labor, agreed on one thing: the appointment of the new secretary of labor would be a crucial indication of the intentions of the administration. Wrote Fidler, "The key to the whole situation is the Department of Labor." Gompers, he predicted, would scheme to have someone sympathetic to him appointed; if Harding resisted and appointed an anti-Gompers unionist such as a representative of one of the railway brotherhoods, he would do much toward destroying the AFL president's power and

[4] Harry Fidler to Hays, Nov. 24, 1920, enclosed in Hays to Harding, Dec. 18, 1920, Harding Papers, Box 655. Unfortunately there is no record of Harding's reaction to Fidler's views. In March 1921 Harding appointed Fidler, an officer in the Brotherhood of Locomotive Engineers, as vice-chairman of the Federal Board of Vocational Education.

toward aligning organized labor with the GOP. Leaders of the open shop campaign adamantly opposed the naming of any union official, since in their view the department under Wilson had been little more than an extension of organized labor's power. Said John M. Glenn, secretary of the Illinois Association of Manufacturers, labor arrogance could be blunted only if Harding refrained from choosing a man "who carries a union card."[5]

Leaders of organized labor, of course, hoped for a friend in the cabinet. Unionists had worked for years for the creation of a separate department devoted to labor matters. Finally established in 1913, under William B. Wilson it had indeed provided organized labor with a voice in the government. Labor officials reacted sharply against postelection rumors regarding the curtailing of some of its functions and sought to persuade the president-elect to follow Woodrow Wilson's precedent by appointing someone active in the labor movement. Gompers himself urged Harding to name a representative of labor, "a man who has had . . . experience [and] contact with the great mass of labor."[6]

Within the GOP there was wide disagreement. Senators Poindexter and Frelinghuysen charged that the department had become an appendage of the Democratic party, declaring that the president ought to eliminate completely the influence of Gompers. To William Howard Taft, however, an AFL man would be acceptable, for the administration had to get along with labor. Although the former president shared some of the apprehension over the growth of union power, he did not fear the naming of a unionist, for Harding, unlike Wilson, would keep him in line. Sutherland concurred, arguing that Harding

[5] *Ibid.*; New York *Times*, Dec. 31, 1920.
[6] William Chenery, "The Department of Labor: An Appraisal," *The Survey*, XLV (Feb. 26, 1921), 763-65; Gompers to Harding, Feb. 7, 1921, Gompers Letterbooks, Vol. 275. See also New York *Times*, Feb. 25, 26, 1921.

should not risk alienating the unions by appointing a known antagonist.[7]

The appointment was one of the last Harding filled and he weighed various choices. Newspapers, unionists, and politicians speculated as to the criteria the president-elect would base his decision on, but Harding did not publicly reveal his thinking. He told Sutherland that he wanted "to combat the socialistic idea and would like to have a strong union labor man." Certainly, a unionist would help to strengthen his position with organized labor, but it would also antagonize a large body of business and antiradical opinion. Nonetheless, the names that most frequently appeared in public discussion were those of unionists or labor sympathizers, such as T. V. O'Connor, president of the Longshoremen's Union; James Duncan, an AFL vice president whom Gompers favored; John I. Nolan, a California congressman who had once been a union official; and Raymond Robins, a reformer and social worker from Chicago.[8]

Sutherland, Taft, Oscar Straus, Nicholas Murray Butler, Charles D. Hilles, and other Republicans made inquiries for Harding about the various candidates. Sutherland felt that Nolan had socialistic tendencies, but he reported that Duncan was free of that stigma. Taft felt that either would be competent and useful to the party in its efforts to get along with labor. Robins' advocacy of recognition of the Soviet Union, his involvement in the progressive union movement, and his outspoken opposition to compulsory arbitration ap-

[7] Poindexter to S. L. Johnson, Jan. 17, 1921, and to Alfred Bickford, Jan. 31, 1921, Poindexter Papers, Series VI, Box 6; Frelinghuysen to Joseph M. Brown, Jan. 18, 1921, Frelinghuysen Papers, File Cabinets; Taft to Charles D. Hilles, Dec. 18, 1920, and to Loyall A. Osborne, Jan. 10, 1921, Taft Letterbooks, Vol. 99; Sutherland to Harding, Dec. 22, 1920, Harding Papers, Box 656.

[8] Harding to Sutherland, Dec. 24, 1920, Harding Papers, Box 656; statement by Raymond Robins, Feb. 1, 1931, in Herman Hagedorn Papers (Manuscript Division, Library of Congress), Box 3; hereafter cited as Hagedorn Papers; Gompers to Duncan, Dec. 28 and 30, 1920, Gompers-AFL Papers, Box 41.

peared to rule him out. The front runner seemed to be O'Connor. Not only had the longshoremen's leader broken with the Democrats to support the Republican ticket but, one railroad executive reported, if the post had to go to a union man, O'Connor was probably more acceptable to businessmen than anyone else.[9]

In the end, Harding rejected all of these possibilities. Seeking to balance the demands of business and the interests of labor, as well as to tap a possible source of political strength, the president-elect chose James J. Davis of Indiana and Pennsylvania. A fraternal order executive, businessman, and former union official, Davis commanded little support from the AFL and other labor groups. Although early speculation had not mentioned him, he had worked actively for the Republican nominees, and Harding had maintained contact with him. Chief among his desirable attributes were his Republican orthodoxy, his continued (although inactive) membership in a union, his business interests, and his leadership in the Loyal Order of Moose, a fraternal organization to which Harding himself belonged. Indeed, this latter factor was apparently a major consideration, for Harding was much impressed with the thousands of telegrams and letters that he received from Davis' Moose supporters.[10]

[9] For various accounts and speculations regarding the appointment of the secretary of labor, see Nicholas Murray Butler, *Across the Busy Years: Recollections and Reflections*, 2 vols. (New York, 1939), I, 399; Straus, "Visit to President-elect Harding . . . December 28, 1920," in Diary Material, 1919-1923, Straus Papers, Box 24; Sutherland to Harding, Jan. 4, 1921, Sutherland Papers, Box 4; A. S. Gilbert to Charles D. Hilles, Dec. 10, 1920, and E. E. Loomis to Hilles, Dec. 29, 1920, Charles D. Hilles Papers (Yale University Library), Box 201; hereafter cited as Hilles Papers; and statement by Raymond Robins, Feb. 1, 1931, Hagedorn Papers, Box 3.

[10] Harding to Davis, Jan. 21 and Feb. 14, 1921, Harding Papers, Box 653; various communications from members of the Loyal Order of Moose to Harding, 1921, Harding Papers, Box 486. The *Moose News* of Dec. 1920 (Cincinnati Lodge No. 2) ran a front-page picture of Harding, a life member of the Marion Lodge. Under the sketch was the caption "Howdy, Pap." Harding Papers, Box 662. In 1920 total Moose membership amounted to nearly 600,000.

Davis, a political unknown at the time of his appointment, was born on October 27, 1873, in Tredegar, South Wales. Emigrating with his parents to the United States in 1881, he grew up in western Pennsylvania. After apprenticeship as an iron puddler, he worked in the steel mills in Pittsburgh and Birmingham. He moved to Elwood, Indiana, in 1893, where he held various offices in the Amalgamated Association of Iron, Steel, and Tin Workers of America, an organization that declined rapidly after the 1892 Homestead strike. Between 1898 and 1907 he held local political offices and then started his organizational work with the Moose. Davis began banking activities in Pittsburgh and founded a jewelry concern which supplied Moose with their pins and insignia. He also ran a real estate service that specialized in building for and renting to Moose organizations. As Supreme Dictator and Reorganizer of the Moose, he succeeded in enrolling many new members, for every one of which he received a commission. Forty-eight years old when he entered Harding's cabinet, Davis' banking, real estate, and fraternal activities had made him wealthy.

Politically, Davis was an orthodox Republican. He had been a Roosevelt candidate for delegate from Pennsylvania to the 1912 GOP convention, but had withdrawn in favor of an organization delegate, and thereafter he remained a party regular. Eventually he served two terms in the United States Senate as a loyal Mellon Republican.[11]

Although Davis maintained membership in the Iron, Steel, and Tin Workers union, he had not been active in the labor movement for fifteen years. Never a militant unionist, he regarded the relationship between worker and employer as a personal one in which unions functioned not as aggressive opponents of capital but as benevolence associations. He gloried in his early days in the steel mills and was fond of reciting the

[11] U.S. Congress, 81st Cong., 2d sess., *Biographical Directory of the American Congresses, 1774-1949* (Washington, D.C., 1950), 1061; New York *Times*, Feb. 27, 1921. See also Davis' obituary in New York *Times*, Nov. 22, 1947.

virtues of self-advancement and good hard work. When a "reformer" once complained to him of the outrageous labor conditions in the steel mills in the 1890s, Davis replied that the workers did not have to toil there. "Nobody forced me to do this," he said. "I do it because I would rather live in an iron age than in a world of ox carts." Extremely skeptical of reformers and intellectuals, he remarked, "I never knew a theorist who wasn't a sick man." Although in principle he was not opposed to strikes, he regarded them as seldom justifying the waste and bitterness they engendered. He admonished the worker to improve himself, to work hard, and to follow the precepts of Benjamin Franklin.[12]

The leaders of organized labor were not happy with Davis' appointment, regarding him as a spokesman for business interests rather than as a champion of labor. Nonetheless, he held a union card, supported collective bargaining, and spoke out against the tendency to equate organized labor with radicalism. Throughout his ten years in the cabinet, he enjoyed cordial relationships with AFL leaders and did not use his position to attack labor. As essentially a political appointee he was useful to the party as a liaison with labor and as an electioneer in labor areas.

The department atrophied in the 1920s, carrying on routine functions such as employment services, statistics gathering, and mediation endeavors through the Conciliation Service, but ceasing to be the key to governmental labor policy. Davis' main role, Calvin Coolidge once remarked, lay in keeping labor quiet. Railroad labor matters were almost entirely beyond Department of Labor jurisdiction because of the separate Railroad Labor Board, and Secretary of Commerce Herbert C.

[12] James John Davis, *The Iron Puddler: My Life in the Rolling Mills and What Came of It* (New York, 1922), 107, 151, 176-77, 180, 185, and 268. See also Joseph Mitchell Chapple, *"Our Jim": A Biography* [of James J. Davis] (Boston, 1928), 249, and Roger W. Babson, *Actions and Reactions: An Autobiography of Roger W. Babson*, rev. ed. (New York, 1949), 191-92.

Hoover became the chief agent of most other labor policies in the Harding and Coolidge administrations. Davis was an effective political speaker, and he kept the department free of scandal while conducting its routine functions. But the Department of Labor declined in prestige and influence under him and, although he occasionally emerged to assert himself forthrightly, his relative inactivity contrasted sharply with the vigor of his predecessor and successors.[13]

While Davis lacked force, Secretary of Commerce Herbert C. Hoover filled the vacuum. Hoover regarded his colleague as an amiable fellow who "had a genuine genius for friendship and associational activities," but he felt that Davis was in charge of labor affairs only "from a technical point of view." Indeed, Hoover had told Harding that he would enter the cabinet only on the condition that he "have a voice on major policies involving labor."[14] His voice proved the dominant one in the labor policies of the Republican administrations.

At the time of his appointment, Hoover was climbing toward a lofty peak of influence and power. Born on an Iowa farm in 1874, he had worked his way through Stanford University and had established himself as one of the foremost mining engineers in the world. A wealthy man before he turned forty, he began to devote his enormous energy and keen intellect to public service. During World War I his work as food administrator, his efforts toward relief in Europe, and his service on the American delegation to the peace conference stamped him as a man of outstanding administrative ability, shrewd judgment, and strong humanitarian sentiment. He was a major figure, for his recent efforts towered impressively above the ruins of the postwar world and his reputation flourished in the same

[13] For labor's opposition to Davis' appointment, see New York *Times*, Feb. 25, 1921. For Coolidge's comment, see Herbert Hoover, *The Memoirs of Herbert Hoover. II: The Cabinet and the Presidency, 1921-1933* (New York, 1952), 101. Davis' predecessor was William B. Wilson and his successor, Frances Perkins, both much more closely identified with the labor movement and social reform than was Davis.

[14] Hoover, *Memoirs*, II, 101.

soil that choked the reputations of many others. Leaders in both the Republican and the Democratic parties courted him, and an eager public listened to this man who claimed no followers but who seemed to radiate such strength and purpose.[15]

His basic intellectual commitment was to "American Individualism," which phrase he believed encompassed the unique virtues and values of American life. The American way was the way of equality of opportunity, of personal spontaneity and freedom, of steady material and social progress through voluntary activity, and of rejection of abstract political and economic dogmas. This way was truly the progressive way, the liberal way, and, since it followed the path already cleared by the forefathers, also the conservative way. It was not the way of "individualism run riot," Hoover declared, but of individualism "tempered with that firm and fixed [American] ideal . . . an equality of opportunity."[16]

In Hoover's view, government had an extremely difficult and delicate function, not simply an activist one. The men in command of the government had to be vigorous but cautious, to be influential but restrained, to urge and promote and publicize but not to coerce. Extremists of the right and of

[15] For Hoover's early life and career the best source is Herbert Hoover, *The Memoirs of Herbert Hoover. I: Years of Adventure, 1874-1920* (New York, 1951). See also Eugene Lyons' uncritical biography, *Herbert Hoover: A Biography* (Garden City, N.Y., 1948 and 1964), chapts. 1-7, and Hoover's obituary, New York *Times*, Nov. 21, 1964. For testaments to Hoover's stature after the war, see Richard Hofstadter, "Herbert Hoover and the Crisis of American Individualism," in *The American Political Tradition and the Men Who Made It* (New York, 1948), 286, and Samuel Haber, *Efficiency and Uplift: Scientific Management in the Progressive Era, 1890-1920* (Chicago, 1964), 156-57. Hoover led the field in the 1920 Michigan *Democratic* primary.

[16] The best summary of Hoover's social philosophy is his slim volume, *American Individualism* (Garden City, N.Y., 1922). The words quoted here are from a 1934 reprinting, pp. 8-9. His views are further outlined in his *Memoirs*, especially vols. II and III. Throughout his long public career, his ideas about government and society were remarkably consistent. See Carl N. Degler, "The Ordeal of Herbert Hoover," *The Yale Review*, III (Summer 1963), 563-64.

the left had oversimplified conceptions of the nature of government and its place in a free society. Reactionaries clung to laissez faire views, rejecting all governmental activity beyond the barest functions. Radicals on the left including not only socialists and communists, but also many misguided liberals regarded coercive government as a panacea that could meet complex social problems through direct controls or regulation. Hoover argued that both were wrong, for government's role was more complex and subtle than either envisioned. The proper function of government was to serve as a focal point for ideas and information; to advise businessmen, workers, and farmers; to promote mutual understanding and cooperation through the encouragement of voluntary associational activity; and to refrain from direct, coercive action except in the most dire emergencies. Nor should government be passive. Its promotional, advisory, and information-dispensing functions would be pursued vigorously. Government officials, with the ability to see the whole picture, would exert strong leadership and would guide and channel the nation's resources and energies. The good society would be achieved not through the police power of the state but through the state's unique ability to gather information and to persuade its citizens to undertake their activities in conformity with that information. Hoover declared, "the government could [best] be an influence . . . not by compulsory laws . . . but by leadership." It was only through this combination of leadership and restraint that the affairs of an increasingly complex and interdependent society could be regulated in a manner consistent with individual liberty.[17]

In addition to this ideological framework, Hoover brought the attitudes and methods of the industrial engineer with him to the Department of Commerce. He was relentless in his pursuit of efficiency and sought to make the department a

[17] The quotation is from Hoover, *Memoirs*, II, 102.

fount of ideas and information for the use of industry, agriculture, labor, and the citizenry at large. A group of young engineers and managers came with him to serve in Washington, and he turned them loose on economic and social problems that reduced production and impeded distribution. With their chief, these young men worked ceaselessly to apply Hoover's ideas, while at the same time shunning the coercive powers of government.

Hoover quickly became a dominant figure in the administrations of Harding and Coolidge. An able and energetic administrator, he was a powerful and often decisive influence in matters of agriculture, transportation, foreign trade, broadcasting, development of resources, industry, disaster relief, and labor. Under Hoover, the Department of Commerce continually expanded its activities, providing expert information and astute leadership, and seeking to infuse American life with the spirit of efficiency and social purpose. "I cannot tell you," wrote Coolidge's private secretary in 1923, "how many things I feel we are dependent on you about."[18]

At the same time, the Department of Commerce became a political platform for its aggressive and dynamic head. His lieutenants, completely loyal to their chief, spread the gospels of efficiency and the efficacy of engineering methods. His own pronouncements and activities gained wide publicity and respect. Bypassing the traditional foci of Republican political

[18] For Hoover's activities in the 1920s, see Lyons, *Herbert Hoover*, chapt. 14, and Hoover's *Memoirs*, II. Secondary accounts that emphasize the limitations of Hoover's approach include Hofstadter, "Herbert Hoover and the Crisis of American Individualism," 289-91, and Arthur M. Schlesinger, Jr., *The Age of Roosevelt*. I: *The Crisis of the Old Order, 1919-1933* (Boston, 1957), 83-87. Accounts that emphasize Hoover's contributions and perspicacity are David A. Shannon, *Between the Wars: America, 1919-1941* (Boston, 1965), 38-44, and esp. William Appleman Williams, *The Contours of American History* (Cleveland, 1961), 425-38. The reliance of the Coolidge administration upon Hoover is indicated in C. Bascom Slemp to Hoover, Oct. 19, 1923, Calvin Coolidge Papers (Manuscript Division, Library of Congress), File 175; hereafter cited as Coolidge Papers.

power, Hoover turned the department into an unorthodox, but extremely effective, vehicle for his political ambitions.[19]

Nowhere were Hoover's political and economic concepts more apparent or actively applied than in the field of labor.[20] Alarmed by the unrest of postwar America and apprehensive over the spread of radicalism throughout the world, he regarded the labor problem as a basic one for American individualism to solve. Here, as in every area of controversy, extremists had readymade solutions. Reactionaries urged the destruction of labor organizations and the relegation of the worker to a subservient and deprived status. Radicals sought a dictatorship of the proletariat, the destruction of private enterprise, or, at very least, the imposition of drastic governmental controls.

These cures were worse than the disease. Properly understood, the roles of labor and capital were complementary, not antagonistic. Properly pursued, the role of government was to bring the two together, not to crush or shackle either. Thus, the government's function in combating unrest, unemployment, and radicalism was not as an author of drastic legislation, but rather as a conductor of scientific studies designed to eliminate waste, inefficiency, and joblessness, as an encourager of cooperation and accord, and as a promoter of a spirit of service on the part of both labor and capital through the removal of barriers of hatred and distrust. The old categories of labor and capital, the old rhetoric about classes and masses, the old assumptions about the inevitability of hostility and strife that had dominated Europe and that threatened America, had to be rejected. The government, personified in the 1920s by Hoover himself, had to work actively to increase production, to promote accord,

[19] Views that emphasize Hoover's political maneuvering in the 1920s are Hofstadter, "Herbert Hoover and the Crisis of American Individualism," 291-93, and Schlesinger, *Crisis of the Old Order*, 87-89. See also Kent Michael Schofield, "The Figure of Herbert Hoover in the 1928 Campaign" (unpublished Ph.D. dissertation, University of California-Riverside, 1966).

[20] Hoover participated (and usually was the most influential figure) in virtually every major labor policy in the decade, and most appointments to labor-oriented posts passed over his desk.

and to educate businessmen, workers, and the public in general to awareness of their responsibilities and their interdependence.[21]

Hoover's view of labor organizations was less clear. In theory, since labor and capital were mutually dependent, there was no need for either militant labor unions or aggressive employer groups. Hoover proposed at various times organizations of workers within factories and businesses which would function through shop committees, whose members would be employees of the establishment chosen by democratic ballot. Since there was no need for militancy, these committees would cooperate with management, representing the workers, but in an atmosphere of accord rather than in one of tension. If to labor leaders Hoover's ideas smacked of open shopism and company unionism, this was just a further indication of the prevalence of the outmoded and irrelevant stereotypes that lingered and that government would try to remove.[22]

These shop committees might be the wave of the future, but in the 1920s there existed strong and well-established labor unions. Hoover certainly had no intention of seeking their destruction or decline. He worked well with their leaders, frequently consulting Gompers, Lewis, William Green, William Doak, and others in the AFL and railroad brotherhoods. Combining a shrewd recognition of existing realities with cautious hope for a better future, Hoover realized that these unions were necessary and important. Public officials, in their efforts to achieve industrial harmony and to promote the idea

[21] Hoover's views on labor are expressed in *American Individualism*, 1-13 and 32-47, and, more concretely, in *Memoirs*, II, 101-108. See also the interesting comments in Herbert C. Hoover, *Principles of Mining: Valuation, Organization, and Administration* (New York, 1909), 161-67.

[22] "Mr. Hoover's Labor Plans," *Literary Digest*, LXVII (Dec. 4, 1920), 12-13. See also Stephen J. Scheinberg, "The Development of Corporation Labor Policy, 1900-1940" (unpublished Ph.D. disesertation, University of Wisconsin, 1966), 140-51. The "shop committee" idea was part of the "industrial democracy" system advocated by Boston businessman Edward Filene and others.

of service, could work with men such as Gompers and Lewis, and would often find them more sensible and cooperative than some members of the business community.[23] Yet these unions had been born in an atmosphere of strife and ill will; all too often their battle-scarred officers represented narrow and selfish interests and used the rhetoric of class conflict. Many businessmen continued to exploit labor, and many labor leaders continued to emphasize antagonism. It was the duty of government to persuade both groups, to encourage understanding and trust, to discourage strikes and hostility.

While the government could work effectively with a Samuel Gompers or a John L. Lewis for the amelioration of difficulties, it would often find that these veterans of labor wars were skeptical of the doctrines of industrial harmony and cooperation. Hoover's attitude reflected both appreciation and restraint. He could say quite sincerely that "our nation is very fortunate in having the American Federation of Labor," for the aggressive forces of radicalism "have been met in the front line trenches by the Federation . . . and routed at every turn." At the same time, this appreciation of American labor's services did not lead him to encourage expansion of the traditional labor unions, rooted as they were in past conflicts.[24]

In the troubled postwar years when Hoover's ideas would be put to a severe test, one of his strongest assets was friend-

[23] There is an extensive literature that emphasizes the eagerness of labor leaders in the 1920s to prove the efficiency and economic usefulness of labor unions and to accept the doctrines of the New Era. See, for example, Milton Lewis Farber, "Changing Attitudes of the American Federation of Labor Toward Business and Government, 1929-1933" (unpublished Ph.D. dissertation, Ohio State University, 1959), chapt. 1; Nadworny, Scientific Management and the Unions, 148; James O. Morris, Conflict Within the AFL: A Study of Craft Versus Industrial Unionism, 1901-1938 (Ithaca, N.Y., 1958), 72-84; and Irving Bernstein, The Lean Years: A History of the American Worker, 1920-1933 (Boston, 1960), 83-108. Countertendencies, however, were powerful as well, as evidenced by the 1922 strikes, labor's hostility toward the courts, and the unions' political ventures between 1922 and 1925.

[24] Hoover's comment on the AFL is in Memoirs, II, 102.

ship with Samuel Gompers. The AFL chieftain opposed Hoover's shop committee ideas, but he realized that the new cabinet member was obviously not a militant open shop advocate. Moreover, Hoover and Gompers had served together on several wartime relief commissions and as delegates to the Versailles Conference, always with mutual respect. Thus, when organized labor began to seek friends in the Harding administration, the secretary of commerce was a likely candidate.

Actually, Gompers had been drawing closer to Hoover even before the election. On September 29 he had met with Hoover at the request of some prominent industrial engineers who wanted the AFL president to urge Hoover to accept the presidency of the Federated American Engineering Societies. After November 2 the two men kept in touch. Both were interested in the social ramifications of the industrial engineering movement. Hoover felt that engineering methods and studies could be of great value in seeking technological solutions to labor problems and therefore in reducing discontent. He introduced to Gompers several of his associates in the industrial efficiency movement and on November 17 he addressed the AFL executive council, explaining the social goals of the engineering societies. For his part, Gompers welcomed these contacts with Hoover and the engineers. He had been an uncompromising critic of early efficiency schemes such as the Taylor system, but he now felt that the narrow clock-watching and speedup aspects of the engineering approach had been repudiated and that liaison with Hoover and his colleagues would be advantageous to the AFL. In particular, Gompers knew that recent engineering studies had been critical of the employer-sponsored movement to reduce wages and that engineering studies had been emphasizing the responsibility of businessmen for recent production difficulties. Thus, the AFL president was receptive to Hoover's overtures, for these would help labor to maintain a politically useful association and to cooperate with a movement whose programs lent support to labor's fight to keep wages up.[25]

Gompers sought to forge other links to the new administration also. While he had no direct contact with Harding, he did confer with people close to the president-elect. Through Ralph M. Easley of the National Civic Federation he was in touch with George Sutherland. A chance meeting aboard a train turned into a lengthy discussion of political affairs with William Howard Taft. Oscar Straus was another Republican who discussed the attitude of the new administration toward labor with both Gompers and Harding.[26]

Nor was the labor movement content to rest its interest on the assumption of friendship within the Harding regime. In November 1920 the AFL executive council appointed a special committee "to devise ways and means of meeting the nation-wide attempt to destroy the American Labor Movement." A special meeting of prominent unionists was held in February 1921 to consider action to regain the public confidence that had been lost since the war and to battle labor's enemies in the corporations and the government.[27] The Harding administration's plans and policies were suspect, so labor's leadership must be prepared for all contingencies.

When Harding was inaugurated in March 1921 the labor picture and the attitudes of many of those about to exercise

[25] "Mr. Hoover's Labor Plans," 12-13; Gompers to Morris L. Cooke, Nov. 20, 1920, and to Hoover, Nov. 30, 1920, Gompers Letterbooks, Vol. 271; entries for Sept. 29, 1920, and Jan. 29, 1921, Gompers engagement books, Vols. 15 and 16, Gompers-AFL Papers; "Conference in Office of President Gompers . . . on the Question of Wage Theory," May 27, 1921, report in Gompers-AFL Papers, Box 57. See also Scheinberg, "The Development of Corporation Labor Policy," 145-46.

[26] Gompers to James Duncan, Dec. 28 and 30, 1920, Gompers-AFL Papers, Box 41; entry for Jan. 28, 1921, Gompers engagement book, Vol. 16, Gompers-AFL Papers.

[27] Report of special committee, Dec. 29, 1920, Gompers-AFL Papers, Box 41; Gompers to Warren S. Stone, grand chief of the Brotherhood of Locomotive Engineers, Feb. 1, 1921, and to S. G. Savage, secretary-treasurer, District 6, United Mine Workers of America, Feb. 13, 1921, Gompers-AFL Papers, Box 41.

power were little clearer than they had been immediately after the election. While organized labor would not be friendless, the shrill cry of antilabor extremism still sounded. The appointment of the secretary of labor, widely predicted as a key to Harding's intentions, only deepened the uncertainty, for Davis was neither a foe nor a committed supporter of organized labor. The secretary of commerce, obviously a major figure in labor policies, voiced mild open shop concepts, but his respect for Gompers was so widely known as to lead some Republicans to accuse him of being virtually an agent of the AFL.[28] The president seemed as vacillating as ever. Laborites knew that he was pledged to take the country back to normalcy, but they did not know what the term meant as applied to labor matters. Thus, as Harding assumed office, the only certainty was that labor leaders and working people in general would have to await the administration's response to concrete situations to determine exactly where they stood.

[28] Fidler to Will Hays, Nov. 24, 1920, enclosed in Hays to Harding, Dec. 18, 1920, Harding Papers, Box 655; Raymond Robins to William Boyce Thompson, Nov. 25, 1920, Robins Papers, Box 17.

4 The Open Shop and Immigration Restriction

THE HARDING ADMINISTRATION was a time of hectic activity in the field of government-labor relations. As Secretary of Labor Davis later recalled his first months on the job, "In those days we worked day and night. . . . It seemed then that the whole universe had business with the Secretary of Labor."[1] While unemployment continued at high levels, the campaigns to deflate wages and to hobble labor unions reached their peaks. Labor strife racked the soft coal fields of West Virginia. Strikes rocked the meatpacking and maritime industries, and the railroad unions chafed under the heavy hand of the Railroad Labor Board.

Of all the issues that faced the new administration in its early days, none were of more immediate importance to organized labor and its ardent foes than the open shop and immigration. If the aggressively antilabor elements within the GOP could secure party support for the open shop movement, they would take a major step toward establishing their influence over labor policy in the coming years. At the same time, these antilabor forces combated efforts to restrict immigration, feeling that the success of the open shop crusade depended in good part upon the availability of cheap foreign labor. After much internal dissension and debate the Republican party rejected proposals to link itself formally to the open shop.[2] Equally to the displeasure of many businessmen and party stalwarts, the GOP sponsored and passed America's first generally restrictive immigration laws. Thus, these early tests of the Harding administration demonstrated that the president would not lead a frontal assault upon organized labor. Still, laborites could not be complacent, for their foes were high in party councils. With antilabor feeling still running high and with labor's officialdom largely excluded from influence within the government, it was a difficult time for the unions, causing one unionist to declare, "The federal administration, while not wholly hostile, is anything but friendly."[3]

In 1921 organized labor faced difficult times. Political defeat in 1920, unemployment, the public reaction against its postwar activities, and the virulence of the open shop drive combined to weaken its influence and to put it on the defensive. Antilabor forces continued to press their views upon Harding. According to Gompers, the war had produced a sort of national nervous strain, which in turn gave rise to numerous unwise proposals. The AFL's president spent much of the year fighting legislation directed against organized labor. He opposed an antipicketing proposal, a measure to allow the importation of Chinese labor into Hawaii, a bill to abolish the federal Board of Vocational Education, and other legislative efforts. Open shop groups urged adoption of antistrike railroad labor legislation, while the Kansas Court of Industrial Relations, with its implication of compulsory arbitration, continued to claim wide support. Moreover, there were repeated assaults upon the Department of Labor in the guise

[1] Davis to E. J. Henning, June 5, 1925, James J. Davis Papers (Manuscript Division, Library of Congress), Box 41; hereafter cited as Davis Papers.

[2] Of course, on occasion members of Harding's administration were able to indulge their antilabor, open shop sympathies. Thus, after his injunction request in the 1922 shopmen's strike, Attorney General Daugherty proclaimed, "So long [as] and to the extent that I can speak for the government . . . I will use the power of the government to prevent the labor unions . . . from destroying the open shop." (Quoted in William E. Leuchtenberg, *The Perils of Prosperity, 1914-1932* [Chicago, 1958], 99.) Daugherty, however, did not always (or even often) "speak for the government," and circumstances such as those surrounding the rail strike were not usual.

[3] John Philip Frey to W. A. Appleton, Nov. 2, 1921, Frey Papers, Box 1.

of reorganization of the executive branch. In all, reported the AFL legislative committee, Congress was "sizzling with reactionary legislation." "Labor," it predicted, "will have to fight mightily [to thwart] the reactionary elements that control the members of Congress."[4]

While few of the legislative proposals became law, the open shop drive proved quite successful. Although the term *open shop* had a variety of definitions, it always meant trouble for organized labor. Businesses pledged to operate under the American plan, which called for nonrecognition of unions and individual bargaining between the employer and the employee. Theoretically a man was free to belong to a union, but the employer would not deal with any labor organization, except, perhaps, one consisting only of workers in the shop, without outside affiliation. Supported by some politicians and businessmen as a means of protecting the nonunion employee, it was usually linked to the yellow-dog contract, signaling an all-out assault upon the very concept of meaningful collective bargaining. Thus, according to a leading open shop advocate, "We will not employ an individual . . . [who] does not sign an individual contract in which it is expressed that he is not and will not become a member of a labor organization while in our employ." Many employers even refused to do business with firms that did not also endorse the American plan.[5]

The movement had gained momentum immediately after the war. Although its focus was upon local conditions, such national groups and corporations as the National Association of Manufacturers, the American Founders' Association, the United States Steel Company, and the Pennsylvania Railroad

[4] Gompers to Frey, June 23, 1921, Gompers Letterbooks, Vol. 280; "Report of the [AFL] Legislative Committee," *American Federationist*, XXVIII (Nov. 1921), 973-74, and XXVIII (Dec. 1921), 1036-41; New York *Times*, Dec. 7, 1921.

[5] Allen M. Wakstein, "The Origins of the Open Shop Movement, 1919-1920," *Journal of American History*, LI (Dec. 1964), 57-59, 98, and 128; Philip A. Taft, *Organized Labor in American History* (New York, 1964), 364.

gave it vital support. By the fall of 1920 almost every industrial center in the country had an open shop organization. "Lined up behind the 'open' shop," one journalist reported, "are 23 national associations of industry, 540 employers' organizations in 247 cities of 44 states, and 1665 local chambers of commerce." A number of cities, including Detroit and Seattle, announced that they had signed up virtually all area businessmen in support of the antiunion drive.[6]

Although the campaign had begun on the local level, many businessmen expected the triumphant GOP to give it political and perhaps even legislative support. At very least open shop leaders expected Harding to endorse antistrike legislation and to speak in favor of wage reductions. To these demands, the president reacted with characteristic ambivalence. He did inform Gompers that it was the workers' duty to accept wage slashes in the deflationary postwar months, and his annual message in December 1921 did contain favorable references to some form of compulsory arbitration, but he shied away from aggressive pronouncements. To Bourne, who urged his endorsement of an antistrike railroad labor proposal, Harding replied sympathetically, "I am not unmindful of the merits of the measure." But, while such legislation might be needed to cope with a threatened rail strike, "I would much rather settle our industrial disputes amicably and promote a spirit of accord."[7] Open shop supporters kept pressure upon the president, finding him, as did Bourne, verbally favorable to their efforts but unwilling to commit himself to action.

Other prominent Republicans were more certain of the desirability of the party's endorsement of the antilabor program. Bourne pledged the Republican Publicity Association to a

[6] Taft, *Organized Labor in American History*, 364; Wakstein, "The Open Shop Movement," 128; "A Battle of Titans," *Current Opinion*, LXX (March 1921), 295-99.

[7] Gompers to Harding, Aug. 19, 1921, Gompers Letterbooks, Vol. 281; New York *Times*, Dec. 7, 1921; Bourne to Harding, May 28, 1921, and Harding's reply, June 1, 1921, Harding Papers, Box 693.

campaign in favor of the open shop and against Samuel Gompers and "the false economic doctrines he espouses." The director of the Bureau of the Budget, Charles G. Dawes, and the attorney general, Harry M. Daugherty, were both vigorous proponents of the American plan. Senator Poindexter sponsored the 1921 antistrike bill, urging businessmen to "get together and make a fight on a reasonable basis for industrial freedom and the country will back you, just as it backed Judge Gary" in his opposition to the steelworkers' union.[8]

Men such as Bourne, Daugherty, Dawes, and Poindexter were eager to link the party directly to the open shop effort. Motivated by politics and patriotism, they felt that the power of labor leaders had to be broken. The strikes and threatened strikes, the radical agitation, the sharp industrial depression, and the whole atmosphere of discord and unrest that pervaded the country endangered the Republic and demanded action. The nation, having defeated the foreign foe, must not fall victim to the internal menace. "The most important problem now confronting us," declared Senator Frelinghuysen, a frequent critic of organized labor, "is . . . shall this continue to be a government of, by and for the whole people, or a government of, by and for a class." Frelinghuysen, disturbed by the Russian Revolution, feared that if the open shop movement failed and labor's power went unchecked, "Sovietism" would replace American institutions.[9]

These open shop enthusiasts constituted a vocal and influential segment of the party. They often proved quite effective in their efforts to chastise organized labor, for many Americans shared their concern. Still, many Republicans considered them extreme and doctrinaire, and their views harmful and inexpedient. Secretary of Labor Davis warned one employers' association against smashing its workers'

[8] New York *Times*, Nov. 7, 1920; Poindexter to Howard Elliott, Aug. 25, 1921, Poindexter Papers, Series VI, Box 2.
[9] Undated memorandum [ca. 1919-1920] by Frelinghuysen, Frelinghuysen Papers.

unions. "Labor unions," he insisted, "are an organic growth of the times." Their destruction would lead to secret societies and to a growth in revolutionary ideas. From Emporia, Kansas, William Allen White denounced the open shop as "a conspiracy to put American laboring men into serfdom," while Secretary of Commerce Hoover encouraged efforts to fight the "obvious attempt to destroy union organization." Even conservatives drew back at the prospect of a holy war against labor under the banner of the American plan. William Howard Taft feared that the extremists among the employers would seek a decisive confrontation with labor, thus provoking even more industrial strife. Sutherland, who shared Taft's view that labor unions were valuable assets but that they should not be allowed to coerce nonunion men, was equally concerned about the militancy of businessmen. After the election he sensed apprehensively a strong "sentiment in our party . . . that the open shop is the only thing to be considered." Many industrialists and their political spokesmen were seeking not simply to protect the rights of nonunion workers but to discriminate against unionists. "I think," he wrote Harding, that "the later attitude would be the substitution of one form of intolerance for another."[10]

Republican leaders were reluctant to endorse the open shop explicitly, but enthusiasm for the American plan remained great. Of interest to many Republicans (including the president) were the antilabor efforts of Charles G. Dawes in Chicago. A rough-and-ready patriot, Dawes was deeply disturbed by the unrest and violence that swept postwar America. So, in the spring of 1923, this Illinois banker, international financial expert, government official, and vice-president-to-be

[10] Davis' speech to the National Hardwood Lumber Association, June 9, 1921, New York *Times*, June 10, 1921; Emporia *Gazette*, April 19, 1921; Hoover to Ralph M. Easley, June 10, 1921, National Civic Federation Papers (The New York Public Library), Box 58; hereafter cited as NCF Papers; Taft to Loyall A. Osborne, Jan. 10, 1921, Taft Letterbooks, Vol. 100; Sutherland to Harding, Jan. 4, 1921, Sutherland Papers, Box 4.

founded in Evanston an organization that he called the Minute Men of the Constitution. With the help of businessmen, patriotic groups, and newspapers such as the Chicago *Tribune*, it sought to promote a spirit of law and order—and to combat the influence of organized labor.

Dawes' purpose was to stand firm against both radicalism and "the arrogance and lawlessness of certain unworthy leaders of special groups." Hoping to awaken the public, he recruited young men (including many veterans), organizing them into "companies." These Minute Men stood for Americanism, providing "a definite field, a definite method and a definite platform," that would rally decent folk in support of American principles.[11]

The main thrust of this quasi-military body was against organized labor. The Minute Men did not specifically advocate the open shop in their platform, since the Supreme Court had decided that the closed shop was not unconstitutional. Still, Dawes' every reference to labor contained attacks upon its leaders. For example, according to Dawes Chicago's labor leaders were largely "gun men and criminals," and he was active in crushing the building trades unions there. Even the most respected labor leaders in the state and nation were targets of his invective. To him the president of the Illinois Federation of Labor, Victor Olander, was merely a labor demagogue, and he accused Samuel Gompers of inciting workers to violence.[12]

Labor leaders attacked the patriotic association, likening it to Mussolini's blackshirts. Dawes welcomed their opposition, for it was "helping to bring about what I want to create—a

[11] Charles G. Dawes to Harding, May 3, 1923, Harding Papers, Box 695; Dawes untitled journal, entries for June 8 and 10 and July 8, 1923, Charles G. Dawes Papers (Deering Library, Northwestern University); hereafter cited as Dawes Papers.

[12] Entry for June 24, 1923; draft of Dawes' letter to Olander, ca. late spring 1923, Dawes Papers, Private Papers, 1923; Dawes to Ralph M. Easley, Nov. 27, 1923, Subject Letter File "Minute men . . . ," all in *ibid.*

square issue between those who believe in law enforcement and those who at heart are against it." When, in the municipal elections of 1923, Chicago labor sought to unseat two local "injunction" judges, Dawes "called the Minute Men into their first battle." He believed that their votes helped to reelect the magistrates, thereby securing a victory for law and order.[13]

Dawes kept Harding informed of his antilabor activities. Soon after he founded the Minute Men, he told the president that "The labor and political demagogues are already keeping their damned mouths shut." Harding appeared not to appreciate the stridently antiunion character of Dawes' patriotic group. Mrs. Harding, he informed the Chicagoan, found the Minute Men's black and white cockade most appealing. He did report that for some reason Secretary of Labor Davis was apprehensive about the effect of the Minute Men upon organized labor's attitude toward the GOP, but he felt that Dawes could easily explain to Davis the patriotic and benevolent nature of the group. At any rate, he was pleased to learn how well Dawes was getting on with the organization and its activities.[14]

Despite his apparent naïveté and his sympathetic words, the president was unwilling to lend direct support to such activities. Harding had made this clear early in 1923 when Dawes and other open shop advocates appealed to him to adopt the open shop as a major issue in the 1924 presidential campaign. While Harding vacationed in Florida, Dawes and a group of prominent Republican businessmen and industrialists conferred with him and urged him to wage his campaign for reelection on the open shop issue. Most of them were not politicians, but all were important contributors of Republican campaign funds and many had been ardent supporters of the president in 1920.

[13] Entries for June 9 and Nov. 4, 1923, Dawes' untitled journal, *ibid*.
[14] Dawes to Harding, April 30 and May 3, 1923; Harding to Dawes, May 3 and 8, 1923, Harding Papers, Box 695.

The New York *Times* reported that they were anxious to have the Republican party come out unambiguously in favor of the open shop.[15]

Throughout the country, businessmen responded warmly to the news of this effort. Finally, after many false starts, they would be able to enlist governmental support in their attempt to put labor in its place. They felt too that the party would aid itself immeasurably in the coming election if it took a strong stand. According to one railroad executive, Harding "will gain strength from the business and agricultural interests if he comes out flatfooted for an open shop." Moreover, he predicted, unorganized workers, resentful of the elitist AFL, would swing to the GOP. Responding to front-page reports in the New York *Times*, hundreds of appreciative businessmen congratulated Dawes. The *Times* called Dawes "the chief spokesman of this movement to President Harding."[16]

Gompers had been aware for some time that these pressures were at work upon the Republican party, but he felt that the issue would be a false one if the party were so unrealistic as to embrace it. The AFL president remarked that if these businessmen did get the party to endorse an open shop plank in the platform, it would inflict upon the divided Republican party another troublesome issue. Although the open shop advocates welcomed Gompers' opposition as a challenge, Harding regretted that the labor problem threatened to intrude into politics. The groups that Dawes spoke for were admittedly prominent in the GOP, but labor cut across party lines and an antilabor appeal in the 1924 election would further fragment the party. Since foreign policy, farm problems, and an impending battle over ship subsidies were splitting the GOP

[15] Entry for Aug. 6, 1923, Dawes untitled journal, Dawes Papers; New York *Times*, April 1, 1923.

[16] New York *Times*, April 1, 1923; Frank H. Alfred to Dawes, April 18, 1923, Dawes Papers, Subject Letter File "Minute Men. . . ." There are scores of similar letters in this file.

already, one journalist remarked that Harding's attitude was "Why lug in another issue such as the open shop."[17]

Harding and the GOP withstood pressure to endorse the open shop. Dawes and Bourne had the president's sympathy, and Daugherty and others were able from time to time to launch attacks upon the unions. But in general the GOP followed the more moderate course of Taft, Sutherland, and Hoover. As with other labor issues, the party revealed a wide spectrum of opinion on the open shop, ranging from Bourne and Dawes on the aggressively antilabor extreme to progressive friends of organized labor such as La Follette, White, and Norris at the opposite end. It had to reconcile as many of these diverse interests as possible. Despite business efforts to gear the party to the open shop drive, it maintained a right-of-center but moderate consensus, allowing the peculiar circumstances of the 1920s to cripple organized labor but usually not actively aiding in the process.[18] The party was a political organism, not a doctrinaire splinter group.

Whether or not the open shop movement entered the political arena, its success depended upon a continuing surplus of labor. If an employer sought to drive out a union and the union resisted and struck, the employer could persevere only if he could readily hire substitutes. The greatest source of cheap, pliable labor in America always had been the immigrant. It was natural then in the postwar economic environment that businessmen should resist efforts to curtail immigration and that organized labor should increase its long agitation for restriction. In the lameduck session of the 66th Congress and in the early months of the Harding administration, the GOP supported sharp reductions in immigration. Moreover, in 1922 Republicans led in renewing the restrictive immigration

[17] New York *Times*, April 2 and 6, 1923; Gompers' editorial, "A National Association of 'Malefactors,' " *American Federationist*, XXX (June 1923), 495.

[18] For the outstanding exception to this statement, see chapter 6.

legislation and in 1924 supported even more sharply limited quotas. In effect, if not in intent, the party supported labor's position, opposing the demands of business and, in the view of many businessmen, hindering the open shop effort.

The debate over immigration, which had occupied the country's attention for over half a century, reached a peak after the war. After the election supporters of restriction felt confident of success, for not only had Harding indicated his belief in restriction, but the victorious GOP contained many who shared his view. In a questionnaire on immigration which the GOP Campaign Information Committee circulated before the convention, most replies from professional people, local political leaders, civic groups, and labor leaders favored restriction, while business spokesmen contended with equal vehemence that such a policy would hurt industry. Typical of the business position was the terse reply to the questionnaire of an American Tobacco Company executive, who wrote "Not enough laborers now." Business groups responded quickly to threats of immigration legislation. In March 1920 the Building Trades Employers' Association of New York City protested that "The main cause of the falling off of production . . . is the existing labor shortage"; they urged that Congress refrain from curtailing overseas supplies. Another business group petitioned Congress in a similar vein, declaring "We need every respectable, ambitious and industrial [sic] person the world can spare."[19]

To open shop sympathizers, there was an intimate connection between restriction and the success or failure of the

---

[19] These three examples of business reaction to immigration restriction are drawn from the following sources, respectively: Questionnaire and replies, ca. spring 1920, Lindsay Papers, Boxes 120-21; resolution from Building Trades Employers' Association to Sen. Miles Poindexter, March 24, 1920, Poindexter Papers, Series VI, Box 15; memorial from National Association of Merchant Tailors to House Committee on Interstate and Foreign Commerce, March 19, 1921, House of Representatives Records (Record Group 233, National Archives), Petitions and Memorials to the House Committee . . . , 67th Cong., 1st sess., 1921.

antiunion campaign. Noting that Congress had been considering anti-immigration bills, John Glenn, secretary of the Illinois Manufacturers Association asserted that these measures would have a powerful effect on his organization's drive. "The final action [by Congress on immigration] will have considerable to do with the success or failure of the open shop movement," he contended. The *Wall Street Journal* insisted that the agitation for restriction was the work of union propaganda, which sought to frighten Congress and the public with lurid descriptions of hordes of destitute Europeans invading the country. Reversing the relationship between the open shop and unrestricted immigration, the *Journal* asked rhetorically "Is there any connection between restricted immigration and the closed shop?"[20]

The 1920 Republican platform had been silent on immigration, but many Republicans sought to commit the party to restriction. Particularly important among these were Congressman Albert Johnson of Washington, whose state had witnessed a resurgence of radical labor activity, and Senator William Dillingham of Vermont, who had consistently warned of the alien menace. They found Harding openly sympathetic to their position. During the campaign he had indicated his support for immigration restriction, and later he assured Dillingham that he would make appointments to the Bureau of Immigration and Naturalization which the Vermont senator would find acceptable.[21]

Johnson did not wait for the change in administrations. Shortly after the final session of the 66th Congress convened in December 1920 he introduced sharply restrictive legislation. On February 19, 1921, the Republican-controlled Congress passed the Johnson immigration bill, but Wilson, who had

[20] Glenn is quoted in New York *Times*, Dec. 31, 1920; *Wall Street Journal*, Dec. 1, 1920. See also the *Journal* of Dec. 6, 9, and 13, 1920.
[21] Chicago *Tribune*, Sept. 15, 1920; Harding to Dillingham, Feb. 20, 1921, Harding Papers, Box 653.

steadfastly opposed similar measures in the past, vetoed it. Hence, the immigration question was one of the first that the 67th Congress undertook in the spring of 1921; on May 19, the Johnson measure, or the First Quota Law, passed. It established a quota of 3 percent per year based on 1910 census figures and was heavily weighted in favor of Northern Europeans. Under its provisions some 350,000 immigrants could enter the country each year, although, since the total from Northern Europe had dwindled and relatively few from that region were likely to emigrate, the bill actually cut immigration more sharply. The Act was due to expire on June 30, 1922, but Congress later extended it until 1924. In that year, under Johnson's leadership again, Congress enacted a permanent restriction law which provided for a 2 percent quota based upon the 1890 census figures, thus sharply reducing both total immigration and the quotas for Eastern and Southern Europe at the same time. The 1924 bill sliced the 1921 figure almost in half.[22]

The debates in Congress over these bills followed the same pattern in 1920, 1921, 1922, and 1924. Proponents of restriction argued along two lines: immigration endangered democratic institutions, and it adversely affected the American laborer, undermining American standards of living. Thus on December 11, 1920, Johnson defended his bill in the House by warning that unrestricted immigration "brings too many who are antigovernment and antiGod," and by charging that a continued influx would lengthen the nation's appalling breadlines. In April 1921 he repeated these arguments, contending that much of the country's labor trouble was traceable to the presence in the labor movement "of aliens without a vote in the United States, who do vote in those organizations, which in turn influence affairs." Criticizing business groups that favored unrestricted immigration, the Republican con-

---

[22] Frank L. Auerbach, *Immigration Laws of the United States*, 2d ed., rev. (Indianapolis, Ind., 1961), 8-10.

gressman charged that they were selfish and irresponsible, interested only in "distribution [of immigrants] in lots of 1,000 f.o.b. at the factory door."[23]

Patriotism, reaction to the war, and popular antagonism toward immigrants were the major factors that enabled the Johnson bill to pass. The AFL and other unions had lobbied for restriction for over forty years without success, but in the postwar reaction, the times were ripe for it. Some Republicans, however, sought to identify restriction as consciously prolabor in intent. In the 1924 debate Congressman Grant M. Hudson of Michigan contended that from its inception his party had always favored well-paid labor; its immigration program followed this tradition. Republican Senator Samuel Shortridge of California averred that in opposing immigration he was speaking for the AFL, which had long urged legislation. Despite these expressions, in general the Republican response in regard to immigration restriction was to the voice of popular demand, fearful of the alien faces and devious doctrines of Europe, rather than to the AFL's demands.[24]

Few Republicans opposed immigration restriction. Those who did represented urban immigrant districts or spoke for powerful manufacturing interests. Congressmen William Vare of Philadelphia and James R. Mann of Chicago voted against most restrictionist measures, asserting that restriction constituted an affront to large groups of Americans and that it choked off the supply of needed labor. The most outspoken and articulate Republican critic was Representative Fiorello La Guardia of New York City. Appealing to the great American traditions of sanctuary for the oppressed and economic opportunity, La Guardia attacked restriction and its chief administration spokesman James J. Davis, charging

[23] *Congressional Record*, 66th Cong., 3d sess., 1920, 60:227, and 67th Cong., 1st sess., 1921, 61:501 and 518.
[24] *Congressional Record*, 68th Cong., 1st sess., 1924, 65:5640 and 5743; John Higham, *Strangers in the Land: Patterns of American Nativism, 1860-1925* (New Brunswick, N.J., 1955), 305-11.

the secretary of labor with hypocrisy and dishonest. Thousands of illegal immigrants entered the country each year with Davis' knowledge, the Italian-American asserted. "There is no fear that these men will be disturbed as long as they continue to work as slaves in the mines and you are Secretary of Labor," he asserted to Davis.[25]

Such attacks did not sway Davis from his belief in restriction. He remained the administration's leading defender of this policy throughout the 1920s. Davis made his plea against unlimited immigration in speeches and articles and in a book entitled *Selective Immigration,* published in 1925.[26] The Department of Labor handled immigration affairs for the country. Indeed, the Bureau of Immigration and Naturalization was by far the most active arm of the department throughout the decade, consistently using well over half of the department's appropriations. Davis found himself dealing largely with immigration affairs, reporting in 1922 that "the time of the Secretary and the Assistant Secretary was almost entirely consumed by . . . matters arising through the Bureau of Immigration."[27]

Davis felt that immigration restriction was the most important policy that the Republicans could foster in labor's behalf. When Congress passed and Coolidge signed the permanent restriction bill in May 1924 the secretary of labor wrote the president, "This is the most important [bill to] which you will attach your signature during your term. History will record it as one of the greatest acts of your administration."

[25] For characteristic antirestriction arguments, see *Congressional Record,* 66th Cong., 3d sess., 1920, 60:178, and 68th Cong., 1st sess., 1924, 65:5933. For La Guardia's views and his scathing attack upon Davis, see La Guardia to Phil Ardissone, April 19, 1928, Fiorello La Guardia Papers (New York City Municipal Records Center), Box 2533; hereafter cited as La Guardia Papers, and La Guardia to Davis, July 3, 1928, La Guardia Papers, Box 2522.

[26] James J. Davis, *Selective Immigration* (St. Paul, 1925).

[27] Merle Fainsod and others, *Government and the American Economy,* 3d ed., rev. (New York, 1959), 169; U.S., Department of Labor, *Tenth Annual Report* (Washington, D.C., 1922), 2.

Coolidge agreed, calling restriction "undoubtedly a protection to the wage earners of this country."[28]

By the mid-1920s, immigration control had become part of the standard Republican formula, along with economy in government, tax cutting, and the tariff. Some business interests still opposed the policy, yet even these found it difficult to attack restriction. One of the chief charges against labor in 1919-1920 had been that radical labor influences were dominating the American labor movement. Businessmen in particular painted this picture of radical and militant labor, and politicians such as Poindexter and Bourne endorsed it. When restriction bills came up before Congress, however, businessmen and their supporters, whether within or outside the party, faced a dilemma. If, as they charged, labor was overly radical, how could a congressman vote against immigration laws that would stop the radical flood? Few disagreed with Senator Matthew Neely of West Virginia in 1924 when he urged restriction in the name of the American people, the American Legion, and the American Federation of Labor. "On every ship that brings immigrants to our shores," he asserted, "come those who . . . formulate plans to capture the American Federation of Labor, use its great power for wicked purposes, and vanquish its able and patriotic officers and leaders."[29] Although America's labor leaders had no intention of allowing radical aliens to take control of their organizations, such sentiments helped to justify the restrictionist policy they sought.

Restriction was a popular policy that soon found its place among the GOP's fixed verities. The party favored and supported it in spite of business opposition and largely regardless of labor's approval. If the policy was popular with labor, Republicans would not hesitate to make political capital; if

[28] Davis speech, Jan. 21, 1924, Davis Papers, Box 40; Davis to Coolidge, May 29, 1924, *ibid.*; U.S., *Annual Address of the President to the Congress of the United States* (Washington, D.C., 1925).

[29] *Congressional Record*, 68th Cong., 1st sess., 1924, 65:6627.

it ran counter to business desires, it was regrettable. Regardless of these two groups, public sentiment and patriotic considerations demanded restriction.

In its response to the intertwined issues of the open shop and immigration, the Republican party early revealed that it was not to be the vehicle for consistent antilabor extremism. Whatever the statements and even actions of zealots such as Bourne, Poindexter, Dawes, and Daugherty, the GOP in general found that a single-minded assault upon organized labor was neither intelligent nor expedient. Party leaders were willing to antagonize the aggressive business interests by failing to meet their demands regarding the American plan and immigration, for in the early 1920s the country was more concerned about dangerous aliens than it was about native labor leaders. Vaguely hostile to the pretensions of organized labor, Americans probably would not have supported a major political attack upon the American Federation of Labor and other long established unions. Labor leaders remained suspicious of antilabor elements within the party, but they were assured that Republicans who were sensitive to labor's political potential and eager to keep the party from unwise extremism usually held the balance of power. Although the handling of the 1922 railroad strike shook this assurance, Herbert Hoover's labor programs helped to rescue the party and administration from the worst effects of even that debacle.

5 The Hoover Approach

THE OPEN SHOP and immigration were largely political issues, but two major industrial labor situations in the Harding administration provided Hoover with chances to demonstrate the efficacy of his concept of governmental action in labor matters. The massive unemployment that troubled the country offered one test of the Hoover approach, and the clamorous debate over the twelve-hour day in the steel industry provided another. The activities of Hoover and his associates with regard to these situations revealed the Hoover approach in practice: The government, led by Hoover himself, gathered information, coordinated the activities of diverse groups and individuals, generated publicity, and applied pressure. Particularly, Hoover and his cohorts sought to avoid the use of legislative or coercive measures. By the end of 1923, the worst of the unemployment had vanished, along with the twelve-hour day, in most steel mills. Critics denied that Hoover's efforts had been decisive, but the secretary of commerce felt confident that the course of events had vindicated his methods of handling industrial problems.

By 1921 industrial engineers and efficiency experts had established themselves as major figures in American life. The Taylor Society, the Federated American Engineering Societies, and similar organizations proclaimed the twin gospels of "Efficiency and Uplift." Hoover, who had been a mining engineer, and others associated with this movement saw such social disturbances as unemployment and labor unrest as primarily technical problems. Seasonal operations, outdated machinery, and failure to adopt modern accounting and marketing methods often produced waste in industry, the most visible sign of which was the unemployed or restive worker. "If one surveys all the industries," Hoover told Samual Gompers, "it will be found that those of high intermittancy [of operation] are the ones where the condition of the workers is the worst, and that they are the areas of most industrial disputes." To the engineer, the charity kitchen and the picket line meant not only human dissatisfaction and misery but also terrible waste and inefficiency. To the industrial engineer, the great problems that confronted society called not for the socialists' slogans or for the standpatters' moralisms, but for diligent inquiry, cost-price formulas, and time-and-motion studies.[1]

Hoover and his associates looked upon the industrial turmoil that faced the country as an opportunity as well as a threat. Radicalism, violence, and employer intransigence were dangerous, of course, but if properly led the government could use the insights of the efficiency experts and engineers to eliminate some of the social problems that had bedeviled the nation for so long. Strikes, unemployment, and dissatisfaction created problems, but they also provided the engineers with proving grounds for their ideas. To Hoover's closest aide, Edward Eyre Hunt, for example, a threatened strike in the New York garment industry offered the government not only a problem but also the "possibility that a first class piece of industrial engineering can be done in the situation."[2]

In 1921 unemployment confronted the nation and created a major challenge for the engineers. Unemployment, despite the frequency of its appearance in the past, had rarely been subjected to systematic study, and statisticians had not perfected methods of collecting and interpreting data. Government officials disagreed as to the precise nature and magnitude

[1] For a recent discussion of the engineering-efficiency movement, see Samuel Haber, *Efficiency and Uplift: Scientific Management in the Progressive Era, 1890-1920* (Chicago, 1964), esp. chapts. 8 and 9. Hoover's remarks are contained in an unsent letter from Hoover to Gompers, fall 1921, Herbert C. Hoover Papers (Herbert Hoover Presidential Library), Box 19; hereafter cited as Hoover Papers.

[2] Hunt to Hugh Kerwin, April 18, 1922, Hoover Papers, Box 413.

of joblessness. In mid-1921 the Bureau of Labor Statistics estimated that as many as six million Americans were out of work, but Davis considered this figure to be unrealistic, since it reflected the general decline in employment after the war and not necessarily the number of people actively seeking work. Other federal reports put the figure variously at 3,500,000 and 4 to 5 million.[3] Available totals usually provided only a lump sum, without regional or occupational differentiations. The methods of the Bureau of Labor Statistics were so primitive and its conclusions so ambiguous that one Department of Commerce official remarked, "When we go to the [Department of Labor] statistics [we find] that they are open to several interpretations." The Department of Commerce found it necessary to glean data from businessmen and local governments to try to discover the configurations of unemployment.[4]

While they disagreed about the nature and extent of joblessness, everyone recognized the seriousness of the situation. At the same time many federal officials, especially in the Department of Labor, felt helpless. While Davis and his associates rejected the moralistic view that unemployment was purely an individual problem and that the worker without a job was necessarily shiftless and unworthy, they did not know what to do. Late in August 1921 the secretary of labor answered a query about combating joblessness by remarking, "I don't know of anything that can be done. . . . You know

[3] The six million figure is from a Department of Labor report quoted in the *Congressional Record*, 67th Cong., 1st sess., 1921, 61:5371, while Davis' explanation is found in his press release, ca. Sept. 15, 1921, Department of Labor Records (Record Group 174, National Archives), File 20/145; hereafter cited as Department of Labor Records. For the other estimates, see Report on the Volume of Unemployment in Sept. 1921, by a subcommittee of the Economic Advisory Committee to the President's Conference on Unemployment, Sept. 20, 1921, Hoover Papers, Box 406; United States, Department of Commerce, *Annual Report: 1922* (Washington, D.C., 1922), 6. See also V. W. Lanfear, *Business Fluctuations and the American Labor Movement, 1915-1922* (New York, 1924), 55.

[4] F. M. Feiker to W. S. Rossiter, Aug. 25, 1921, Department of Commerce Records (Record Group 40, National Archives), File 81650; hereafter cited as Department of Commerce Records.

about that as I do." He did, however, see some possibilities in the acceleration of planned public works projects.[5]

Hoover and his cohorts in the Department of Commerce and in the engineering societies were more sanguine. In 1920 and 1921 the Federated American Engineering Societies, with the support of the Taylor Society, had conducted a survey of waste in industry.[6] Their conclusion that industrial unrest and unemployment were often the products of poor management, intermittent operations, and wasteful manufacturing processes led them to believe that programs of modernization and planning could deal effectively with unemployment. With Hoover as secretary of commerce, engineers such as Lawrence T. Wallace, executive secretary of the Federated Engineering Societies, and Morris L. Cooke felt that the time had come for the government, in conjunction with the engineers, to undertake comprehensive studies of unemployment and its relationship to industrial inefficiency. As Cooke remarked, "the great *advantage* of a season of acute unemployment is that only during such a time can we get that measure of public attention which is needed to effect ultimate solutions."[7] To the engineers joblessness was not merely a problem; it was also a challenge and an opportunity.

In August 1921 after some preliminary studies by the Department of Commerce, Hoover suggested to Harding the appointment of "a Presidential Commission of men representative of all sections" to study unemployment and to recommend means of fighting it. With Harding's approval,

[5] Davis to Sen. Joseph Frelinghuysen, Aug. 26, 1921, United States Conciliation Service Records (Record Group 280, National Archives), File 165/358; hereafter cited as USCSR. See also Assistant Secretary of Labor E. J. Henning to Charles Evans Hughes, July 25, 1921, Department of Labor Records, File 20/145.

[6] Federated American Engineering Societies, *Waste in Industry* (New York, 1921).

[7] Morris L. Cooke to Edward Eyre Hunt, Sept. 6, 1921, Hoover Papers, Box 410. See also Jean Cristie, "Morris Llewellyn Cooke: Progressive Engineer" (unpublished Ph.D. dissertation, Columbia University, 1963), 45-54.

Hoover immediately began to recruit businessmen, engineers, academic experts, and labor leaders for service on the President's Conference on Unemployment. Secretary of Labor Davis was to share in the work and direction of the conference, but, aside from making suggestions for appointments, he deferred almost completely to his more able colleague.[8]

The establishment and work of the conference owed much to the previous findings of the industrial efficiency movement, and especially to the Taylor Society and the Federated American Engineering Societies. The latter's publication *Waste in Industry* provided a frame of reference for the conference, and a number of engineers served on it or offered advice and suggestions. While the focus was upon immediate reduction of existing unemployment, the project by its very nature had more far-reaching implications. Hoover and the engineers saw it as a sort of experiment in which they could test the assumptions that previous studies had formulated. As the first direct federal effort to alleviate unemployment, its methods and recommendations could not help but have a lasting impact. In addition, Hoover viewed its work as a test of a democratic, individualistic society's ability to resolve modern economic and industrial problems through voluntary coordinated activity, rather than through governmental compulsion. The work of the president's conference, then, was to be a unique blend of private initiative, federal leadership and persuasion, and engineering know-how.[9]

[8] Hoover to Harding, Aug. 20, 1921, Harding Papers, Box 285; Hoover to Owen Young, Aug. 27, 1921, Department of Commerce Records, File 81650. Davis could not be present at the opening of the conference in mid-September because he had to attend several fraternal conventions in the Middle West. He felt he could not cancel or postpone his engagements. Davis to Hoover, Sept. 19, 1921, USCSR, File 165/358.

[9] There are numerous communications in the Hoover Papers, esp. in Box 410, to and from engineers and efficiency experts reflecting their interest in and influence upon the conference. See esp. an untitled report enclosed in Lawrence T. Wallace, executive secretary of the Federated American Engineering Societies, to Edward Eyre Hunt, Oct. 19, 1921, Hoover Papers. See also Herbert Hoover, *The Memoirs of Herbert Hoover. II: The Cabinet and the Presidency, 1921-1933* (New York, 1952), 44-46.

In addition to the emphasis upon industrial engineering and scientific management, a spirit of "uplift" ran through the work of the conference. Besides suggesting specific solutions to problems and making recommendations to citizens, businessmen, and government, some participants felt it necessary to instill in the unemployed and in the public a mood of confidence and cheerfulness in the face of adversity. One report prepared for the conference urged that the unemployed be grouped into clubs, which would help to infuse them with self-respect and confidence "through the spirit of song in the midst of good cheer, and wholesome communion every Sunday morning." Good fellowship, food supplied by charitable organizations, and religious activities would help to dispel the gloom that had infected some of the men on the streets and breadlines. Reports to the conference also emphasized the necessity to alert the public to the need to help the unfortunate and to remove the stigmas that middle-class Americans often attached to joblessness. Otto Mallery of the Industrial Board of Pennsylvania, a frequent and influential participant, urged the adoption of slogans, such as "Improve the Home Town and Give Work to the Workers." He called upon communities and charitable groups to "Use 'four minute men,' movies and community singing and other war-time methods in raising funds," as well as to stage dramatic tableaux "of the story of unemployment and the possibilities of success."[10]

Sloganeering and uplift occupied only part of the conference's time. The more important job of finding concrete methods of reducing joblessness began in September 1921 under the direction of Hoover and Hunt, who served as secretary to the conference. Among those Hoover recruited were Owen D. Young of the General Electric Company, labor leaders such as James P. Noonan, president of the AFL Brotherhood of Electrical Workers, and John Donlin, president of

[10] "Mass Psychology Statement Prepared for Mallery by Fedoux [?]," fall 1921; "First Memorandum, Sept. 13th, [1921]," by Otto T. Mallery. Both in Hoover Papers, Boxes 414-15.

AFL Building Trades Department, and academicians and economists such as Samuel McCune Lindsay, Leo Wolman, Wesley Mitchell, and E. R. A. Seligman. Mallery, whose background was a blend of social work, administration, and interest in labor matters, also served on the advisory committee. Prior to taking his assignment, he had submitted a memorandum entitled "Suggestions for Relieving Unemployment under the Guidance of the Department of Commerce," which provided a basis for the conference's discussion, although parts of it were too far-reaching for acceptance. Mallery urged a sweeping program, emphasizing the need for public works construction as a stimulus to employment. He envisioned the federal government as playing a major role in relief, for he urged quick congressional appropriations for public works, an accelerated federal roadbuilding program, and federal aid to local and state public works projects. As a last resort, if these expedients proved ineffective, he advocated "a Federal out-of-work donation of $10.00 per week minimum" to unemployed workers.[11]

Hoover, of course, deplored the last suggestion; "governmental doles and other fallacious remedies based upon the practices of European governments" were not acceptable.[12] Other points found more favorable reception. For example, the conference endorsed the principle of accelerating public works construction in order to increase employment. The conferees thought that the government should not undertake new construction merely to create jobs, but when depression struck it should hasten projects already decided upon.

Consistent with Hoover's view, the conference concluded that the proper role of the federal government was that of an

[11] A list of the members of the advisory committee, which had been working with Hoover since May, is in Hoover Papers, Box 406. For the general conference, some 300 "leaders from production, distribution, banking, construction, labor, and agriculture" were chosen. Hoover, *Memoirs*, II, 44. There is a copy of Mallery's memorandum in Lindsay Papers, Box 144.

[12] Department of Commerce, *Annual Report: 1922*, p. 6.

adviser, coordinator, and supporter, not an initiator. The economic advisory committee declared that the major effort must rest with local communities. The committee emphasized the importance of local self-help prjoects, and it urged citizens to take a personal interest in eliminating unemployment. For example, families might undertake needed house repairs, giving work to the needy. Insisting that individuals bear the prime responsibility in the fight against joblessness, the advisory committee warned communities that, while "public works will serve as a partial substitute for private relief and charity," individual good works were still extremely important. The conference as a whole echoed the advisory committee's suggestions and added several, such as tariff increases, lowered railroad freight rates, retrenchment in government spending, and undefined aid for chaotic conditions in coal and agriculture.[13]

None of its legislative recommendations became law directly as a result of the conference. Congress did raise tariffs, but this was the Republican party's preannounced policy anyway. Still, some of its nonlegislative proposals were translated into action. The federal government set up federal-state-local committees to coordinate efforts to combat unemployment, and it worked through these groups and through industry to encourage a work-sharing program, through which workers voluntarily rotated jobs in periods of slackened business.[14] The conference submitted to Congress a proposal to adjust

[13] Report of the Economic Advisory Committee to the Unemployment Conference, Sept. 26, 1921, Lindsay Papers, Box 144; Tentative Conference Recommendations, enclosed in R. S. Emmet, Hoover's secretary, to Arthur Cook, Davis' secretary, Oct. 11, 1921, USCSR, File 165/358B. See also Philip Klein, *The Burden of Unemployment: A Study of Unemployment Relief Measures in Fifteen American Cities, 1921-1922* (New York, 1922), 57-60, and Leah Hannah Feder, *Unemployment Relief in Periods of Depression: A Study of Measures Adopted in Certain American Cities, 1857 through 1922* (New York, 1936), 296-97.

[14] Harding to Hoover, May 22, 1922, Department of Commerce Records, File 81560; Department of Commerce, *Annual Report: 1922,* pp. 6-7; Hoover, *Memoirs,* II, 46.

public works construction to the state of the economy, envisioning "the execution of about 80 per cent of the usual annual average of federal public works during years of active industry and the postponement of about twenty per cent for execution during years of depression," which would "be used as a safety valve."[15] Newspapers, labor leaders, and engineers considered this recommendation a major step toward evening out employment, but the bill died despite their support. Throughout the decade, Davis, the unions, and many employers continued to support this measure, but Congress failed to act. Thus, in 1928 in response to a Senate resolution concerning public works, Davis, disappointed at Congress' repeated failure to enact the recommended legislation, replied, "I do not recall an instance where there was 'proper timing for the inauguration of public works.' "[16]

In 1922 the economy began to accelerate, reducing unemployment and inaugurating the prosperity of the decade. The findings and recommendations of the conference probably had little to do with the upswing.[17] Its main contribution was to focus national attention for a short time on the problem of unemployment. Few economists and fewer public officials thought in terms of massive public works programs, planned deficits, or calculated tax cuts as means of triggering economic growth, for they failed to appreciate the key role of the consumer. In the early 1920s, for example, some politicians and economists wanted to cut corporate taxes and to replace the lost revenue through a highly regressive national sales tax, a measure that would have decreased buying power. Thus, the conference's emphasis on local and individual self-help and

[15] Hunt to Gen. R. C. Marshall, Jr., Nov. 28, 1921, Hoover Papers, Box 413; Mallery to Sen. William Kenyon, Feb. 3, 1922, United States Senate Records (Record Group 46, National Archives), 67th Cong., 2d sess., 1922, Papers Relating to Senate Bill 2749.
[16] Davis to Charles G. Dawes, March 24, 1928, Davis Papers, Box 43.
[17] George Soule, *Prosperity Decade: From War to Depression, 1917-1929*, Economic History of the United States, Vol. IX (New York, 1947), 111.

its unwillingness to contemplate massive federal aid, lower-bracket income tax reductions, or planned deficit spending were proper and predictable given the state of economic thinking.

Whatever its limitations, the conference aroused much interest and favorable comment. Its activities and recommendations received wide publicity and its very existence demonstrated a new view of the federal government's role in the alleviation of economic distress. The chief recommendations such as the better planning of public works, the elimination of waste and duplication, and the federal coordination of state, local, and private efforts represented precisely the ideas of Herbert Hoover and the influential engineering societies. If these proposals and programs contributed little to America's return to prosperity, they reflected a keen awareness of the government's role in a complex, interdependent economy. Moreover, with all its warnings about the dangers of governmental activity, the conference was decidedly closer in spirit to Franklin D. Roosevelt's New Deal than to Grover Cleveland's response to the depression of the 1890s. So far as Samuel Gompers was concerned, it had done what the labor movement could properly have expected of it. "In all its procedure," he declared approvingly, "the Conference was guided by the fact that it was not authorized to attempt to overturn existing theory and practice but was epected to meet the problem . . . through existing agencies." Within these reasonable limits, "the Conference was rich in results."[18]

Hoover agreed. In 1924 he reflected on the hard times that had greeted the Harding administration in 1921. "Distress prevailed in every city, soup lines had been formed," he recalled.

[18] Report of Samuel Gompers to AFL executive council, Nov. 7, 1921, enclosed in Florence C. Thorne to Hunt, Nov. 7, 1921, Hoover Papers, Box 406. For more critical commentary, see William L. Chenery, "The President's Conference and Unemployment in the United States," *International Labour Review*, V (March 1922), 359-76, and Feder, *Unemployment Relief*, 344-46.

Then he described the vigorous response of the Republican party. "Credit and Confidence were restored in the business world. An organized campaign for employment was initiated. . . . And the whole country mobilized to provide emergency employment."[19] In Hoover's view the government had done what it properly should have, and no more. It neither sought out functions nor established an elaborate bureaucracy. It had simply identified a problem, mobilized available resources, coordinated private efforts, and curtailed its activities when prosperity returned. By late 1923 a sharply lowered rate of unemployment and a lack of permanent federal agencies and bureaus created to cope with unemployment indicated to Hoover, as well as to many others, the success of his approach.

Hoover's efforts to find effective means of coping with labor problems were not confined to his leadership of the conference on unemployment. Even as that body met, he began to work for the elimination of the twelve-hour day in the steel industry, once again using the prestige of his office, his administrative talents, and the ideas and influence of his engineering associates. Indeed, the Hoover approach was even more success-ful in his campaign to reduce working hours than it was in the assault on joblessness, for by late 1923 President Harding, responding to the persistent prodding of his gifted subordinate, had persuaded the steel industry to replace the twelve-hour (two-shift) day with the eight-hour (three-shift) system.

For years labor policies of the steel operators had been notoriously exploitative. In 1920 half the men toiled a twelve-hour day and over 25 percent worked a seven-day week. Ethnic rivalries, employer arrogance and ruthlessness, and extreme antiunion measures combined with low pay and often squalid living conditions to create an explosive atmosphere among the more than 300,000 workers in the country's most significant industry. Periodically reformers and publicists had attacked these conditions, often with considerable public support, but

[19] Statement of Herbert Hoover, 1924, in Mills Papers, Box 2.

the war, the steel strike of 1919, and the successful Red-baiting tactics of the manufacturers had momentarily diverted public attention. Then, late in July 1920 the Interchurch World Movement released its *Report on the Steel Strike of 1919*, which reminded Americans that dreadful conditions still prevailed, and attacked with particular force the twelve-hour day as an anachronistic and barbaric institution. Overwhelmingly favorable response greeted the report, and the movement to abolish the long working day gathered force, despite the determined efforts of the steel industry to discredit its critics.[20]

By 1921 the twelve-hour day was a major public issue, claiming the attention of an administration concerned with industrial unrest and unemployment. Republicans had to act cautiously in matters relating to the powerful steel industry, but President Harding could not ignore the outcry against labor conditions in the mills. So as Hoover began to work for the abolition of the long working day, the president cautiously lent his support, even if he did not exercise bold leadership.[21]

Outside the government, others worked for the same result. The Interchurch World Movement continued its criticism of the steelmakers, publishing a report in 1921 entitled *Public Opinion and the Steel Strike*. Many businessmen felt that the steel industry's position was untenable and harmful and that the continuance of the twelve-hour day promoted industrial

[20] Interchurch World Movement, Commission of Inquiry, *Report on the Steel Strike of 1919* (New York, 1920); David Brody, *Steelworkers in America: The Nonunion Era* (Cambridge, Mass., 1960), 270-75. See William Finley McKee, "The Social Gospel and the New Social Order, 1919-1929" (unpublished Ph.D. dissertation, University of Wisconsin, 1961), 126, for a discussion of the Interchurch World Movement and the steel industry's attacks upon it.

[21] Brody gives a good outline of the major events in the twelve-hour controversy in *Steelworkers in America*, but he virtually ignores Hoover. Hoover's *Memoirs*, II, 103-104, contain an account that ignores virtually everyone except Hoover. Andrew Sinclair, *The Available Man: The Life Behind the Masks of Warren Gamaliel Harding* (New York, 1965), 255-56, attributes primarily political motives to Harding in the affair.

unrest. Industrial engineers demonstrated in several studies that the industry could abandon the long working day with relatively little difficulty. Serving as a link between all these opponents of the twelve-hour day was professor Samuel McCune Lindsay of Columbia University. Lindsay served on the conference of unemployment, was an unofficial but influential adviser to Republican leaders, and had important contacts with engineers, churchmen, academicians, New York business and financial leaders, and Judge Elbert Gary and other steel executives. In the year-long effort to persuade the steel industry to abandon the twelve-hour day, Lindsay was a major figure, for he arranged conferences, funneled information to both government and industry, and used his acquaintances with businessmen to keep pressure upon the industry.[22]

Opponents of the twelve-hour day lashed out against it for a variety of reasons. Virtually all of them asserted that an enlightened and humane society could not tolerate such conditions. The engineers emphasized that waste and inefficiency resulted from long hours, little rest, and general fatigue. As a member of the conference on unemployment, Lindsay was disturbed by circumstances that forced some men into idleness while others toiled twelve hours a day. He argued that the elimination of the twelve-hour day would produce "results of . . . incalculable value to the general economic situation." He also stressed the social value of a shorter workweek. Under present circumstances, he pointed out, the workers' long day "frequently means fourteen to fifteen hours per day absence from their families or from any possibility of engagement in community activities." Not only would shorter hours benefit

[22] Interchurch World Movement, Commission of Inquiry, *Public Opinion and the Steel Strike* (New York, 1921); H. B. Drury, "Three Shift System," *Independent Management* (Jan. 1, 1921), 63-67. Lindsay's efforts are described in a series of letters from Lindsay to Hoover throughout 1922 and 1923 in Hoover Papers, Boxes 191 and 313. For a typical expression of business support for the eight-hour day, see Clarence H. Howard of the Commonwealth Steel Company to Hoover, June 10, 1922, Hoover Papers, Box 313. See also Hoover, *Memoirs*, II, 103.

the economy, but the worker would be a better citizen and a more active member of the community.[23]

Hoover, of course, agreed with all these sentiments, but he thought also of the value of demonstrating the efficacy of his methods of handling industrial problems. It was important to show that the government could obtain a significant social benefit without resort to restrictive legislation. He knew that if the administration failed to act, the conditions that had precipitated the 1919 strike would still be at work. Moreover, there was the threat of congressional action, which he considered unnecessary, but which the public might demand if his methods failed. His main problem, he felt, was to persuade Judge Gary, who as head of United States Steel led the defense of the existing system, and the other steel executives to do what was best for them. Thus, the secretary of commerce had to maintain pressure while forestalling congressional action, hoping to prod the steelmakers to "take action which will give the steel industry credit for initiative instead of waiting until they are smashed into by some kind of legislation."[24]

At first Hoover thought that Gary might voluntarily recommend the shorter workday at the annual meeting of the United States Steel Corporation on April 17, 1922. When Gary failed to make such a move, the secretary of commerce urged Harding to invite the steelmakers to a White House dinner conference to discuss the matter. Hoover advised the president to make public the nature and intent of the conference; not only would an announcement fix public attention on the twelve-hour day, but it "would [also] place a certain moral pressure on these gentlemen to take action." The date for the dinner was set at May 18.[25]

[23] Lindsay to Harding, Feb. 21, 1922, Lindsay Papers, Harding Folder; Lindsay to Hoover, May 17, 1922, Hoover Papers, Box 313.

[24] Hoover, Memoirs, II, 103-104; Hoover to John V. M. Reynders, May 22, 1922, Hoover Papers, Box 313.

[25] Hoover to Harding, April 8 and May 4, 1922, Hoover Papers, Box 313.

Meanwhile in New York Lindsay busily recruited support
for the eight-hour day. He conferred with Gary and other
executives, seeking to persuade them of the moral, economic,
and public relations benefits of voluntary adoption of the three-
shift system. Although unable to change Gary's mind, he
made efforts to influence leaders of "big business or banking
interests with important influence in the circle of steel men,"
especially cultivating financiers such as Felix Warburg and
Mortimer L. Schiff. He planned to attend the annual meeting
of the American Iron and Steel Institute on May 27, and he
felt that a change in the executives' attitudes was possible.
"I am very anxious," he told Hoover, "to get some pressure
from Washington to bear on that meeting."[26]

The forty-one steel men who assembled on May 18 for the
White House dinner conference found the secretary of commerce armed with reports, studies, and statistics to justify the
abandonment of the twelve-hour system. Gary and Charles
M. Schwab of United States Steel called Hoover's views
"unsocial and uneconomic," but they found the president
anxious for the conference to result in some action relative to
the twelve-hour day. Yet, while Harding was eager to eliminate
a two-shift system, he was equally eager not to antagonize
the steel executives. Prior to the meeting, Harding had opposed
Hoover's wish to publicize the meeting because "I would
infinitely prefer to announce a thing accomplished than to
make public the intention to seek the accomplishment." Gary
found the president to be cautious, even deferential; the judge
reported to his fellow steel executives that Harding "did not
intend to insist unduly, but if he could be helpful in bringing
about the abolition of the twelve-hour day, it would be very
pleasing to him." Still, the continuing publicity and the
president's interest in the question led the steel men to agree
to appoint a special committee to investigate the matter.

[26] Lindsay to Hoover, April 8 and May 15, 1922, Hoover Papers,
Box 191.

"Disheartened" and "in less than a good humor," Hoover left the meeting and told the White House reporters about the meeting and the steel men's special committee.[27]

Lindsay was convinced that the meeting and Hoover's bold publicizing of it would help to assure the elimination of the twelve-hour day. Several days after the dinner conference, he spoke with Gary and reported that the widespread favorable editorial comments in newspapers throughout the country had impressed the industrialist. The professor predicted that the special committee would realize "how keen and widespread is the interest and public demand that something be done," and would act accordingly.[28]

Events proved Lindsay too optimistic. Gary appointed a committee with himself as chairman, but it was in no hurry to issue a report. Steel spokesmen continued to attack their critics and to emphasize the need for more permissive immigration laws before they could contemplate a reduction in hours. While the Steel Institute committee made no public announcement during the year after its formation, there was every indication that its report would be as unsympathetic to the eight-hour day as the steel executives had been early in the year.[29]

Throughout 1922 and early 1923 Hoover, perhaps anticipating an unfavorable response from the committee, "kept the pot boiling in the press." He began also to make use of his associations in the engineering societies. Horace Drury and other engineers had been studying the technicalities of the

[27] Hoover's account is given in *Memoirs*, II, 103-104; Harding's remarks are contained in Harding to Hoover, May 10, 1922, Hoover Papers, Box 313. Gary is quoted in Brody, *Steelworkers in America*, 273.

[28] Lindsay to Hoover, May 17 and 27, 1922, Hoover Papers, Box 313.

[29] Brody, *Steelworkers in America*, 273; New York *Times*, Dec. 24, 1922, and April 17, 1923. For the steelmakers' continuing efforts to discredit the Interchurch World Movement's *Report*, see McKee, "The Social Gospel and the New Social Order," 126. The Iron and Steel Institute helped underwrite and circulate attacks upon the *Report* such as one by Marshall Olds, *Analysis of the Interchurch World Movement Report on the Steel Strike* (New York, 1923).

abandonment of the long working day and had published studies justifying the change. As president of the Federated American Engineering Societies, Hoover was aware of these reports and he urged the engineers to summarize and consolidate their findings for public dissemination. In November 1922 the Societies completed their report. Even Hoover expressed surprise at the "unanimity of the whole engineering profession in their demonstration that from a technical point of view there is no difficulty with what was obviously necessary from a social point of view." The secretary of commerce then wrote a foreword to the report for Harding's signature in which he had the president again condemn the twelve-hour day as detrimental to "good citizenship" and to "business and economic stability."[30]

Meanwhile Lindsay continued his efforts from New York. As a director of the Cabot Fund of Boston, which had helped to finance the publication of the report, he edited the engineers' report. He alerted Governor Gifford Pinchot of the steel-producing state of Pennsylvania to the report and sought to secure his support for the eight-hour day movement. All the while he continued his efforts to persuade his business and financial friends to influence the steel executives. In the spring of 1923 he and Hoover held a luncheon conference with such outstanding industrialists and financiers as Owen Young, Dwight Morrow, and Robert P. Lamont. There they presented and explained the engineers' report in an effort to bring indirect pressure to bear upon Judge Gary and his colleagues. By the spring of 1923 signs were favorable: the engineers' report had been favorably received; many business-

[30] Hoover, *Memoirs*, II, 103-104; Samuel Gompers, *Seventy Years of Life and Labor*, ed. Philip A. Taft and John Sessions (New York, 1957), 320-21; Hoover to Harding, Nov. 1, 1922, and enclosed draft of foreword to the Engineering Societies' report on the twelve-hour day, Hoover Papers, Box 313. The citation for the report is Committee on Work Periods in Continuous Industry of the Federated American Engineering Societies, *The Twelve-Hour Shift in Industry* (New York, 1922). See also Cristie, "Morris Llewellyn Cooke," 49-50.

men had shown interest in the eight-hour proposal; the government was firmly committed; and there was continuing public and press interest. Lindsay hoped that a personal meeting with Gary before the Iron and Steel Institute committee was to report in May would finally lead to a favorable response from the steel manufacturers.[31]

Despite all these efforts, the steel men proved obdurate. On May 25, 1923, at the annual meeting of the American Iron and Steel Institute, Gary and Schwab presented the report of the committee appointed the previous year. In it, the steel executives insisted that the agitation against the twelve-hour day was not supported by the workers and asserted that a reduction in hours would be neither feasible nor beneficial to the men. Conversion to the three-shift system would require 60,000 unobtainable workers and would raise steel prices 15 percent. If the government really wanted to reduce the workweek in the steel mills, the report declared, it would remove restrictions on immigration.[32]

Coming after a year of agitation and public discussion, the report of the steel institute shocked the advocates of the eight-hour day. Hoover would not be denied, however. He charged that the report disclosed "an inability to grasp the great ground swell of social movements among our people" and urged Harding "not [to] allow this matter of fundamental social importance to drop." He continued to apply pressure, asking the steel industry to stipulate specific conditions under which they would agree to abandon the twelve-hour day. On June 13 he drafted a letter of reply for Harding to send to

[31] Lindsay to Gifford Pinchot, Jan. 31, 1923, Gifford Pinchot Papers (Manuscript Division, Library of Congress), Box 250; hereafter cited as Gifford Pinchot Papers. Lindsay to Hoover, March 22, 1923, Hoover Papers, Box 191.

[32] Copy of the American Iron and Steel Institute Committee on the Proposed Total Elimination of the Twelve Hour Day *Report*, presented at the annual meeting, May 25, 1923, in Amos R. E. Pinchot Papers (Manuscript Division, Library of Congress), Box 144; hereafter cited as Amos Pinchot Papers; New York *Times*, May 26, 1923.

Gary. The twelve-hour day, he reiterated, should be made obsolete. While appearing to take at face value the steel committee's reasons for failure to eliminate the two-shift system, Hoover's letter sought to wring from Gary the admission that it was at least theoretically desirable to abandon the long day. If Gary refused to grant this point, the steel industry would further isolate itself. If he did grant the desirability of reducing hours, Hoover felt that he should agree "that before there shall be any reduction in staff or employees . . . through any recession of demand for steel . . . that then the change should be made from the two shifts to the three shifts basis."[33]

This letter, sent on June 18 over Harding's signature, placed the steel men in a difficult position. While Gary continued to cling to the twelve-hour day, the president had attacked the executives' stand in a communication that was sure to become public. If the steel executives agreed with the contention of Hoover and Harding that the twelve-hour day was indeed harmful and obsolete, they would in effect be announcing that they permitted private gain to weigh more heavily than social goals. Moreover, they could read in the letter the veiled threat of more strenuous government action: Hoover and Harding might "still entertain the hope that these questions . . . should be solved by action inside the industries themselves," but it was obvious that the government was not going to abandon the fight until the eight-hour day had been secured. The Hoover-Harding letter conclusively revealed the steel industry's isolation from the main currents of American opinion and forced Gary into a reply that would either be unpopularly rigid or publicly inconsistent.[34]

Although Gary himself held tenaciously to the twelve-hour day, the Hoover-Harding letter and the secretary of commerce's relentless campaign won victory. Late in June, the Steel

[33] Hoover to Harding (draft), May 26, 1923, Hoover Papers, Box 313; Hoover to Harding, June 13, 1923, with enclosed draft of letter to be sent by Harding to Gary, n.d., *ibid*, Box 243.

[34] Harding to Gary, June 18, 1923, Hoover Papers, Box 313.

Institute committee held another meeting and capitulated. On June 27 Gary informed Harding, then on a western trip, of the decision: aware of public feeling and impressed with Harding's letter of June 18, he said, "we are determined to exert every effort . . . to secure in the iron and steel industry . . . a total abolition of the 12-hour day at the earliest time practicable." Taking advantage of an apparent loophole in Harding's June 18 letter, he added, "We think it can be brought about without undue delay when, as you stated, 'there is a surplus of labor available.' "[35]

If Gary hoped through this qualification to delay or evade the conversion to an eight-hour day he was mistaken. On July 5, Harding spoke at Tacoma, Washington, and incorporated a major statement, written by Hoover, regarding the steel situation. He congratulated the industry on its "important step," which "will heal a sore in American industrial life which has been the cause of infinite struggles and bitterness for over a generation." Gary and the Steel Institute committee may have considered their new stand to be tentative and qualified, but Harding's remarks provided them with an imperative to create the conditions favorable to the introduction of the three-shift system. Further committing them to action, on July 5 Hoover released the Harding-Gary correspondence of June 18-27. By the end of 1923 virtually the entire industry, led by United States Steel, had moved to the eight-hour day, with few of the adverse consequences that the steel executives had predicted.[36]

[35] Gary to Harding, June 27, 1923, *ibid.*

[36] Note headed "Written by Mr. Hoover on July 4, 1923 and incorporated in the President's address at Tacoma, Washington on July 5, 1923," Hoover Papers, Box 313. The copies of the Harding-Gary correspondence of June 1923 in the Hoover Papers (Box 313) bear a note indicating that they were released to the press by the Department of Commerce on Hoover's authority. The Harding-Gary correspondence of June 18 and 27, together with Harding's Tacoma remarks, are published in James W. Murphy, reporter and comp., *President Harding's Last Speeches* (n. p., 1923), 290-95. For the actual shift to the eight-hour day, see Brody, *Steelworkers in America*, 274.

The capitulation of the steel industry constituted a major victory for the Harding administration and for Herbert Hoover in particular. The secretary of commerce had shown how voluntary efforts, coordinated and publicized by the government, could bring about a major social change in the face of powerful opposition. With justifiable pride Hoover later remarked that "owing to public opinion and some pushing on our part, the twelve-hour day was on the way out in American industry." This was achieved, he declared, "without the aid of a single law."[37]

The reduction of the workweek in steel showed that Hoover's approach, to this industrial problem at least, was as effective as legislation could have been and more effective than the steel strike had been. Together with his vigorous activity on behalf of the unemployed and his willingness to use the knowledge and influence of private groups and individuals for social purposes, the struggle with the steel executives revealed the Hoover approach at its most effective: the government, if well led and if vigorous and unrelenting enough, could indeed bring about desirable social and economic changes without resort to coercion.

Hoover's activities won him wide respect and support. Such a combination of vigor, intelligence, persistence, and knowledge of the public mood had rarely been seen in Washington. Yet the same qualities that enabled him to produce results also raised important questions. The conference on unemployment, after all, had not been a major factor in the business upturn, despite Hoover's publicity to the contrary. If the government acknowledged its responsibility in combating unemployment and mild measures produced no results in a future economic crisis, the citizenry might well expect the government to take far more vigorous action. The elimination of the twelve-hour day was an impressive achievement, but despite the untenable

[37] Hoover, *Memoirs*, II, 103-104. Neither Hoover nor anyone else seems to have remembered Professor Lindsay's important role in bringing the twelve-hour day to an end in the steel mills.

position of the steel manufacturers, the sentiment of an aroused public, the work of the churches, and the efforts of the government, it had taken two years to accomplish. In this case, industry's case had been unusually weak and the government's commitment unusually strong. Could the unskilled workers who manned most of America's economy expect similar results in the future? Some unionists and social critics argued that Hoover's success in the steel controversy emphasized, rather than obviated, the need for unionization, for workers needed power of their own to apply in situations in which there was no Herbert Hoover, no engineers' report, and no agitation by churchmen. Finally, although Hoover feared the resort to legislation in such matters, his power to publicize, to manipulate, and to influence could be dangerous, perhaps more dangerous than governmental power derived from law and limited by legislation. Certainly, there were those such as Albert J. Beveridge in the Republican party who feared that through his bold activities Hoover was building up an organization with strong financial support to further his own political ambitions.[38] In short, while Hoover's approach was high-minded, responsible, and effective, it also smacked of paternalism and expediency, and was dependent upon favorable circumstances for success.

Still, such reservations seemed ungenerous in 1923. With Hoover leading the way, the Harding administration had made important advances in labor affairs. Neither president nor cabinet nor party had revealed a passion for social justice, but, despite lingering antilabor extremism in the GOP, Hoover's policies had benefited the American worker. By mid-1923 scandal and general incompetence were pushing the administration to the verge of collapse, but in labor matters, largely because of Hoover's efforts, it had made significant contributions which even the disastrous handling of the 1922 coal and railroad strikes could not completely discredit.

[38] Beveridge to Raymond Robins, June 1, 1922, Robins Papers, Box 18.

6 Industrial Crisis of 1922

IN THE SPRING and summer of 1922 the most explosive strikes of the 1920s shook the country. In April more than 500,000 coal miners left their jobs. On July 1, about 400,000 railroad shopcrafts workers struck. Throughout the summer coal stocks dwindled, transportation sputtered, and violence flared, as America seemed, in the words of James J. Davis, to be "on the verge of industrial collapse." From Washington, at the height of the trouble, Mrs. Harding wrote, "The days are most trying, and I have made up my mind that the days of the war had no harder problems to meet than the present time."[1]

Indeed, the 1922 strikes proved exceedingly difficult for her husband and his administration. As coal shortages grew and as commerce suffered, pressures mounted for Harding to act, but Harding found the strikes extraordinarily complex and ambiguous. Moreover, his closest advisers were sharply divided. Throughout the strikes, Harding pursued an erratic course, at times following the counsel of moderates such as Hoover and Davis, and at times acting upon Attorney General Daugherty's advice to move against the strikers. These members of the cabinet worked at cross-purposes, while the befuddled president provided only sporadic and inconsistent leadership. The result was damaging to organized labor, the public, and Harding's administration and party.

Throughout late 1921 and early 1922 members of the administration were deeply concerned about the serious labor difficulties that threatened. The coal miners' contracts would expire on March 31, and the resentment of the railroad unionists against the carriers and the Railroad Labor Board grew. Hoover attempted to bring the railroad workers and the managers together for conferences, and Davis—and even Harding himself—sought on several occasions to arrange for negotiations in the coal industry. All these efforts failed and the arrival of spring brought the Harding administration face to face with the country's worst industrial crisis since the 1890s.[2]

The soft coal strike occupied the immediate attention of the administration, for curtailment of bituminous coal production would have a major national effect.[3] At the heart of the soft coal problem that gave rise to the labor difficulties lay a great paradox: the United States had vast supplies of bituminous coal, yet shortages, unsteady prices, and intermittent operations plagued the industry and created labor unrest.

Bituminous coal was the nation's industrial fuel, and the public in many areas relied upon it for domestic heating as well. Many states mined soft coal, but seven—Pennsylvania, West Virginia, Illinois, Ohio, Kentucky, Indiana, and Alabama —accounted for 85 percent of the nation's output. Bituminous coal marketing was ruthlessly competitive, with hundreds of

[1] James J. Davis, "A History of Strikes," unpublished manuscript, 1941, in Davis Papers, Box 37; Mrs. Harding to Charles D. Hilles, July 28, 1922, Hilles Papers, Box 203.

[2] Edward Berman, *Labor Disputes and the President of the United States*, Columbia University Studies in History, Economics, and Public Law, whole number 249 (New York, 1924), 215-17; memorandum dated Jan. 4, 1922, on union-carrier conference to be held at Hoover's home on Jan. 7, and Hoover to Hon. Samuel H. Sibley, Feb. 2, 1922, Hoover Papers, Box 249.

[3] The anthracite strike began at the same time as the bituminous coal strike and ended shortly after. It was a complicating factor, since reduced supplies of hard coal made the soft coal shortages more damaging. Moreover, the specter of 155,000 hard coal miners on strike contributed to the general sense of crisis. Still, the anthracite strike was not so serious as the soft coal strike, for homes did not have to be heated in the spring and summer. See Robert H. Zieger, "Pinchot and Coolidge: The Politics of the 1923 Anthracite Crisis," *Journal of American History*, LII (Dec. 1965), esp. 567-68, and "Senator George Wharton Pepper and Labor Issues in the 1920s," *Labor History*, IX (Spring 1968), 167-70.

companies fighting for profits in an often overcrowded market-place. The great need for industrial fuels during the war had intensified competition, contributing to the erratic nature of soft coal demand. Periodically, as during the war or during strikes, marginal, high-cost mines opened up to exploit the momentary demand. Then, as normal conditions returned, these mines closed, often with much unemployment and hardship, revealing the root problems of the industry: too many mines and too many miners. Although there were several big bituminous coal producers, including companies controlled by the Mellon and Rockefeller families, the overall pattern was one of easy entrance, cutthroat competition, high incidence of failure, wasteful production, and prolonged periods of unemployment and partial employment.[4]

Incomplete unionization greatly complicated and intensified this instability. In the early 1920s the United Mine Workers of America contained only about 30 to 50 percent of the soft coal workers in the major production areas. The Central Competitive Field, which included the mines in Ohio, Indiana, Illinois, and many in Pennsylvania, was the heart of union membership, while the nonunion mines flourished in the regions extending south from central Pennsylvania to northern Alabama, along the Appalachians.

The operators in the unionized fields and the union had

[4] There is a vast amount of literature on the soft coal problem in the 1920s. Particularly useful are Walton H. Hamilton and Helen R. Wright, *The Case of Bituminous Coal* (New York, 1925), 166-209; Waldo E. Fisher, *Collective Bargaining in the Bituminous Coal Industry: An Appraisal* (Philadelphia, 1948), 20-26; Isador Lubin, *Miners' Wages and the Cost of Coal: An Inquiry into the Wages System in the Bituminous Coal Industry and Its Effects on Coal Costs and Coal Conservation* (New York, 1924), esp. 3-4; and A. T. Shurick, *The Coal Industry* (Boston, 1924), 270-73. See also United States Coal Commission, *Report of the United States Coal Commission*, 5 parts (Washington, D. C., 1925); Edward Eyre Hunt and others, eds., *What the Coal Commission Found* (Baltimore, 1925); and Helen R. Wright and Isador Lubin, "Wage Rates in the Bituminous Industry," ca. April 27, 1923, United States Coal Commission Records; hereafter cited as USCCR (National Archives, Record Group 68), Drawer 20.

established an elaborate bargaining process. By 1900 the two parties had achieved a degree of rationalization and order in this intensely competitive region. With the stimulation of production occasioned by the war, however, the nonunion Appalachian fields began to expand production. The United Mine Workers had sought repeatedly to extend unionization to these fields and continued their efforts in the 1920s. The nonunion operators, almost invariably with the support of local and state authorities, resisted organization bitterly and even violently.

The great problem of the union in the 1920s was to maintain its hold on the Central Competitive Field while unionizing the southern fields. Throughout the decade, John L. Lewis, president of the UMW proclaimed this dual policy of "no backward step" in the unionized fields and organization of the Appalachian areas. With a few exceptions, the union was unsuccessful in its southern efforts. This failure was largely due to the vigorous union-smashing of the nonunion operators and the authorities in the states concerned, but critics of Lewis in the UMW contended that he was too concerned about the Central Competitive Field to devote sufficient funds or organizers to the southern effort.[5]

Free from union wage scales, the Appalachian operators paid their miners considerably less than northern operators. Wages constituted well over half of coal production costs, so the antiunion operators enjoyed an enormous competitive

[5] Wright and Lubin, "Wage Rates in the Bituminous Industry"; an adequate history of the UMW has not as yet been written, nor is there an adequate biography of John L. Lewis. Helpful, though, are the following: John Brophy, A Miner's Life, ed. John O. P. Hall (Madison, Wis., 1964), 133, 140-44, 154, and 189-92; A. F. Hinrichs, The United Mine Workers of America and the Non-Union Coal Fields, Studies in History, Economics, and Political Science of Columbia University, whole number 246 (New York, 1923); Rex Lauck, John L. Lewis and the International Union United Mine Workers of America: The Story from 1917-1952 (n.p., 1952), 23-44; and William E. Akin, "The Mineworkers' Struggle for Collective Bargaining: 1927-1935" (unpublished M.A. thesis, University of Maryland, 1963), chapt. 1.

advantage. Hence, after the war the Appalachian fields encroached steadily upon Central Competitive markets, aided, the union and the northern operators charged, by railroad freight differentials favorable to the southern fields. At the turn of the century, the northern region had produced most of the nation's soft coal and had employed most of the miners; by 1923 nonunion areas produced 65 percent of the bituminous coal and employed two-thirds of the miners. The mines in the Central Competitive region competed with each other; in addition, the region as a whole competed on unfavorable terms with the southern fields. To the operators, this meant shrunken markets and eventual bankruptcy; to the union it meant either accepting wage reductions in order to remain competitive or facing unemployment as Appalachian coal drove northern coal from the markets. Arguing that if the union accepted wage reductions, the nonunion operators would simply lower their wages further, Lewis chose to fight the battle for the high wage scale that the government had helped to arrange in the union areas in 1920 rather than heed the operators' call for lower wages. The upshot was labor strife, more unemployment, fewer markets, and a knotty dilemma for a national government committed to prosperity.[6]

With a former UMW official, William B. Wilson, as secretary of labor, the Democrats had enjoyed a period of relative stability in the coal industry. After the war, however, the UMW, which had agreed to a freeze on wages during the conflict,

[6] Wright and Lubin, "Wage Rates in the Bituminous Industry." Wage differentials between the southern and northern mines are discussed in Rush Greenslade, "The Economic Effects of Collective Bargaining in Bituminous Coal Mining" (unpublished Ph.D. dissertation, University of Chicago, 1952), 22 and 66, while the freight rate advantages enjoyed by the nonunion areas are described in Edward T. Devine, *Coal: Economic Problems of the Mining, Marketing and Consumption of Anthracite and Soft Coal in the United States* (Bloomington, Ind., 1925), 285, and Harvey C. Mansfield, *The Lake Cargo Coal Rate Controversy: A Study in Governmental Adjustment of a Sectional Dispute,* Columbia University Studies in History, Economics and Public Law, whole number 373 (New York, 1932).

demanded higher wages and a reduced workweek. In the fall of 1919 negotiations failed, and Lewis prepared to lead his militant miners off their jobs. On November 1, 1919, about 400,000 unionized soft coal miners struck in the face of an injunction that Attorney General Palmer secured under the wartime Lever Act. Although Lewis capitulated to the threat of federal force, many strikers refused to heed his appeals to resume work and the strike dragged on. Finally, in December the miners agreed to a government-sponsored compromise that called for a 14 percent wage increase, to go into effect in 1920; they returned to work, but the problems of overdevelopment and diminished markets remained to bedevil the industry.[7]

The agreement was due to expire on March 31, 1922. The postwar depression and the reduced demand for soft coal had weakened the UMW's activities in the southern fields, and its leaders were determined to be successful in their negotiations with the northern operators over the new contract. Since the operators in the Central Competitive Field also faced economic crisis after the war, they sought to abrogate the longstanding regional bargaining procedure and to deal with the union on state and even local levels within the Central Competitive Field, hoping through this device to force the union to agree to wage reductions. Realizing that the state and local bargaining would indeed operate to reduce wages and to weaken the union, and feeling that the very existence of his organization was in the balance, Lewis refused to bargain on these levels and insisted that the operators honor the 1920 contract, which called for the traditional regionwide negotiations.[8]

Every effort of the Harding administration to settle the dispute stumbled over the rock of this controversy. Beginning in October 1921 Harding, Davis, and other administration

[7] Stanley Coben, A. Mitchell Palmer: Politician (New York, 1963), 177-83.
[8] Berman, Labor Disputes, 215-17.

officials tried to bring the two parties together under the terms of the old contract. Since the operators felt that even to confer on the Central Competitive basis would weaken their stand for subregional negotiations, they resisted all these attempts. Ten days before the contract expired Harding admitted defeat, declaring, "I doubt if there is anything which the Administration may do to prevent a suspension of mining activities in the union fields." For the failure to bring about negotiations, Davis placed the blame squarely on the operators, since they refused to honor the existing contract's negotiation procedures.[9]

From the beginning, the administration sought to bring about a conference, but at first it viewed the situation as temporary and not yet critical. "The President and myself," said Davis, "have had neither legal right nor personal desire to dictate [a settlement]." The Department of Labor offered its mediating services, but Hugh Kerwin, chief of the conciliation service, characterized the attitude of the department as being "wholly one of watchful waiting." Hoover declared, "My own personal view . . . is that all big movements of this kind must pass through certain stages before any constructive remedies can be undertaken." Since public deprivation was unlikely for several months, assertive governmental action would only worsen the situation.[10]

In the early weeks of the strike, the major efforts of the administration were to insure a sufficient supply of soft coal to industry and public institutions and to restrain prices. In March the United States Geological Survey had declared that a shutdown of twelve weeks would create critical shortages of bituminous coal, and as early as mid-May the Department of Commerce began to receive reports of price profiteering, spur-

[9] New York *Times*, Feb. 28 and March 31, 1922; Harding to Albert B. Fall, March 21, 1922, USCCR, Drawer 12.

[10] New York *Times*, March 31, 1922; Richard Emmet, Hoover's secretary, to Hoover, April 1, and Hoover to Mayor of Detroit James Couzens, April 18, 1922, Hoover Papers, Box 360. Kerwin is quoted in Emmet's letter.

ring Hoover to action. Hoover emphasized repeatedly that the government had no formal powers with which to combat price increases and that he opposed proposals to create price-fixing authority. While he did seek to commit nonunion operators to a policy of restraint, he characterized any agreements between himself and cooperative coal operators as simply friendly understandings that had no legal standing. Still, he collected and circulated coal price figures, exposing unscrupulous operators to unfavorable publicity, and he urged coal consumers who felt that they were being overcharged to appeal to his department for whatever relief it could offer through such publicity and through appeals to the offending operators. In early June Hoover reported that, while the Department of Commerce could seek only voluntary price restraint, "The result so far has been to halt the rise and to secure considerable reductions."[11]

To deal with the related problem of coal shortages, Hoover encouraged the production of nonunion coal. On May 31 he told a group of West Virginia coal operators that their supplying of nonunion bituminous coal amounted to a patriotic duty, so great was the public need. According to these operators, Hoover added "that he was not concerned with any labor or wage problems, but was interested only in the problem of preventing a severe loss to the Nation." Encouragement of nonunion efforts would have two effects, he hoped: not only would it help to supply public demands, but it would provide a powerful impetus for settlement in the Central Competitive region. The UMW and the Central Competitive operators, of course, resented Hoover's program, arguing that it exacerbated

11 United States Geological Survey, "The Coal Supply in the Event of a General Strike, April 1," March 8, 1922, in George Otis Smith notebook, USCCR, Drawer 12; Hoover press release, June 2, 1922, and Hoover to Harding, June 5, 1922, Department of Commerce Records, File 80769. See also Hoover to Borah, June 9, 1922, Borah Papers, Box 213. By mid-July, however, the situation had changed. Voluntary price restraint "is rapidly breaking down," Hoover declared. (Hoover to Harding, July 19, 1922, Hoover Papers, Box 354).

the conditions that had led to the strike. Nonetheless, Hoover felt that the government's three-part policy of refusal to intervene directly in the strike, price restraint, and encouragement of nonunion production offered the best hope of protecting the public and indirectly promoting settlement. To Lewis, he denied that this plan was designed to penalize the Central Competitive operators and miners; it was simply the best method of dealing with a difficult situation and, he remarked, "I protest against your pounding the non-union operators over my back."[12]

Throughout the spring the administration maintained its policy of caution in the bituminous coal dispute. Then, on June 21 violence erupted in Williamson County, Illinois. Striking miners clashed with strikebreakers, killing at least twenty. Civilian authorities lost control and bloody labor warfare raged. Newspapers throughout the country described the battles, and members of the administration began to work more actively for an end to the strike. "Surely," Davis said, "no better argument can be advanced for the settlement of these disputes around the conference table, than the dead bodies of a score or more of American workmen."[13]

Even as the bituminous coal strike exploded into violence, railroad labor matters came to a head, contributing enormously to the administration's sense of urgency. On July 1, more than 400,000 shopcrafts and other nonoperating employees walked off their jobs in the first nationwide railroad strike since 1894. *Labor*, the organ of the railroad unions, reported that the strike was "as near 100 percent perfect as it is possible to be," and claimed that by July 15, 600,000 railroad men had gone out,

[12] Coal operators' advertisement in Charles Town, W. Va., *Daily Mail*, June 4, 1922, in USCCR, Drawer 16; Hoover to Lewis, June 14, 1922, Hoover Papers, Box 190.

[13] John D. Hicks, *Republican Ascendancy, 1921-1933* (New York, 1960), 70; Paul M. Angle, *Bloody Williamson: A Chapter in American Lawlessness* (New York, 1952); "The Illinois Mine Massacre," *Literary Digest*, LXXIV (July 8, 1922), 5-7. Davis is quoted in Berman, *Labor Disputes*, 219.

at least 100,000 of whom were not members of the unions that
had called the strike.[14]

The strike was as much a protest against the Railroad Labor
Board as it was against the railroads themselves. The unions
had never favored the board and looked upon it as a precursor
to industrial courts and compulsory arbitration. In addition,
Harding had appointed to the labor sector of the board two
men, Walter McMenimen and E. F. Grable, whom the railroad unions opposed.[15]

Labor criticized the board because it was flagrantly unfair
to the workers. While the body often voted for the unions,
their charge was justified because of the unequal implementation of board decisions. For example, it had abrogated the
national agreements that covered all unionized train-service
employees and that had been instrumental in the growth of the

[14] *Labor*, July 1 and 15, 1922. There were sixteen standard railroad
labor organizations at this time, five consisting of workers who operated
the trains and the other eleven of men who serviced and maintained the
engines, cars, tracks, and stations. The operating railroad men had been
organized early and their prestigious organizations commanded great
respect. These brotherhoods were not directly affiliated with the AFL,
although they did at times cooperate with that organization. The other
eleven unions were weaker and more recently organized, their growth having been much stimulated during the period of governmental operation.
These unions were part of the AFL's Railway Employees Department.
While the two bodies of railroad unionists had much in common—joining
together, for example, to publish *Labor*—they had many separate interests
also, especially since the more prestigious and established brotherhoods
were often unwilling to support their less fortunate colleagues. Seven of
the nonoperating rail unions—the blacksmiths, the boilermakers, the
machinists, the carmen, the electrical workers, the sheetmetal workers, and
the stationary firemen—struck in July 1922, although many of the clerks
and maintenance-of-way employees joined the strike of their own accord.
See Elwin W. Sigmund, "Federal Laws Concerning Railroad Labor Disputes: A Legislative and Legal History, 1877-1934" (unpublished Ph.D.
dissertation, University of Illinois, 1961), chaps. 4-8, and Robert H.
Zieger, "From Antagonism to Accord: Railroad Labor Policy in the
1920s," *Labor History*, IX (Winter 1968), 25-28. Leo Troy, "Labor
Representation on American Railways," *Labor History*, II (Fall 1961),
295-300, discusses effects of government control on nonoperating unions.

[15] In addition to Sigmund and Zieger, cited above, see Harry D. Wolf,
The Railroad Labor Board (Chicago, 1927), 214-65, and Leonard A.
Lecht, *Experience Under Railway Labor Legislation* (New York, 1955),
chaps. 1 and 2.

nonoperating unions. In addition, the board ordered successive wage slashes in 1920 and 1921, arguing that the employees had to sacrifice to bear their share of the postwar economic distress. The unions had accepted reluctantly most of these decisions, although they successfully forestalled the implementation of some. However, when the board ruled against powerful railroads, as it did on several occasions, the carriers ignored the decisions without penalty, creating a sense of outrage among the employees and unions. Thus, although the board sanctioned wage reductions for shopcrafts and maintenance-of-way workers in June 1922 the strike was actually a product of these grievances, coupled with the board's apparent inability to make the railroads abide by decisions unfavorable to them.[16]

The president responded immediately. Erroneously regarding board decisions as legally binding, Harding declared his determination to force both parties to accept them. White House spokesmen denounced the strike as virtual contempt of government. Shortly after the strike began, Harding reinforced his position by supporting the board in a resolution that it passed, condemning the strikers as outlaws and encouraging the carriers to strip them of seniority rights, thus inviting the railroads to employ strikebreakers. Although he privately admitted that the failure of the carriers to adhere to board decisions lent justice to the employees' grievances, and although he encouraged efforts to settle the dispute through negotiation, the sanctity of board decisions remained the basis of his personal attitude.[17]

[16] In addition to sources cited in notes 14 and 15 above, see Philip A. Taft, *The AFL in the Time of Gompers* (New York, 1957), 471-72, and John R. Commons and others, *History of Labor in the United States. IV: Labor Movements*, by Selig Perlman and Philip A. Taft (New York, 1935), 517-20.

[17] New York *Times*, July 1, 1922; Railroad Labor Board Resolution, July 3, 1922, USCSR, File 165/277B. For Harding's awareness of the grievances of the strikers, see Harding to Sen. Atlee Pomerene, July 31, 1922, Harding Papers, Box 61. Harding's endorsement of the RLB resolution and his public criticism of the shopmen is expressed in a presidential proclamation, July 11, 1922, printed in Berman, *Labor Disputes*, 229-30.

Harding's cabinet was sharply divided. Daugherty denied that there was justice in the employees' case and sought repeatedly to persuade the president to take drastic action. He held that agents of the Soviet government had called and dominated the strike, and he set about immediately to dispatch federal marshals and to build a case for the use of injunctions. Entirely opposed to this view, Davis spoke for the railroad workers. It was wrong, he felt, to criticize them for disregarding one of the board's decisions, for the railroads had continually ignored them with impunity. Labor and management alike regarded the federal agency as powerless and unwieldy, he claimed. To punish the unions, which had been more faithful to board decisions than were the carriers, was unfair. Davis tried to find a compromise formula, meeting often with Bert Jewell, the president of the AFL Railway Employees' Department, and other labor officials. Taking another approach, Hoover sought to enlist the aid of moderate· railroad executives such as Daniel Willard, president of the Baltimore and Ohio, in behalf of a settlement that would treat the unions equitably.[18]

As July progressed, the nation began to feel the impact of the strikes. Harding attempted to form some unified policy, but, he complained, "It is a very great menace to have two great nation-wide strikes on hand at one time." The railroad strike began to affect the nation's transportation system and to slow soft coal deliveries. In mid-July George Otis Smith,

[18] Daugherty's view of the strike is expressed in Harry M. Daugherty (in collaboration with Thomas Dixon), *The Inside Story of the Harding Tragedy* (New York, 1932), 127-40. See also Daugherty to Harding, July 29, 1922, Harding Papers, Box 61, and U.S., Department of Justice, *Appendix to the Annual Report of the Attorney General of the United States for the Fiscal Year 1922* (Washington, D.C., 1924), which contains most of the correspondence and documents regarding Daugherty's view of the strike and his efforts to defeat it. For Davis' views, see Davis to Rodney Brandon, July 20, 1922, Davis Papers, Box 39, and New York *Times*, July 23, 1922. Hoover's attitude is revealed in *The Memoirs of Herbert Hoover. II: The Cabinet and the Presidency, 1921-1933* (New York, 1952), 105-106.

director of the United States Geological Survey, issued a memorandum which stated flatly that nonunion soft coal production simply was not adequate, even though the administration had encouraged the Appalachian operators continually. In order for the country to escape a disastrous fuel shortage, Smith declared, the shopmen's strike had to come to a swift conclusion and the unionized bituminous coal areas had to resume production. Coupled with the administration's concern about the congressional elections, this stark notice of the failure of the nonunion coal areas to supply the nation adequately made action imperative.[19]

Throughout much of July, the president wavered between Daugherty's position and that of Hoover and Davis in his response to the industrial crisis. His initial reactions showed considerable sympathy for the strikers in both disputes. He had on several occasions criticized the Central Competitive operators for failing to negotiate with the UMW as the expired contract required, declaring for example on June 28 that "the mine operators made the colossal blunder in declining the requested conference prior to the time of the strike." Moreover, on the several occasions he corrected antilabor spokesmen who sought to place the entire blame for the rail strike on the unionists. It was hardly fair to single out the shopmen, he insisted, for the railroads had frequently ignored Railroad Labor Board decisions that pertained to them. He noted that "There has been a very strong protest in behalf of business men in favor of getting through with the railroad strike, cost what it may," but he rejected this advice, for, as he told Senator Atlee Pomerene, "I very much fear . . . that peace and restored transportation would be a very long way off if we undertook to bring it about from the viewpoint of those

[19] Harding to Russell R. Whitman, July 31, 1922, Harding Papers, Box 61; George Otis Smith memorandum, "Could the Non-Union Fields Meet the Country's Requirements for Coal?" ca. July 15, 1922, USCCR, Drawer 12.

who speak alone for the operators."[20] Consistent with these sentiments, the early efforts of the administration in both strikes evinced some concern for labor's demands and grievances.

Even before the outbreak of the railroad strike, the administration renewed its efforts to settle the bituminous coal strike. The confusing situation defied the efforts of Davis and Hoover, the chief agents of the government. The primary problem was to establish a level upon which negotiations could take place. The mine operators and the National Coal Association insisted upon district and local negotiations, arguing that competition and unfavorable market conditions for soft coal rendered obsolete the 1920 scale and the whole concept of the four-state Central Competitive region as a cohesive bargaining unit. Declared J. H. Pritchard of the Southern Ohio Operators' Association, the traditional bargaining arrangement had helped to cause "extreme poverty and business depression throughout the mining districts of Southern Ohio." In response to local conditions and to circumstances that had changed since the 1920 agreement, the Southern Ohio Operators would propose a new wage scale in the district that would compensate for the competitive advantages that the Appalachian mines enjoyed. Of course, Lewis rejected this view, for he realized that new arrangements would certainly mean wage reductions. The UMW leaders emphasized repeatedly that state and sub-district conferences were unacceptable to the union and that "The holding of state conferences would destroy the joint inter-state movement that has existed . . . for twenty-four years." Lewis feared that sub-regional negotiations would drive

[20] Harding's criticism of the soft coal operators is in Harding to Pomerene, June 28, 1922, Harding Papers, Box 175. His comments on the carriers' abuse of the Railroad Labor Board occur in three separate letters, all dated July 31, 1922, to Pomerene, to Sen. George Wharton Pepper, and to Russell R. Whitman, Harding Papers, Box 61. See also Andrew Sinclair, *The Available Man: The Life Behind the Masks of Warren Gamaliel Harding* (New York, 1965), 256-57.

union miners' wages down to the lowest common denominator in the union fields and encourage even lower wages in the south. In addition, Lewis faced challenges to his leadership within the UMW. From one side, Frank Farrington, president of the Illinois (district 12) UMW, favored district negotiations as a means of consolidating his strength in the UMW's strongest district and of contesting Lewis' hold on the national presidency. From the other side, militants in the western Pennsylvania and upper southern fields criticized the national leadership for not pressing the unionization campaign into the nonunion areas of Pennsylvania, West Virginia, and Kentucky. John Brophy, who was seeking to organize these soft coal miners, angrily charged that Lewis' fixation with the Central Competitive Field constituted an abandonment of the newly organized miners. The union president, Brophy charged, was too eager to come to an agreement with the Central Competitive operators and thus to leave the newly organized workers outside the region to the mercies of the ruthless nonunion operators.[21]

Thus, the first problem of the administration was to get the parties to agree to some common principles upon which to start negotiations. Gradually Hoover, usually the source of the basic ideas regarding the strikes, formulated a general approach to the bituminous coal situation. First, he contended that while district negotiations were probably inevitable, regional talks were necessary at the outset to get the two parties to the negotiation table, with the understanding that such a conference would merely serve the purpose of defining the terms of subsequent conferences. Secondly, some form of arbitration

[21] For the operators' view, see Pritchard to Lewis, Dec. 27, 1921, along with similar communications from Central Competitive mineowners, in UMW *Journal*, Jan. 15, 1922. Lewis' view is summarized in Akin, "The Mineworkers' Struggle for Collective Bargaining," chapt. 1, while the words quoted are in UMW *Journal*, March 15, 1922. For the Lewis-Farrington antagonism, see UMW *Journal*, March 15, 1922, Brophy, A *Miner's Life*, 191, and Philip A. Taft, *Organized Labor in American History* (New York, 1964), 400.

was highly desirable, even though the union resisted this device. Finally, he declared that the administration could not stop with temporary settlement of the current dispute. Some way had to be found out of the coal dilemma. Hoover contended that some sort of federal investigatory and mediatory commission was needed not only to moderate future disagreements but also to study the entire coal problem and to recommend long-range, fundamental solutions.[22]

Shifting his focus from encouragement of nonunion production and price restraint, Hoover formulated and communicated these recommendations to the president between the middle of June and the middle of July 1922. After the Herrin violence, he began to organize a White House conference of miners and operators to discuss their demands in the context of his general approach. On June 26 Davis lunched with Lewis, Hoover conferred with A. M. Ogle of the National Coal Association, and the two parties committed themselves to a meeting with Harding on July 1. Summarizing his limited expectations for a settlement, Hoover informed the president of his efforts: "I have the feeling that the only thing we could hope to succeed in at this meeting is the acceptance of some kind of machinery for continued negotiations, and I have the feeling that we must insist on public representation in such machinery."[23]

During the first two weeks of July, representatives of the union and the operators met periodically with government officials. The UMW continued its insistence upon the Central Competitive Field as the basic bargaining unit, while the operators submitted proposals that provided for district level bargaining and for arbitration. After listening to both sides Hoover concluded on July 5 that no agreement would be

[22] Hoover's views are expressed in a series of letters and memoranda to Harding during June and July 1922. See Hoover to Harding, June 17, 26, July 5, 14, 1922, Hoover Papers, Box 243.

[23] Hoover to Harding, June 26, 1922, Hoover Papers, Box 243; New York *Times*, June 27, 1922.

reached by the parties themselves, and that the administration needed to make definite proposals. Harding met with them and on July 10 submitted a plan whereby the miners would return to work under the terms of the 1920 contract. The president would appoint a commission that would survey the entire coal situation and would suggest changes in the structure of collective bargaining and in wage rates consistent with its findings. The miners tentatively accepted this compromise, for it left intact both the 1920 wage scales and the Central Competitive Field bargaining unit. Some operators lent their support, but *Coal Age*, an organ of the coal operators, attacked the president's plan, claiming that "There has been no parallel to this since the passage of the Adamson law six years ago." In addition, the Mellon coal interests of Pittsburgh opposed it, sealing its fate. Hoover and Harding tried variations of this proposal, but to no avail. Increasingly they turned to arbitration as a solution, feeling that so long as the mines resumed output, inquiry by an impartial tribunal could settle the remaining difficulties. The UMW, while willing to accept a governmentally appointed body with recommendatory powers, would not agree to arbitration, at least without a definite understanding as to the subjects to be arbitrated.[24]

The president and the secretary of commerce placed great faith in arbitration. Harding regarded it as a device desirable in itself and could not understand why the unionists objected to it. Even at that late date he had not grasped the fundamental importance of the Central Competitive Field to the

[24] For the basic plan of the operators, and for Hoover's view of the need for federal involvement, see Hoover's telegram to Harding, July 5, 1922, Hoover Papers, Box 243. For the July 10 proposal, which reflected Hoover's influence, see Berman, *Labor Disputes*, 220-21. For the operators' reaction, see *Coal Age*, XXII (July 13, 1922), 43, reprint in Frelinghuysen Papers, Coal Box 6. Hoover's support for arbitration is seen in a letter to Harding, July 14, 1922, Hoover Papers, Box 243. Despite his abhorrence for compulsion, Hoover as early as 1909 had shown enthusiasm for compulsory arbitration of labor disputes. See Herbert C. Hoover, *Principles of Mining: Valuation, Organization, and Administration* (New York, 1909), 168.

union, for on July 24 he told Governor Alexander J. Groesbeck of Michigan that the UMW was opposed to district or local arrangements and that "This *apparently is one of the issues involved*, and one which must be definitely settled."[25] Thus, it was with justice that John Brophy, the dissident unionist, criticized the administration for insisting upon arbitration without even understanding the issues involved. Harding, he recalled, "seized upon the magic word 'arbitration,' and used it in all his proposals and suggestions." The UMW leaders sought repeatedly to define the terms of arbitration. Would, for example, the concept of the Central Competitive Field be subject to arbitration? Would arbitration extend to the newly unionized fields outside the Central Competitive Field? But "Harding simply clung to the empty generality about arbitration, showing no consciousness that the desirability of the procedure would depend on how it was used."[26]

By July 17, Harding concluded that the government's efforts had failed. For this he blamed the UMW, since it had been primarily responsible for the rejection of the last administration proposal. Thus, in his statement acknowledging the fruitless-ness of his administration's efforts, he declared that the strike would continue, "owing to the refusal of mine-workers and a minority of . . . [the] operators to accept the proposed arbitra-tion."[27] This statement presaged more drastic action. In the middle of July, with coal shortages growing acute, with the rail strike vastly complicating matters, and with the subtleties of collective bargaining beyond his grasp, the president abandoned his administration's earlier position that the mine owners had been responsible for the failure of negotiations and now launched a vigorous campaign to discredit the UMW and to break the back of the union's effort.

On July 18, Harding inaugurated his assault upon the union

[25] Harding to Groesbeck, July 24, 1922, Harding Papers, Box 174. Emphasis added. See also *The New Republic*, XXXI (Aug. 9, 1922), 292.
[26] Brophy, *A Miner's Life*, 189-90.
[27] Harding statement, July 17, 1922, Harding Papers, Box 174.

with a telegram to 28 governors of soft coal producing states. Noting the failure of negotiations, Harding encouraged them to provide assurances to coal operators that the states would protect the right of men to work. In effect Harding was urging the mines in the union areas to resort to strikebreaking. Moreover, he pledged "the assurance of the prompt and full support of the Federal Government whenever and wherever you find your own agencies of law and order inadequate to meet the situation." Simultaneously, the Department of War issued orders for corps commanders to be ready for domestic crisis duty in the strike-torn areas.[28]

Harding's plea for strikebreakers had little effect. The governors and coal operators were overwhelmingly favorable, but almost all reported that miners were simply not available. "Practically all of our ninety thousand qualified mine workers . . . are unionized and ceased work on April first," Acting Governor Fred E. Sterling of Illinois reported. Laws in many states, including Illinois, required the licensing of miners. Since licensed miners were almost all members of the UMW, this law in effect prevented the mines from operating. Harding admitted that such laws were safety measures and hence probably in the public interest, but, he declared to Sterling, "you may face a condition in Illinois which will require the repeal of such a law. The simple truth is that Americans must have fuel."[29]

From the middle of July until the middle of August, the administration reverted to its pre-Herrin policy. Hoover undertook with indifferent success the task of propping up the

---

[28] Harding press release (text of telegrams to 28 state governors), July 18, 1922, Harding Papers, Box 174; Berman, *Labor Disputes*, 222.

[29] The replies of the governors are in Harding Papers, Box 174. Typical is that of Gov. Arthur M. Hyde of Missouri, July 19, 1922. Some governors, including Albert C. Ritchie of Maryland and Cameron Morrison of North Carolina, replied unfavorably, claiming that state and federal sanctioning of strikebreakers would constitute a grossly unfair antilabor act. For the Sterling-Harding exchange, see their letters dated July 24, 1922, Harding Papers, Box 175.

sagging programs of price restraint and encouragement of non-union production. Davis limited himself to keeping the door open to renewal of negotiations while he praised the president for his high-minded and altruistic approach to the strike. When a critic claimed that Harding's efforts to defeat the strike would drive wages down, the loyal secretary protested, "Harding is a kind man in every respect." Without making clear just how the defeat of the UMW, to which the administration was now committed, would help to keep wages up, Davis declared that Harding "has always advocated that the workers receive a wage that is sufficient to make their house a home and life worth living."[30]

Throughout the rest of July and August, Harding lashed out repeatedly at the United Mine Workers. Resentful over Lewis' refusal to bargain on the subregional level and over the UMW president's opposition to arbitration, Harding attacked the union leader and his organization publicly and privately. He regarded the UMW's refusal to settle in local areas as contempt for the public interest and indicated that "it will be necessary for government to challenge the authority of the mine workers to tie up the entire country." He declared, "It is not for me to criticize Mr. Lewis . . ., [but] I think he has handled the situation with very little diplomacy and less discretion." Harding characterized the mineworkers' chieftain as defiant and uncompromising. He accused the union of trying "to freeze the American people into submission." Throughout his month-long assault, he clung to the assumption that it was a few unscrupulous leaders who stood in the way of local settlements, apparently even at this late date unable to understand the union's determination not to abandon a bargaining arrangement that had prevailed for a quarter of a century, "I cannot believe," he wrote, "that the thoughtful, loyal mine

[30] For Hoover's efforts, see Hoover to Harding, July 19, 1922, Hoover Papers, Box 354, and Department of Commerce mimeographed announcement, July 25, 1922, USCCR, Drawer 16. Davis' views are expressed in Davis to A. W. McMillen, July 24, 1922, USCSR, File 170/1633B.

workers throughout the country mean to imperil the welfare of the people of the United States."[31]

As the administration's program in the soft coal strike degenerated into an assault upon the UMW, a similar pattern developed in the shopmen's strike. With thousands of skilled machinists and maintenance employees off their jobs, locomotives broke down and train service became uncertain in some areas. Transportation failure made more critical the coal shortage, and demands for assertive action confronted the heavily burdened president. William Allen White urged Harding to move decisively, for under the impact of the crisis his administration was "drifting toward bankruptcy." Charles D. Hilles, a conservative Republican and former national chairman, called upon the president to move directly against the strikers in both disputes. Hilles usually opposed vigorous use of federal authority, but he informed Mrs. Harding that the situation was critical and "There are many precedents for red-blooded action on the part of the Chief Executive."[32]

Throughout July and into August conflict raged within the administration over the shopmen's strike. Daugherty continued to press upon Harding his reports of violence and drastic transportation breakdown. The attorney general sent federal agents to gather information against the strikers and sent federal marshals to protect railroad property. Hoover and

[31] Harding to Gov. Robert D. Carey of Wyoming, July 31, and to Gov. Warren T. McCray of Indiana, July 27, 1922, Harding Papers, Box 174; Harding to Stanley Washburn, July 24 and 27, 1922, Washburn Papers, Box 1. Secretary of Labor Davis joined in the verbal assault upon Lewis, accusing him (in an unsent letter, at least) of sabotaging a settlement. "I know of no way for adjusting the difficulty except on the principle of give and take . . . ," Davis declared, but "you have stubbornly and autocratically refused to consider such a possibility." (Davis' unsent letter addressed to Lewis, July 27, 1922, Davis Papers, Box 39.) Thus, apparently even Davis was unaware of the great significance that the UMW attached to regionwide bargaining.

[32] Sigmund, "Federal Laws," contains an account of the disruption of train service (142-43). For White's plea for action, see Emporia Gazette, Aug. 1, 1922, and for Hilles', see Hilles to Mrs. Harding, Aug. 1, 1922, Hilles Papers, Box 203.

Davis, however, were equally adamant, and, for the time being, their counsel was more influential. Hoover particularly regarded the strike as an unfortunate result of the unwieldy Railroad Labor Board. He could not blame the unionists and could not understand why the carriers and their advocates insisted upon making the strike a basic question of principle. He sought to end the dispute quickly and equitably, to get the trains and nonunion soft coal moving, and to resume his work of ameliorating labor-management antagonism. He sought constantly to persuade businessmen and railroad officials that the strike ought to be settled with a minimum of rancor. Late in the strike, a note of weariness and resignation crept into his remonstrances to antilabor advocates. Thus, he told one, "If the American people . . . believe that there is a great moral principle involved upon which a hundred million shall make a sacrifice, they, no doubt, can have their way about it."[33]

Later in July a compromise settlement appeared likely. Davis pressed the unionists' viewpoint at cabinet meetings and with Harding's approval he went to Chicago to confer with Jewell. Davis found the unionists ready to come to an agreement, but, the AFL railroad labor leader informed the secretary, while the unions were entirely willing to settle, the Association of Railway Executives, the carriers' association, had now erected a major obstacle to a compromise: they insisted upon removing seniority rights from striking employees. The carriers contended that under the encouragement of the July 3 Railroad Labor Board resolution they had hired thousands of nonunion workers. Since in their view and apparently in Harding's the unionists were in effect striking in contempt of the government, these new workers were performing a patriotic and essential function. If the railroads had to honor the seniority claims of strikers when the strike ended, the costs would force them to discharge most of these replacements, thus in effect rewarding

[33] Hoover to Robert Withington, Aug. 26, 1922, Hoover Papers, Box 253.

disloyalty and punishing patriotism. The unionists charged that their foes were thinking of more practical matters. If the strike ended with the destruction of seniority, the carriers would be able to choose from an oversupply of workers, thus virtually naming their own terms. Moreover, without protection of seniority the right to strike was meaningless. Since no legislation prohibited railroad strikes, the unions were acting in a manner entirely consistent with the normal pattern of labor-management relations. It was the employers, with their insistence upon stripping strikers of seniority rights, who were seeking to change drastically the balance of power between the two parties and who would, if successful, pit worker against worker, reduce wages, and force the railroad men into company unions. Since the seniority question had not been part of the original grievances, and since retention of seniority was fundamental to labor unions, the railroad unionists regarded the carriers' policy as a gratuitous and basic attack upon their very existence.[34]

Davis thought that even this controversy could be reconciled. Out of his conversations with Jewell grew an administration proposal. Late in July the president suggested that both parties agree to a resumption of work on a *status quo* basis, with the employees accepting the wage reduction and the carriers abandoning their position on seniority and dropping law suits against strikers. Both sides would agree to abide by future Railroad Labor Board decisions and, the president indicated, he would expect the carriers to begin adherence to past decisions that they had hitherto ignored. By August 1 the unions were

[34] For indications of the carriers' stand on seniority and the vigor with which they held it, see W. H. Chandler and J. H. Beck, president and executive secretary respectively of the National Industrial Traffic League, to members of the League (Circular No. 461), July 28, 1922, copy in Hoover Papers, Box 253, and telegram from Employers' Association of North Jersey to Sen. Joseph Frelinghuysen, July 31, 1922, Frelinghuysen Papers, Railroad Strike folder. For the unions' view, see New York *Times*, July 23, 1922, and Department of Labor, notes (by Davis?), July 28, 1922, uscsr, File 170/1553A.

willing to accept such terms, for without the direct support of the powerful operating brotherhoods they could not hope to win. Moreover, the strike had already depleted their meager resources. Harding's terms were not really favorable to them, for the carriers had only to concede a point that had not been part of the original grievances while the unions had to accept the wage cut, which had been among their original reasons for striking. Nonetheless, reeling under the strain of the strike, they accepted, although not without noting to the president their unhappiness with such a settlement.[35]

It remained for the administration to persuade the carriers to agree to these terms. On July 31, Harding made public a letter to Thomas Dewitt Cuyler, chairman of the Association of Railway Executives (ARE), which outlined the administration's plan. Seniority, he realized, was a problem, but "It has seemed to me that the proposition that the order of things on the day the strike began be restored . . . will leave to the managers only the difficult problem of dealing with the new men employed." Looking at the dispute from "the larger viewpoint," the president contended that the resumption of transportation and the recognition of the Railroad Labor Board would far outweigh the temporary problem of seniority. Harding expressed strongly his desire to end the strike quickly. Since acceptance of the compromise by the unions was certain, if the managers rejected it "they will be obligated to open direct negotiations or assume full responsibility for the situation."[36]

Hoover traveled to New York to persuade the ARE to agree to the proposal, but the executives were in no mood to compromise. They knew that the AFL railroad unions could not hold out long. They were determined to crush the strike,

[35] Telegram from various labor leaders to Harding, Aug. 2, 1922, uscsr, File 170/1553A.

[36] Harding to Cuyler, July 31, published in the New York *Times*, Aug. 21, 1922. This memorandumlike letter was probably written by Hoover for Harding's signature. A typescript copy is in the Hoover Papers, Box 253.

to chasten the rebellious workers, and to undermine the influence of the AFL unions among their workers. To them, an important principle was involved in the seniority question. As one business group telegraphed Hoover, "If the railroad presidents break their word now no one in the future will believe the industrial leaders when a strike is on and all industry will be at the mercy of labor unions." The secretary knew that conservative opinion was paramount, but he was unprepared for the flat and uncordial refusal with which the ARE greeted the president's plan. The railroad men treated him with outright hostility, for many of them were angry with the secretary for his support of a moderate solution. They rejected the administration's settlement plan by a nearly unanimous vote. Hoover, convinced that "their social instinct belonged to an early Egyptian period," returned to Washington. As he left New York, one executive expressed the carriers' determination to cripple the unions and break the strike. "Acceptance of President Harding's proposal," asserted president Samuel Felton of Chicago and Great Western Railroad, "would result in complete demoralization of America's transportation system." Denouncing governmental interference, Felton sounded the keynote of the carriers' program: "We must have discipline," he insisted.[37]

Until this point, the Harding administration had shown considerable sympathy toward the unions. Harding had repeatedly emphasized the responsibility of the carriers for creating labor antagonism toward the Railroad Labor Board, and Davis and Hoover had actively sought a compromise solution that would at least preserve the AFL unions. Indeed, Harding's initial reaction to the ARE's refusal to accept his

[37] The telegram cited (from Herman H. Hettler and John M. Glenn, officers of an Illinois businessmen's organization, to Hoover, ca. Aug. 1, 1922, Hoover Papers, Box 253) is typical of many that government officials received, not only from railroad men but from other businessmen and groups. Hoover's comments about the carriers and his account of the meeting are in *Memoirs*, II, 105-107. For Hoover's trip and the carriers' intransigence, see New York *Times*, Aug. 1, 2, 1922.

plan seemed to follow this pattern, for he quickly complained to Cuyler that while the unions had accepted the plan, "the majority of your membership will accept no friendly negotiations to end the strike."[38]

Whatever good will Harding had had for the unions, however, quickly evaporated. On August 4, he informed one unionist that the strike was completely inexcusable. Faced with carrier intransigence, he now turned to a new formula that would, he hoped, appease the railroad executives. Since seniority remained at the core of the managers' opposition to his former plan, Harding now called "on the striking workmen to return to work, and . . . upon the carriers to assign them to work, and . . . upon both workmen and carriers . . ., to take the question in dispute [i.e., seniority rights] to the Railroad Labor Board for hearing and decision, and a compliance by both with the decision rendered." In effect, Harding was asking the unions to accept arbitration by the Railroad Labor Board on the question of seniority. To the president, this plan had the dual advantages of ending the strike and having the tough problem solved by an impartial tribunal, but, just as in the coal strike, he apparently failed to understand the meaning of his proposal. The unions had struck in part in protest over the personnel and activities of the board. Moreover, they blamed the board's July 3 resolution for encouraging the carriers to recruit strikebreakers and for allowing them to raise the question of seniority in negotiations. Thus, they felt that it was hardly reasonable for the president to expect the unions, which traced their grievances directly to this body, to entrust their interests and especially their precious seniority rights to it for arbitration. On August 7, shortly after Harding offered this plan, they rejected it flatly.[39]

---

[38] Harding to Cuyler, Aug. 4, 1922, Harding Papers, Box 62.

[39] Harding to Timothy Shea, Aug. 4, and B. F. Bush, president of the Missouri and Pacific Railroad, Aug. 8, 1922, Harding Papers, Box 62; Harding to Cuyler, Aug. 7, 1922, Hoover Papers, Box 253; Berman, *Labor Disputes*, 233.

With the rejection of these two proposals and with the coal strikes still unsettled, the administration seemed utterly unable to cope with the deepening crisis. Harding had been devoting "something more than ninety percent of my time . . . to the industrial situation," he complained. Senator Peter Norbeck of South Dakota, after a visit to the distressed chief executive, reported, "It is just as necessary to mention the strike[s] when you go to the White House as it is to speak about the weather when you meet your neighbor." Still, results were meager. The coal deficit grew, and a member of the Interstate Commerce Commission reported that a complete transportation breakdown impended.[40]

Faced with this crisis and with the threatening political effects of the strikes, Harding, unable to persuade the railroad and coal operators to accept compromises, sought to force settlements through an assault upon the unions. On August 18 Harding addressed a joint session of Congress on the labor crisis. He described the peril to the nation resulting from the intertwined disputes: declining rail transportation choked off the supply of coal, already dangerously low. He then outlined the efforts of the administration to bring about settlements. In both the soft coal and the railroad strikes, Harding declared, both sides had refused to take heed of the public interest. He indicated that the mine operators and the carriers had been guilty of this, the former for failing to negotiate under the expired contract and the latter for their intransigence on the seniority issue. But, he insisted, the prime responsibility belonged with the labor organizations. In the coal strike, for example, after his arbitration plan was refused, he offered federal protection for men who wanted to work. "But little or no new production followed. The simple but significant

[40] Harding to Gov. John J. Blaine of Wisconsin, Aug. 31, 1922, Harding Papers, Box 174; Norbeck to C. M. Henry, Aug. 8, 1922, Peter Norbeck Papers (University of South Dakota Library); Mark Potter to Sen. William E. Borah, Borah Papers, Box 223.

truth was revealed that . . . the country is at the mercy of the United Mine Workers."[41]

Since the president had been criticizing the union for several weeks, his comments about the coal strike were not surprising. His attack upon the rail unions, however, constituted a significant reversal of the administration's public position. Whereas only two weeks before, the refusal of the carriers to accept a compromise on seniority had angered the president and his secretary of commerce, he now lashed out at the train employees. Drawing upon the lengthy reports that Daugherty had been sending him for several weeks, Harding described instances of violence and the desertion of passenger trains in isolated areas. He accused the rail strikers of "cruelty and contempt" and of having "conspired to paralyze transportation." "There is," he charged, "a state of lawlessness shocking to every conception of American law and order." Admitting that carrier violations of Railroad Labor Board decisions had triggered understandable grievances among the shopmen, he insisted that "they had a remedy without seeking to paralyze interstate commerce."[42]

Although he favored strengthening the Railroad Labor Board, Harding was not now asking Congress for special powers or for emergency legislation. His message was a report to the Congress and to the public. Yet it was more, for in passing over so lightly the responsibility of the carriers and operators and in emphasizing so starkly the truculence of the unionists, he was in effect committing the government to an antilabor public position. Here was notice that the federal government, hitherto thwarted in its efforts to reach settlements, would turn upon the strikers.

Even while Harding was denouncing the UMW, its leaders were meeting with bituminous coal operators from the Central

[41] U.S., *Address of the President of the United States to the Congress, August 18, 1922* (Washington, D. C., 1922).
[42] *Ibid.*

Competitive Field in Cleveland. Davis kept in close touch with the discussions and although Harding felt that his personal intervention would be useless, the conferences had the support of the administration. With the operators gradually abandoning their insistence upon district negotiations and arbitration, the two parties evolved a compromise. On August 30, they announced an agreement wherein they would resume operations under the terms of the old contract. They asked the president to appoint a commission to study the entire coal industry and to recommend changes in the contracts and wage scales.[43] This was essentially the same plan that Harding had proposed and the union had accepted on July 1.

In the railroad strike, however, the carriers, reinforced by Harding's public assault upon the unions, remained immovable. Cuyled contended that in accepting the president's substitute proposal of August 7 (which would have turned the seniority dispute over to the Railroad Labor Board), "a large majority [of the railroad companies] have literally complied with the President's request [for a settlement]." Letters and telegrams from businessmen and other citizens were sent to Harding, Hoover, and other officials urging firmness against the unionists. While most of these did not predict, as did one outraged businessman, that if the carriers had to abandon their position on seniority "the whole foundation of our civilization must crumble," all agreed on the need for a stalwart stand against labor.[44]

Hoover continued to resist these pressures, but the president

[43] For the federal role in the Cleveland meetings, see New York Times, Aug. 2 and 6, 1922; Hoover to Davis, Aug. 11, 1922, Hoover Papers, Box 360; and Berman, Labor Disputes, 223-24. For Harding's attitude, see George Christian, Jr. (Harding's secretary) to John S. Jones, Harding Papers, Box 174. The concurrent anthracite strike was settled largely through the work of Sen. George Wharton Pepper of Pennsylvania in separate negotiations that he and Sen. David Reed, also of Pennsylvania, presided over. See Zieger, "Senator George Wharton Pepper," 167-70.

[44] Cuyler to Sen. William E. Borah, Aug. 22, 1922, Borah Papers, Box 223. For the pressures upon Hoover and other administration officials, see Hoover Papers, Box 253. The dire quotation is from Robert Withington to Hoover, Aug. 23, 1922, Hoover Papers, Box 253.

fell more and more under the influence of Daugherty. The attorney general declared that the approach of Davis and Hoover "meant a surrender of principles of government which could not be yielded." He kept Harding informed of reports from federal marshals and attorneys of bombings and violence. With Mrs. Harding seriously ill and with the transportation crisis growing ever worse, Harding gravitated increasingly toward his friend's viewpoint. Thus, on August 19, the day after his speech to Congress, Harding instructed Daugherty, "At any time you have an intolerant [sic] situation, where it is desirable for the federal government to intervene with armed forces please let me know so that the matter may be immediately taken up."[45]

By late August, the unions, in desperate straits, were willing to settle on virtually any terms that would preserve seniority rights. Some railroads, eager to bring the costly dispute to a conclusion, accepted this provision and gradually drew closer to the unionists, under the prodding of Hoover.[46] Many of the carriers, however, remained intransigent, vowing to crush the strike and to curb the influence of the troublesome unions. They found Daugherty, and increasingly the president himself, extremely cooperative. The attorney general had already secured some local injunctions and had dispatched 3,250 federal marshals to protect railroad property. Finally, on September 1, despite advice to the contrary of his aides in the Department

[45] Daugherty and Dixon, *Inside Story*, 129-30; Daugherty to Harding, Aug. 19, 1922, and Harding to Daugherty, Aug. 19, 1922, Harding Papers, Box 61. See also Department of Justice, *Appendix to the Annual Report of the Attorney General*, 1-7.

[46] An agreement that preserved seniority rights—known as the Willard-Jewell or Baltimore Agreement—was reached on Sept. 13. In all, the AFL Railway Employees Department secured settlements on 112 roads under this agreement, and settlements with another 64 under a modified version. At least 130 carriers, including some of the largest, would not accept it. See Edward Keating, *The Gentleman from Colorado: A Memoir* (Denver, 1964), 482; Taft, *Organized Labor in American History*, 380; *Labor*, Sept. 16, 1922; and Harding to Willard, Sept. 21, 1922, Harding Papers, Box 62. See also Hoover, *Memoirs*, II, 105-107.

of Justice, he asked Federal Judge James Wilkerson of Chicago
to issue a restraining order to curb the activities of the strikers.
This document and the preliminary injunction itself, which
followed three weeks later, were among the most far-reaching
labor dicta to which the federal government had ever resorted.
Among other things, they prohibited union officials from
"picketing or in any manner by letters, circulars, telephone
messages, word of mouth, or interviews encouraging any person
to leave the employ of a railroad."[47]

Having struck this blow against "the increasing threat
against civilization," the attorney general, shrugging off alleged
plots against his life, journeyed to Chicago to present the
government's case before Judge Wilkerson. On September
23, Wilkerson, with whom Daugherty found a sympathetic
audience, issued a preliminary injunction, under which federal
officers set about to prosecute union officials who continued
their strike activities.[48]

Despite its menacing language and its sweeping prohibitions,
the Daugherty-Wilkerson injunction soon backfired. As labor
attorney Donald Richberg remarked, it was "an injunction
to prevent the settlement of a strike." It had little impact on
the course of the strike, for by September many workers had
either drifted out of the railroad industry or were in the
process of coming to terms with their employers, either under
the moderate provisions of the Baltimore Agreement or under
terms dictated by the hostile carriers. For the rest, the
injunction was so extreme as to inspire ridicule rather than
awe: a cartoon in *Labor* pictured an ineffectual little fellow
bearing the label "injunction." The caption employed the

[47] Taft, *Organized Labor in American History*, 378. For the bill in
equity, Daugherty's injunction request, and Wilkerson's grant of a temporary injunction, see *U.S. v. Railway Employees Department* . . . (N.D.
Illinois, Sept. 22, 1922), 283 F 479.

[48] Daugherty and Dixon, *Inside Story*, 132; Berman, *Labor Disputes*,
238-39. In addition to the Daugherty-Wilkerson injunction, federal courts
issued nearly 300 local injunctions during the strike. See Sigmund,
"Federal Laws," 141.

words of Artemus Ward: "He's an Amoosin' Little Cuss."[49]

If the injunction did little to end the strike, it did have a resounding impact within the Republican party. Coming at the end of an antilabor drift in the dual strikes, it appeared to be the work of a united and determined administration, but Daugherty and Harding found that it was profoundly unpopular in the party and especially among the members of the cabinet. Far from being the avowed policy of the administration, said Assistant Secretary of Labor Edward J. Henning, "apparently not a living soul in the Cabinet even knew that the move was contemplated." His chief, Davis, affirmed this impression, contending that Daugherty had acted entirely on his own and that the cabinet had not been informed of his intentions. Indeed, said the secretary, "It is a question as to whether the President knew about it." Hoover, who had worked so long to bring the parties in the strike together, declared that he was "outraged by its obvious transgression of the most rudimentary rights of man." Secretary of State Charles Evans Hughes heartily agreed with him; together they confronted Daugherty at a cabinet meeting, with Harding frequently supporting them.[50]

Republican senatorial critics also lashed out at the injunction. The two most prominent Senate constitutionalists, Borah of Idaho and Pepper of Pennsylvania, attacked it. Said Borah, such pernicious invasions of the Bill of Rights and of common justice could quickly "break down the courts of the country."

[49] Donald Richberg, My Hero: The Indiscreet Memoirs of an Eventful But Unheroic Life (New York, 1954), 117; Labor, Sept. 9, 1922. According to Perlman and Taft, about 225,000 strikers went back to work under favorable terms and about 175,000 had to join company unions. See John R. Commons and others, History of Labor in the United States. IV: Labor Movements, by Selig Perlman and Philip A. Taft (New York, 1935), 521-23. The strike smoldered throughout 1922, 1923, and into 1924 on some railroads. For its aftermath on the Pennsylvania Railroad, see Zieger, "Senator George Wharton Pepper," 170-76.

[50] Henning to John D. Denison, Sept. 7, 1922, USCSR, File 170/1553A; Davis to Lorenzo Dow, March 23, 1923, Davis Papers, Box 39; Hoover, Memoirs, II, 47-48.

He had often supported organized labor, but when Senator Pepper, the newly appointed conservative Republican from Pennsylvania, voiced a similar opinion, it was readily apparent that Daugherty's action had split the party deeply. Speaking to the Philadelphia Chamber of Commerce on September 22, the former corporation lawyer criticized the use of injunctions, telling his audience of businessmen, "If we insist upon interpreting the courts to masses of citizens as mere obstacles to industrial justice we . . . shall be straining government to the breaking point."[51] Organized labor, resentful over the arbitrary assault upon its interests, could feel somewhat compensated by the reaction that the injunction had triggered, a feeling not diminished by the resolution introduced in the House by independent Republican Congressman Oscar Keller for the impeachment of Daugherty for his role in the shopmen's strike.[52]

The repercussions of the injunction went even further. Daugherty had issued the injunction allegedly to uphold the authority of the Railroad Labor Board and to assert the power of the federal government to deal decisively with strikes, as well as to thwart the Moscow-directed "conspiracy to overturn the government itself" that he perceived the strike to be. Yet the ultimate effect of the strike and the injunction was to unleash intensive criticism of the board and of the courts. The drive to abolish the Railroad Labor Board reached a peak in the years after the 1922 strike, and the Railway Labor Act of 1926, which abolished the board, received impetus from the hostility generated in 1922 by the Railroad Labor Board. Moreover, the injunction highlighted the role of the courts in labor disputes and was an important factor in leading many people, including conservatives and friends of the courts such as Pepper, to urge judicial restraint in labor affairs. The Norris-

[51] Borah to Ray N. Castle, Sept. 14, 1922, Borah Papers, Box 214; Pepper's speech reprinted in *Men and Issues: A Collection of Speeches and Articles* [by Senator Pepper], comp. Horace Green (New York, 1924), 61. the breaking point."[51]

[52] New York *Times*, Sept. 12, 1922.

La Guardia Act of 1932 had many origins; Daugherty's injunction in 1922 was not the least of them.[53]

Another adverse effect of the injunction was to antagonize organized labor politically. Labor leaders focused on the injunction and evaluated the administration's entire labor record in terms of it. This dramatic action with its naked threat to organized labor overshadowed the positive achievements of the administration. Unionists saw it as part of the long and harmful history of federal intervention in labor disputes through the courts. In the fall of 1922, the unions were deeply involved in antiadministration progressive politics; "'Remember Daugherty' Is the Rallying Cry for Election Day," headlined *Labor*.[54]

The Harding administration's performance in the 1922 industrial crisis warranted this antagonism. The president had vacillated dangerously and ultimately had proved unwilling to treat unions and employers on equal terms. He regarded the mine operators and the carriers' refusal to compromise as regrettable; he regarded the miners' and railroad workers' refusal to compromise (in both cases after acceptance of his initial proposals) as justifications for direct attacks. Ignoring the advice of those in his cabinet who had labor's respect, he

[53] Daugherty and Dixon, *Inside Story*, 133. For the impact of the 1922 strike and injunction upon the courts and the Railroad Labor Board, see chaps. 9 and 11 below. See also Zieger, "Senator George Wharton Pepper," 177-82, for Pepper's role in the anti-injunction movement; and Zieger, "From Antagonism to Accord," 34-36, for the demise of the Railroad Labor Board.

[54] The attitudes of Gompers and D. B. Robertson, president of the Locomotive Firemen and Enginemen, are revealed in the New York *Times*, July 1 and 17, 1923, respectively. *Labor's* anti-Daugherty appeal is in its Nov. 4, 1922, issue. On the other hand, the very fact that Davis and Hoover had worked with some success to effect a moderate solution on some railroads led some carriers and businessmen to denounce the administration for its prolabor role. "I have heard it remarked by staunch Republicans," complained one businessman in reference to the Baltimore Agreement, "that it amounted to the Republican Administration's patting union labor on the back and saying: 'Go to it, old boy, you haven't lost all your friends, even if Wilson and McAdoo are sidetracked.'" (W. H. Wallace to Davis, Jan. 1923, USCSR, File 165/277B.) See also New York *Times*, April 1, 1923.

had allowed his attorney general to perpetrate a drastic injunction, which ultimately threatened the courts, the Railroad Labor Board, and the Republican party a good deal more than it did the unionists. Nor did Hoover escape responsibility for the course of events. Generally a moderate influence, the secretary of commerce nonetheless relied upon the nonunion mines to satisfy the nation's coal needs. Not only was his program ineffective, but through it he sanctioned, in effect, the arbitrary and often violent antiunion methods of the Appalachian operators. His silence in midsummer seemed to lend tacit consent to the president's anti-UMW outpourings.

Still, despite the assault upon the mineworkers and the injunction, the 1922 strikes had revealed no concerted and pervasive antilabor policy. The coal strikes, after all, were settled on terms generally favorable to the UMW,[55] with the encouragement of the administration. And if the injunction injured some unionists and served as a symbol of governmental antagonism for many more, Hoover's and Davis' long work for a moderate settlement had much influence upon the Baltimore Agreement, which helped to rescue some of the unions and to preserve the jobs and seniority of many railroad workers. The most vigorous antilabor actions and statements were more the result of frustration and despair than of preconceived policy, and even Daugherty's injunction was far more a reversion to the intense antiunion feelings of the immediate postwar months than it was a characteristic example of the labor attitudes and policies of the Republican administrations of the 1920s.

[55] The UMW and the AFL claimed that the settlement was a union victory. See UMW *Journal*, Aug. 15, 1922, and "All Hail Victorious Miners," *American Federationist*, XXIX (Oct. 1922), 761-63. Insofar as the traditional bargaining procedure was preserved, they were right. But the problems of overdevelopment and southern competition remained unsolved and would lead to disastrous consequences for the union in the next few years. Moreover, Brophy claimed that in securing the agreement which embraced mines producing only 10 percent of the national tonnage, Lewis was in effect abandoning the fledgling Appalachian unions. See Brophy, *A Miner's Life*, 191-92.

7 Transition

WHEN WARREN HARDING died on August 2, 1923, Calvin Coolidge became president. Coolidge's succession occurred just as a major crisis in the anthracite coal industry was developing. Thus, even while the nation mourned Harding, the new chief executive faced a knotty and dangerous labor situation, which immediately began to assume significant political overtones, for many political observers regarded the impending strike as the first test of Coolidge's leadership abilities. The slight Vermonter met the challenge effectively, if undramatically. By resisting the public clamor for executive action, Coolidge successfully avoided the unpleasant repercussions that followed the strike's settlement, leaving for Governor Gifford Pinchot of Pennsylvania, who finally brought the dispute to an end, the onus for the price increase for hard coal that accompanied the settlement. In the 1923 anthracite coal crisis Coolidge showed much aplomb, a keen sense of political reality, and great reluctance to become involved, as Harding so often was, in labor controversy. As a result the new president helped to secure control of his party, to strengthen his claim for the 1924 nomination, and to set the pattern of relative tranquillity and moderation in government-labor relations that prevailed throughout the rest of the 1920s.

When he died Harding bequeathed to his successor important unresolved labor problems. The Harding administration, it is true, had confronted such issues as the open shop, immigration, unemployment, and the twelve-hour day, but other and more dangerous difficulties remained. The 1922 strikes had ended, but unrest in the railroad and coal industries lingered to threaten the national government and the Republican party. The controversy over the role of the courts in labor affairs had reappeared during the Harding years, and by 1923 this issue was a major element in the mounting progressive-labor criticism of the GOP. And, perhaps most important, Harding's administration had been too brief and his counsel too divided for it to have formulated a unified labor policy. Both the open shop approach of Daugherty and the engineering-moderate approach of Hoover had won some victories, but Calvin Coolidge entered the White House without a commitment to any particular policy.

Even if the labor scene had been quiet, the new president faced a difficult task. The corruption and inefficiency of his predecessor's government would soon burst upon the party, and if Coolidge had the advantage of being unimplicated in the sordidness of Harding's term, he had the liability of the obscurity that was often a vice president's lot. By no means certain of his ability to control the party and to assure his 1924 nomination, the new president could contemplate with discomfort the inability of most previous vice presidents to attain their parties' nominations for full terms—and even the dour Vermonter's strongest supporters did not compare him to the one exception, Theodore Roosevelt. In the words of one academic observer, Coolidge "was not a bad man—but just nobody." The professor went on to wonder, as did many Americans in the summer of 1923, "Has he any chance of nomination next year?"[1]

Adding to his general difficulty was a serious labor crisis. By

[1] Samuel Eliot Morison to Albert J. Beveridge, Sept. 28, 1923, Beveridge Papers, Box 245. Two recent articles discuss Coolidge's precarious position in 1923. See Robert H. Zieger, "Pinchot and Coolidge: The Politics of the 1923 Anthracite Crisis," *Journal of American History*, LII (Dec. 1965), 566-81, and Robert James Maddox, "Keeping Cool with Coolidge," *Journal of American History*, LIII (March 1967), 772-80. On Coolidge's career, see Claude M. Fuess, *Calvin Coolidge: The Man from Vermont* (Boston, 1940) and Donald R. McCoy, *Calvin Coolidge: The Quiet President* (New York, 1967).

the time of Harding's death, negotiations between the United Mine Workers and the anthracite coal operators had broken down and the nation faced its second successive hard coal strike. This impending walkout held serious implications for Republicans. Unless Coolidge acted decisively a long strike might occur, damaging his party in the populous northeastern states, which relied largely upon hard coal for domestic heating. But if the former governor of Massachusetts could arrange a quick settlement in the name of the public interest, he could capture much public support and could early demonstrate his ability to function as president.

There was ample precedent for vigorous presidential intervention in coal difficulties. The Wilson administration had dealt directly with the coal troubles that followed the war, and Harding had been deeply involved in the 1922 strikes. To many observers the most arresting precedent was Theodore Roosevelt's intercession in the 1902 hard coal strike. Roosevelt, the last vice president to become president, had faced a startlingly parallel situation and had emerged from it with public acclaim and political prestige. To many Republicans, the lesson for Coolidge seemed plain, especially since he had achieved whatever national prestige he possessed with his dramatic action in the 1919 Boston police strike. On the other hand, if he faltered in this first test of his leadership, dissident elements within his party were ready to challenge him and were prepared to contest his right to the nomination.[2]

The dispute that faced Coolidge and the nation grew from a hard coal industry that was in decline in the 1920s. Widespread use of soft coal and fuel oil threatened the supremacy of this long-burning, high-heat coal which was found almost exclusively in northeastern Pennsylvania. Yet, even though

[2] For the 1902 strike, see Robert H. Wiebe, "The Anthracite Strike of 1902; A Record of Confusion," *Mississippi Valley Historical Review*, XLVIII (Sept. 1961), 229-51. For the police strike, see Frederick Manuel Koss, "The Boston Police Strike of 1919" (unpublished Ph.D. dissertation, Boston University, 1966).

anthracite might ultimately become a luxury fuel, the director of the United States Geological Survey asserted that "it has won a place . . . in our national standard of living that makes it a necessity of life." With thousands of home furnaces designed exclusively for anthracite, people throughout the northeast depended upon hard coal and were deeply concerned over the possibility of another strike.[3]

The threatened walkout was a continuation of labor troubles that had plagued the industry since the end of the war. Early in the century the UMW had organized the anthracite miners and had established itself in the celebrated strike of 1902. Between 1905 and 1920 labor peace had prevailed, but an interruption had almost occurred in 1920. The 1922 strike, although overshadowed by the soft coal and railroad strikes, had revealed deep splits between the operators and miners and had been settled only after intensive negotiations and the intervention of Pennsylvania's Republican senators, George Wharton Pepper and David A. Reed.[4]

The 1922 settlement had been a patchwork affair. Basic issues such as wages, hours, the checkoff, and the declining use of hard coal had not been resolved, although as part of the agreement the operators and miners had requested the establishment of a federal investigatory body to study the coal industry. Congress responded in September 1922 by creating the United States Coal Commission (USCC), upon the recommendations of which the parties in the coal industry would presumably act to make basic readjustments in labor relations. However, by August 1923 the commission had not yet completed its studies and had not yet made recommendations. Thus, in 1923 the issues that caused the 1922 strike

[3] George Otis Smith to Sen. Walter E. Edge, May 20, 1921, USCCR, Drawer 16.

[4] "Wage Agreements in the Anthracite Industry," typescript report, n.d., USCCR, Drawer 43; Robert H. Zieger, "Senator George Wharton Pepper and Labor Issues in the 1920s," *Labor History*, IX (Spring 1968), 167-70.

were not resolved by the machinery created to deal with them.[5]

About 155,000 miners worked the Pennsylvania fields, virtually all of whom were members of the UMW. Unlike the chaotic bituminous coal industry, there were only a few anthracite companies, with eight large concerns controlling over 70 percent of the total output.[6] In 1923 as in the previous year, the union demanded higher wages, reforms in work rules, and, above all, the checkoff, whereby the employer would automatically deduct union dues and turn them over to the UMW. The checkoff was an important point of prestige for the union, as well as a means of simplifying bookkeeping and maintaining membership. To the operators, who represented powerful eastern banking and railroad interests, it symbolized union power and arrogance. The coal companies were determined to prevent the checkoff and to insure their high rates of profit. It was over these specific issues that the union and the operators had clashed in 1922 and again confronted each other in 1923, but beyond these problems lay the fundamental malaise of an industry gradually declining in importance.[7]

Recognizing the consequence of a walkout, Republicans began early to persuade the new president of his duty to act quickly. Only three days after Harding's death, one Massachusetts congressman wrote Coolidge, contending that the strike offered him "a wonderful opportunity to render a great service" to the nation and party. Other Republican representatives called publicly for assertive action and assured their constituents that Coolidge would not disappoint them.

[5] "Wage Agreements in the Anthracite Industry."

[6] Typescript copy of USCC Preliminary Report, Jan. 15, 1923, p. 5, USCCR, Drawer 2.

[7] In addition to *ibid.*, several studies are helpful in describing the complex problems of the anthracite industry in the 1920s. See esp. Jules I. Bogen, *The Anthracite Railroads: A Study in American Railroad Enterprise* (New York, 1927), chapt. 9; Tze-Kang Hsiang, "Competition of Substitute Fuels in the Anthracite Industry" (unpublished M.A. thesis, University of Pennsylvania, 1947), 1-3, 88, and *passim.*; and A. T. Shurick, *The Coal Industry* (Boston, 1924), 207-208, 242, and 275.

Senator Walter E. Edge of the coal-consuming state of New Jersey sought to convince the president that the country would support him in firm action, informing Coolidge, "When an Executive . . . somewhat exceeds his authority in order to provide the public with necessities of life," public opinion invariably comes to his defense.[8]

Private citizens and the press also turned to the chief executive for protection against a coal shortage. All New England looked to him to save it from the hardship of a winter without coal, declared one editorialist, while the New York *Tribune* recalled his 1919 dictum that "There is no right to strike against the public safety," asserting to its readers that Coolidge would be as vigorous as president as he had been as governor. Senator Edge informed Coolidge that public opinion would enthusiastically support a vigorous exercise of presidential authority. Indeed, one distraught businessman begged the president to follow his stand against the AFL in 1919 with an even more dynamic one against the UMW: "Declare martial law," he demanded. "Seize the mines, draft men to work . . . Give them Hell."[9]

Such widespread and ringing pleas for dramatic and aggressive action indicated that the nation did not know its new president very well. Superficially, it did seem that he was a foe of organized labor and a crusading defender of the public interest. He had indeed issued the rebuke to Samuel Gompers in 1919, and it was true that many delegates at the 1920 convention had supported his nomination in recognition of this popular act. Nonetheless, a closer examination of his public career would have revealed that his outstanding attribute was not action but patience. Moreover, inspection of his

[8] Frederick W. Dallinger to Coolidge, Aug. 5, 1923; Edge to Coolidge, Aug. 9, 1923, Coolidge Papers, File 175; Washington *Post*, Aug. 9, 1923; Philadelphia *Evening Bulletin*, Aug. 11, 1923.

[9] Philadelphia *Evening Bulletin*, Aug. 7, 1923; New York *Tribune*, Aug. 14, 1923; George Otis Smith, Newspaper Clipping Book, USCCR, Drawer 40; Edge to Coolidge, Aug. 9, 1923, and Ambrose Clark to Coolidge, Aug. 23, 1923, Coolidge Papers, File 175.

political life would have indicated that he rarely challenged any large and powerful group of voters, such as organized labor. Thus, in 1919 far from acting with dispatch, he had allowed the Boston situation to deteriorate to the point of chaos before he revealed his position and sent in the National Guard. Antilabor enthusiasts might interpret his telegram to Gompers as a personal stand against organized labor, but Coolidge had intended no such commitment. Thus, shortly after the election, in which labor issues had been prominent, Coolidge set the record straight when he addressed a group of businessmen in Boston and pointedly warned them against antilabor activity. After leaving the presidency, he once remarked, "It seems to me public administrators would get along better if they would restrain the impulse to butt in or be dragged into trouble. They should remain silent until an issue is reduced to its lowest terms, until it boils down to something like a moral issue." The desperate situation in Boston in 1919 fulfilled this requirement, but in 1923 he would not let the press, irate businessmen, and politicians who wanted to escape responsibility by throwing the burden onto him push him into hasty action.[10]

Still, the strike called for some response. On August 11, Hoover recommended that the president use the United States Coal Commission to mediate the dispute. Although Congress had established this body in 1922 to study the coal industry and not to mediate its labor disputes, Hoover hoped that the stature of its members and its impartial character would help to bring the dispute to swift conclusion. Coolidge heeded his cabinet member's advice and quickly sent George Otis Smith, a member of the commission, to discuss the coal strike with its chairman, John Hays Hammond.[11]

[10] Coolidge's comments on the value of inaction are quoted in William Allen White, *A Puritan in Babylon: The Story of Calvin Coolidge* (New York, 1938), 433. See also McCoy, *Calvin Coolidge*, 83-94, 119-21, and 174-76.
[11] Hoover to Coolidge, Aug. 11, 1923, Coolidge Papers, File 175;

At first the coal commission seemed to have the matter well in hand. On August 15, its members met with anthracite operators and UMW leaders in New York to negotiate a settlement, and Hammond's early statements were encouraging. After two days of conversations, however, the commission acknowledged that it could not lead the parties to a settlement. The conference disbanded on August 17, with Hammond lecturing the miners and operators about the dire consequences to the public and to the industry that a strike would bring. Its mission a failure, the members of the commission dispersed, with Hammond going to Washington to report to Coolidge.[12]

Now the administration's position seemed more precarious than before, for Coolidge had actively committed himself in search of settlement and had apparently failed. Rather than stepping up the tempo of action, however, the chief executive began to withdraw from the fray. Hammond, who had been confident before the negotiations, now muted his assurances to the public, reporting on August 21 that the administration would wait until all hope of bilateral agreement had been exhausted before it would consider additional steps. Whereas newspaper speculation had included the possibility of a special session of Congress or government seizure of the mines, the press now reported only that the government would rely upon urging the public to adopt substitutes for anthracite and upon readying plans for the distribution of those fuels. Republicans braced themselves for the adverse political consequences of a walkout, but Coolidge appeared unconcerned. Indeed, the president told his aides to refer all questions about the rapidly

New York *Times*, Aug. 13, 1923. Actually, some members of the commission were quite hostile to the UMW. On Aug. 11 the commission had drafted (but did not send) an open letter to the anthracite miners, urging them to bypass the union and return to work (USCCR, Drawer 18).

[12] George Otis Smith, "Minutes of Daily Meetings," entries for Aug. 16, 17, 1923, USCCR, Drawer 1; John Hays Hammond to the President and Congress, Aug. 17, 1923, Coolidge Papers, File 175B; Harrisburg *Patriot*, Aug. 16, 17, 1923.

approaching strike to Hammond or to Pennsylvania authorities. "As far as he was concerned," remarked Senator Pepper, "the strike was over."[13]

If Coolidge appeared to have abandoned the quest for settlement, Governor Gifford Pinchot of Pennsylvania could not afford inactivity. The Keystone State mined virtually all the nation's hard coal, it consumed much anthracite, and coal disputes meant economic difficulty and social unrest in the state. Moreover, the strike held political implications for Pinchot. In the 1922 primaries he had swept to a surprise victory over the orthodox Republican candidate and in November he had overwhelmed his Democratic adversary. A Bull Moose progressive who was deeply unhappy about the recent course of GOP politics, Pinchot aspired to a United States Senate seat and perhaps to a progressive-supported Republican presidential nomination. Certainly, many progressives viewed their newly successful colleague of Armageddon days as the logical candidate in 1924 in place of the accidental Calvin Coolidge. At any rate, if progressives in the party had any chance to challenge the Old Guard and to make a bid for control, the summer of 1923 was the best time: As the Harding record began to fall under scrutiny, the new president, unsure and unimpressive, was vacillating shamelessly in a major labor dispute in the home state of a recently successful progressive governor. Conversely, of course, a labor and consumer disaster in Pennsylvania would erode Pinchot's base of power, discrediting his tenuous progressive candidacy.[14]

[13] The changing newspaper reports can be followed in Smith, Newspaper Clipping Book. See Philadelphia *Evening Bulletin*, Aug. 13, 1923, and Harrisburg *Patriot*, Aug. 22, 1923. Hammond's comments are revealed in Smith, "Minutes," entry for Aug. 21, 1923. Pepper's observation is in George Wharton Pepper, *In the Senate* (Philadelphia, 1930), 75-76.

[14] For some of the political implications of the strike for Pinchot and Coolidge, see Mark Sullivan in the New York *Tribune*, Aug. 12, 1923, and the Philadelphia *Evening Bulletin*, Aug. 14, 1923. See also William R. Hingston, "Gifford Pinchot, 1922-1927" (unpublished Ph.D. dissertation, University of Pennsylvania, 1962), 172-80, as well as Zieger, "Pinchot and Coolidge," 575-76.

After meeting with Coolidge and Hammond on August 23, Pinchot became convinced that the federal authorities would not move except to advertise the use of substitute fuels. He returned to Harrisburg determined to act personally to secure a settlement, without references to the feeble federal efforts. The governor grew angry when reporters referred to him as Coolidge's special mediator, since he felt that he was moving in to fill a vacuum left by the retreating president. Thus, he continually emphasized that he was acting solely as the chief executive of his state and that he was in no sense an agent of the president. He asked for little help from federal officials, who in turn were extremely wary about implicating the administration in Pinchot's efforts.[15]

Having committed himself, Pinchot put aside other state business and devoted himself to arranging a settlement. On August 27, he addressed representatives of the UMW and the central committee of anthracite operators, voicing the Rooseveltian progressive concern for the defense of the public from class interests. Thereafter he met daily with the two parties, constantly trying to resolve differences.[16]

Pinchot's plan for settlement included support for most of the union's demands. The operators would agree to full recognition of the union, and both parties would pledge

[15] Pinchot's account of his meeting with Coolidge is in "Address by Governor Pinchot at Conference of the American Academy of Political and Social Science," Philadelphia, Nov. 16, 1923, mimeographed copy enclosed in Gifford to Amos R. E. Pinchot, Nov. 18, 1923, Amos Pinchot Papers, Box 45. For Pinchot's insistence that he was acting on his own, see Harrisburg *Patriot*, Aug. 27, 28, 1923, and Philadelphia *Evening Bulletin*, Aug. 28, 1923. For the role of coal commission staff members, see memorandum from F. G. Tryon to Hammond, Sept. 4, 1923, and report by David L. Wing and F. G. Tryon to the Commission, n.d., both in Hoover Papers, Box 351. Tryon stated, "The Commission may rest assured . . . that we acted solely as statisticians or engineers, and not as advisers, and particularly that we did not express approval of the wage increase proposal by Governor Pinchot."

[16] Address by Gifford Pinchot to Operators and Miners, Aug. 27, 1923, in "Minutes of Sub-Committee of Anthracite Operators and Mine Workers, 1923," mimeographed booklet, pp. 31-33, USCCR, Drawer 1.

themselves to maintaining machinery for collective bargaining. Pinchot's proposal provided for a 10 percent wage increase for the miners and a compromise on the checkoff, wherein representatives of the union would be present at payday to collect union dues, but the operators would not automatically deduct and turn them over to the union officials. The governor contended that wholesalers and the anthracite railroads, which reaped enormous profits from the coal-carrying trade, could absorb most of the extra cost of production of coal. Consumer prices, he admitted, might rise slightly and temporarily, but he pledged himself to avert a significant increase.[17]

Pinchot could not prevent the walkout, and on September 1 the United Mine Workers struck the anthracite fields. However, the governor continued with his efforts, meeting continually with the two parties. Finally, on September 7, he announced a settlement, effective when the rank-and-file miners ratified it, along the lines that he had been urging since his intervention. Thus, the strike was over almost as quickly as it had begun, to the satisfaction of householders and Republican politicians.[18]

Pinchot's success contrasted sharply with Coolidge's inactivity, and it appeared to many observers that the president had made a mistake in allowing Pinchot to engineer the settlement. Even before the agreement, the New York *Times* reported that some Republicans felt that Coolidge had "made a tactical political error in turning over the settlement" to the governor. After the strike ended, congratulations poured in upon the progressive, and speculations regarding his presidential aspirations and prospects circulated widely. One major eastern newspaper declared that Pinchot had emerged as "a very

[17] Pinchot's settlement plans are described in Harrisburg *Patriot*, Sept. 8, 1923. For his determination to prevent price increases, see Philadelphia *Evening Bulletin*, Sept. 8, 1923.

[18] For the announcement of the settlement, see Harrisburg *Patriot*, Sept. 8, 1923.

distinct and vital national figure." Surely, the Baltimore *Sun* predicted, he would "be in the minds of the people and the politicians when the nomination is made." The Governor's reform-minded and highly informed brother Amos asserted that the strike settlement had made Gifford "the only person in the country that stands a show of taking the nomination away from Coolidge," while a friend declared that the time had come to "talk about making governors presidents."[19]

Such speculations, however, underestimated the president. On September 7, Coolidge sent Pinchot a telegram congratulating him for his successful efforts in the "very difficult situation in which I invited your cooperation," thus neatly implying that the Pennsylvanian had been simply an agent of the president. But when Pinchot sought to implicate the administration in his unsuccessful struggle to hold consumer prices for hard coal down, Coolidge declared that federal action would usurp legitimate functions of the state, thus parrying Pinchot's move to involve him in the unpleasant aftermath of the strike settlement. Soon, the enthusiasm for Pinchot melted as coal prices rose and as the governor's attempts to secure vigorous federal support and the cooperation of governors of anthracite-consuming states to restrain prices failed. The public began to notice the hard part of the coal settlement, and Republicans now aware of the wisdom of Coolidge's inaction continued to rally to the president's banner.[20]

[19] New York *Times*, Aug. 26, 1923; Baltimore *Sun* editorial quoted in "The Hard Part of the Hard Coal Settlement," *Literary Digest*, LXXVIII (Sept. 22, 1923), 8; Amos to Gifford Pinchot, Sept. 27, 1923, Amos Pinchot Papers, Box 45; Gilson Gardner to Gifford Pinchot, Sept. 26, 1923, Gifford Pinchot Papers, Box 246.

[20] Coolidge to Pinchot, and Pinchot reply, Sept. 7, 1923, Coolidge Papers, File 285. Pinchot's refusal to release Coolidge's telegram to the press touched off a heated debate among supporters of the governor and the president as to who had been responsible for the settlement. See M. Nelson McGeary, *Gifford Pinchot: Forester-Politician* (Princeton, 1960), 309-10, and Zieger, "Pinchot and Coolidge," 574. For the governor's attempt to prevent price increases, see Zieger, "Pinchot and Coolidge," 577-78. See also "The Hard Part of the Hard Coal Settlement."

Hopes of unseating Coolidge in 1924 soon vanished. "The country," remarked William Allen White, "is reactionary—against labor, middle class conscious." A decade earlier, the editor declared, Pinchot's strike settlement would have made him "a heroic figure," but "Now the tide is washing out."[21] Instead of enabling the progressives to capture the party through decisiveness and daring, the 1923 anthracite strike merely indicated the feebleness of Republican progressivism and the expediency of inaction. And Calvin Coolidge had emerged as a wise and patient statesman, instead of as the vacillating and uncertain cipher that he had appeared to be.

The 1923 anthracite strike was part of the recurring theme of labor problems in the coal industry in the 1920s. In addition, though, it played an important part in the success of Calvin Coolidge. Coming into office with an antilabor reputation and faced with a major strike in an important industry, Coolidge had triumphed by doing nothing. Avoiding positive action and allowing the burden to fall upon a rival's shoulders, he had launched his reputation for commonsense and reasonableness; he had replaced the myth of Coolidge the strikebreaker with that of Silent Cal, the shrewd tactician.[22]

His reaction to the coal crisis helped to set the pattern of his response to labor issues during his years in office. Far from encouraging antilabor extremists, Coolidge largely let labor alone, and even bent to its wishes when that seemed necessary. The contrast with his late predecessor was obvious. As Senator Pepper remarked, Harding had responded to labor crises as a "warm-hearted, impulsive man, who was ready to throw himself into the breech" and to do what he thought right, even if the situation was ambiguous and the facts

[21] William Allen White to Pinchot, Sept. 11, 1923, Gifford Pinchot Papers, Box 255.

[22] Thus, wrote journalist William Hard, "The myth of Calvin Coolidge as a 'union buster' is itself 'busted.' . . . The White House is not only producing no action against unions, but no words against them." ("The Hard Part of the Hard Coal Settlement," 8.)

uncertain.   Coolidge, on the other hand, avoided action
wherever possible, viewing each situation with canny aloofness,
and shunning rash and dramatic acts and pronouncements.[23]
Clearly, Coolidge's desire to settle and calm and his eagerness
to avoid trouble would provide a far more hospitable climate
for the labor views of Herbert Hoover than for the opinions
of Harry Daugherty and other open shop advocates.

[23] Pepper, *In the Senate,* 71, 75.

8 Labor, Progressives, and Republicans

THE REPUBLICAN PARTY from 1919 to 1924 wrestled with the labor problem amid frequent and dangerous industrial crises. Adding still another dimension to the GOP's efforts to produce a labor policy was the revival of the progressive movement and the association of prominent labor groups with it. The insurgent political activities of laborites and progressives between 1922 and 1925 produced sharp criticism of the Republican party's labor policies and forced Republicans, progressives, and unionists to reevaluate their conceptions of the role of labor in politics. While efforts to forge a permanent labor-progressive party failed, labor leaders effectively used their involvement with progressive politics as a means of encouraging in the GOP a move favorable view of their legislative demands.

Throughout the 1920s labor issues and labor organizations were of basic importance to progressives in their various efforts to redefine their purposes and programs and to regain the influence they had held before the war. Belief in some of labor's goals—such as an anti-injunction enactment—served as a "litmus for liberals in the twenties."[1] Moreover, even in its weakened position, organized labor remained one of the most powerful and articulate mass movements with a reformist bent in America. True to the undogmatic, individualistic tradition of their movement, progressives reacted to the importance of organized labor in progressive politics with a variety of responses, ranging from antilabor extremism to close cooperation. Whatever his particular view of the labor movement, however, the progressive could not ignore its vast significance in postwar progressive action.

While progressives debated the proper function of organized labor in reform, unionists were playing a major role in the early political opposition to the Republican party. Laborites led in the formation of the Conference for Progressive Political Action, which in turn formed the basis for Senator Robert M. La Follette's progressive candidacy in 1924. Yet even though insurgent politics threw progressives and laborites together, such an alliance was comfortable for neither group. Most progressives, adhering to the public interest background of their movement, rejected or resented the participation of professional labor unionists in reform leadership. Organized labor, never enthusiastic about political activity, slackened its support for independent political action. Meanwhile, as the uncertain coalition foundered, the Republican party campaigned vigorously and effectively in 1924 to attract labor votes. The election of 1924 represented the peak of organized progressive politics, the end of significant third party activity, and the last major·effort of organized labor to engage in direct political revolt.

In the 1920s, as before the war, "progressivism" was an undefinable and multifaceted movement. The term *progressive* applied at various times in differing contexts to agrarians and urbanites, New Nationalists and New Freedomites, traditionalists and modernists, engineers searching for efficiency and reformers thirsting for social justice, and to defenders of the public interest as well as to spokesmen for special interest groups. At one time or another, the progressive movement embraced farmers, laborites, engineers, social workers, intellectuals, bankers, businessmen, and, of course, politicians. And if the troops in the progressive army were a diverse lot, its objectives were equally varied. Monopoly, political corruption, working and living conditions, adulterated foods, waste

1 Dean Acheson, *Morning and Noon* (Boston, 1965), chapt. 6.

of resources, immigration, prison conditions, poverty, prohibition—the list of progressive goals and grievances was virtually endless. Progressivism was a broadly based, vigorous, moralistic movement of men and women who were persuaded that much was wrong with American society, but who were equally convinced that evil conditions would yield to determined effort, publicity, strong and vigilant governments, and democratized political procedures.

While progressivism had achieved a high level of moral protest and consisted of a rich mixture of ideas and personalities, it had never attained doctrinal or political unity. Freewheeling and individualistic, it lacked the cohesion that doctrine provides. Embracing a wide variety of people and groups, it often relied upon moralistic rhetoric to conceal differences in objectives, methods, and personalities. The year 1916 had witnessed perhaps the greatest degree of progressive unity, when a wide variety of reformers had supported Woodrow Wilson, but the war and the intrusion of foreign policy as the dominant national political issue shattered this imperfect coalition.

By 1920 progressivism had both succeeded and failed. It had exposed and publicized defects in American society. It had dominated political thought and practice for two decades and had elected hundred of legislators, numerous governors and mayors, and two of the country's most powerful and dynamic presidents. It had secured major national legislation as well as important state and local reforms concerning government, railroads, conservation, banking, agriculture, labor, education, and social welfare. Yet as the nation faced the critical postwar period, it found this reform movement virtually leaderless and even more divided than before.[2]

[2] The literature on progressivism is vast and growing. Particularly important and indicative of the variety of both progressivism and interpretations of the movement are the following: Richard Hofstadter, *The Age of Reform: From Bryan to F.D.R.* (New York, 1955), chapts. 4-6; Robert H. Wiebe, *Businessmen and Reform: A Study of the Progressive Move-*

Throughout the 1920s progressivism remained largely without cohesion and leadership. A number of factors worked to weaken this once-dominant movement. The success of past programs, the death of Theodore Roosevelt and the illness of Woodrow Wilson, the impact of the war, the debate over foreign policy, rapidly changing economic and political circumstances, and the powerful pull of traditional party loyalties helped to spawn a variety of progressive programs, but at the same time to fragment further the already divided progressive movement.[3]

Disunity and lack of leadership struck hard at Republican progressivism. Many Republicans harked with nostalgia back to 1912 and sought to revive the spirit of the Bull Moose crusade. Others, upon whom the war and questions of foreign policy had had a profound impact, now emphasized American nationalism and unity above all things, including social reform. To members of both of these groups, the death of Theodore Roosevelt early in 1919 had come as a terrible shock, for both looked to the former president for leadership: in the words of Harold Ickes, "When Colonel Roosevelt was alive he, better

ment (Cambridge, Mass., 1962); George E. Mowry, *The Era of Theodore Roosevelt: 1900-1912* (New York, 1958), esp. chapt. 5; Arthur S. Link, *Woodrow Wilson and the Progressive Era, 1910-1917* (New York, 1954); Gabriel Kalko, *The Triumph of Conservatism* (New York, 1963); Samuel Haber, *Efficiency and Uplift: Scientific Management in the Progressive Era, 1890-1920* (Chicago, 1964); J. Joseph Huthmacher, "Urban Liberalism and the Age of Reform," *Mississippi Valley Historical Review*, XLIX (Sept. 1962), 231-41; and John Braeman, "Seven Progressives," *Business History Review*, XXXV (Winter 1961), 581-92.

[3] For the alarums and diversions of progressivism in the 1920s, Arthur Link's article, "What Happened to the Progressive Movement in the 1920s," *American Historical Review*, LXIV (July 1959), 833-51, is basic. Other useful discussions include William E. Leuchtenberg, *The Perils of Prosperity: 1914-1932* (Chicago, 1958), chapt. 7; Howard Zinn, *La Guardia in Congress* (Ithaca, N.Y., 1959), 259-74; Lawrence W. Levine, *Defender of the Faith, William Jennings Bryan: The Last Decade, 1915-1925* (New York, 1965), esp. 176-81 and 293-95; Paul W. Glad, "Progressives and the Business Culture of the 1920's," *Journal of American History*, LIII (June 1966), 75-89, and John D. Hicks, *Republican Ascendancy, 1921-1933* (New York, 1960), chapt. 4.

than any one else, could interpret to the Progressives what the Republican party stood for." While Bull Moosers and some aggressively nationalistic progressives searched for leadership, still other reformers in the party asserted their claims as progressive spokesmen and formulated programs of various descriptions to which reform-minded people were urged to rally.[4]

The political campaign of 1920 had imposed some unity. Failing to gain control of their party, most Republican progressives felt that driving the Democrats from power was more important than the degree of progressivism of their own party's nominees. Thus, one progressive, although he contemptuously dismissed Harding as "pathetically without color, atmosphere, ideas or the background of knowledge about affairs generally," served on the candidate's staff. William Allen White had worked diligently for a progressive ticket, but after the convention he concluded that "Harding and Coolidge look good to me. There is no excuse for a bolt, no excuse for being sore." The Democratic administration had alienated many Republican progressives and the return of the GOP to power seemed to set things in their proper order again. Thus, James R. Garfield, son of the assassinated president and a 1912 follower of Theodore Roosevelt, felt his doubts about Harding dissipate as he walked into the White House to call upon the new president on the day after his inauguration. "For the first time in 8 years," he exalted, "the gates are open."[5]

Many prewar progressives, with varying degrees of enthusiasm, continued to support Harding and Coolidge, but for others the gates did not long remain open. As the conservatism of the Republican administration grew increasingly obvious,

[4] For Ickes remarks, see Ickes to Raymond Robins, Jan. 10, 1919, Robins Papers, Box 16. The varieties of progressivism in the 1920s are described in Glad, "Progressives and the Business Culture."

[5] Judson Welliver to Borah, July 1, 1920, Borah Papers, Box 199; Emporia *Gazette*, June 14, 1920; entry for March 5, 1921, James R. Garfield Diaries (Manuscript Division, Library of Congress).

progressives became more and more outspoken and rebellious against party orthodoxy. Throughout the 1920s Republican progressives kept up a steady barrage of criticism and held themselves in readiness to engage in independent political action.

For these dissidents the times were hard. While their perception of social evils and their desire for national improvement remained acute, they soon found that the expanding economy and restless society of the postwar decade were diverting middle-class America from reform. After a decade and a half of deep involvement in public business, Americans returned with a will to private pursuits. Business, technology, art, and entertainment flourished, but reform languished. Thus, with the old avenues of reform blocked, progressives had to find new ones.

Not everyone shared in the prosperity and excitement of the 1920s. Reformers pointed to vast social problems and to large areas of blight in American life. Of all the relatively disadvantaged and excluded, however, the farm and labor groups offered the best hope of progressive activity. Representing millions of Americans, farm and labor leaders could supply funds, organs of protest, and votes. Still, prewar progressivism had been middle class in nature, largely avoiding identification with specific interest groups. The farm legislation and, to a lesser extent, the labor enactments passed during Wilson's administration had dented this tradition somewhat, but throughout the 1920s most progressives of the prewar period continued to think in terms of public-interest reform, rather than in terms of social and economic legislation designed explicitly for one or another group, no matter how disadvantaged or deserving.

Progressive hesitancy to work with laborites for reform had strong roots in the prewar period. The attitude of most progressives toward organized labor had been cautious and at times even hostile. The primary menace to America, of course, had been the privileged monopolist and his corrupt political henchmen, but the mere fact that workers were exploited by this combination was no assurance that huge labor unions could not be equally power hungry and corrupt. San Francisco reformers had discovered the Union Labor party at the heart of their city's misgovernment. In Chicago in 1903 Ray Stannard Baker had "found that organized labor and organized capital had joined forces and formed what was in effect a complete monopoly in various industries, thus enabling them to prey upon the public." Even the New Nationalist program, with its acceptance of large aggregations of economic power, regarded labor suspiciously, partly because of the working force's polyglot composition and its potential for destructiveness in times of trouble.[6]

Progressives, it is true, had much sympathy for the plight of the toiler and they often exposed evil conditions and sought legislation favorable to workers. However, typically the prewar progressive had emphasized paternalistic and legalistic relief for labor. Progressives had supported child labor legislation, had railed against factory and tenement conditions, and had opposed labor injunctions. Organized labor, partly because of its own predilections, had not been a leading element in most prewar progressive political movements, nor did progressives characteristically seek out explicit labor support.[7]

But in the 1920s circumstances were different. Reform-

[6] For discussions of the progressive view of labor, see Mowry, *The Era of Theodore Roosevelt*, 101-103; Wiebe, *Businessmen and Reform*, 157-58; and David W. Noble, *The Paradox of Progressive Thought* (Minneapolis, 1958), 152-56, 170-73. The quotation is from Ray Stannard Baker, *American Chronicle: The Autobiography of Ray Stannard Baker* (New York, 1945), 173.

[7] The repugnance of American labor for political action, of course, was as responsible for this condition as was progressive unwillingness to work with labor. See Marc Karson, *American Labor Unions and Politics: 1900-1918* (Carbondale, Ill., 1958), chapt. 2. At times in heavily urban states progressive-labor coalitions did form and were influential. See Irwin Yellowitz, *Labor and the Progressive Movement in New York State, 1897-1916* (Ithaca, N.Y., 1965), chapts. 5-6.

minded politicans and intellectuals could not afford to disregard or to patronize labor if progressive action was to be effective and broad based. No longer able to rest exclusively upon middle-class foundations, progressivism had to consider the possibilities of interest group politics as a vehicle for reform. Progressives had to reevaluate their relationship to workers and their unions which together constituted one of the largest, most powerful, and most frustrated interest groups in the nation.

Among Republican progressives there were a variety of responses to labor's role in reform politics. Some progressives, such as Robert M. La Follette, Gifford Pinchot, Fiorello La Guardia, and George W. Norris were willing on occasion to share with laborites the direction and control of progressive political action, realizing that unionists constituted so important a segment of reform strength that their leaders would necessarily define the terms of their involvement.[8] However, most progressives associated with the GOP continued either to regard labor with suspicion and alarm, or to view it as a junior partner in progressive action. Essentially, Republican progressivism maintained its prewar identification with middle class, public interest reform, despite some efforts to effect a labor-progressive coalition.

Far from working with the unions, some progressives of the prewar period reacted sharply against postwar labor turbulence and identified organized labor as a menace to American institutions. Men such as former Senator Jonathan Bourne, Jr., of Oregon and Senator Miles Poindexter of Washington consistently attacked the power of unionism in America. Both

[8] The commitment of even these Republican progressives to labor-oriented reform politics was tenuous. La Follette is discussed in this chapter. For La Guardia, see Zinn, *La Guardia in Congress*, 145-49; for Pinchot, see Robert H. Zieger, "Pinchot and Coolidge: The Politics of the 1923 Anthracite Crisis," *Journal of American History*, LII, (Dec. 1965), 580; and for Norris, see Norman L. Zucker, *George W. Norris: Gentle Knight of American Democracy* (Urbana, Ill., 1966), 94-97.

of these men from the Pacific Northwest had supported Theodore Roosevelt in 1912, and before the war Poindexter had compiled the most progressive voting record of any United States senator. Yet the conflict had revealed a strong strand of nationalism in these men, and the postwar labor militancy, particularly evident on the West Coast, had convinced them that organized labor presented a direct threat to America. Bourne headed the open shop Republican Publicity Association, the main purpose of which was to discredit the American labor movement, and Poindexter conducted his campaign for the Republican presidential nomination in 1920 on the twin issues of hostility toward the League of Nations and antagonism toward labor unions.[9]

Somewhat less vehement than Bourne and Poindexter, but still sharply critical of labor, were progressives such as Albert J. Beveridge and James R. Garfield. One of the stalwarts of prewar progressivism, Beveridge was an important advocate of child labor legislation. But when he emerged in 1920 as a major figure in the Republican victory and when he sought election to the United States Senate in 1922 he revealed deep suspicion of the labor movement. Thus, he accused organized labor of promoting a lackadaisical and slovenly attitude toward workmanship. Of workers in general and the labor movement in particular, he charged, "The spirit is wrong and that's the great trouble with the country; and it makes the 'labor problem' insoluble while it lasts. And the labor problem is the big problem." The passage of the Adamson Act in 1916 had particularly shocked the former senator, and after this "surrender" to labor's power he vowed to fight "these labor bosses," just as he had fought "the banded bandits of capital" previously.

[9] For the views of Bourne and Poindexter, see Albert Heisy Pike, Jr., "Jonathan Bourne, Jr., Progressive" (unpublished Ph.D. dissertation, University of Oregon, 1957), 240-42, and Howard Allen, "Miles Poindexter: A Political Biography" (unpublished Ph.D. dissertation, University of Washington, 1959), 489, 493, 496-97, and 595. Poindexter's remarkable voting record is discussed in Allen, "Miles Poindexter," 616.

In his 1922 campaign for the United States Senate, Beveridge did not seek the support of labor groups, and in fact he openly criticized this special interest group and appealed to the voters to elect him as a man beholden neither to the power of capital nor to the minions of labor.[10] Garfield, another Bull Moose Republican, declared that he had "steadfastly been against special legislation, whether it be for capital, agriculture, or labor." With organized labor gathering political strength, Garfield drew comfort from his feeling that most workingmen were "hard-headed, sober-minded, law-abiding citizens," who would repudiate the efforts of pretentious labor politicans to use the labor vote for radical purposes.[11]

Men such as Poindexter, Garfield, and Beveridge, however, were in the minority. Most progressives occupied a broad area of middle ground between those who saw labor as a menace and the few who openly welcomed its political influence. The most powerful representative of this viewpoint among Republican progressives was Senator William E. Borah of Idaho. Borah sympathized with the grievances of the worker and thought labor organizations generally beneficial. His relationships with groups such as the AFL, the UMW, and the railroad brotherhoods were cordial and mutually respectful. Yet in most cases he opposed legislative solutions to labor problems, even those advanced by these organizations. "I have never been a supporter of labor legislation simply because it is labor legislation," he declared. He had voted against the labor provisions of the Clayton Act and against the Adamson

[10] Beveridge to Raymond Robins, June 1, 1922, Robins Papers, Box 18; to William Allen White, Dec. 6, 1922, White Papers, Box 70. For his reaction to labor in 1922, see Beveridge to Samuel Eliot Morison, Nov. 20, 1923, Beveridge Papers, Box 245. In his letter to White, the Indianan claimed that he was "about the only fellow left in the whole country who stands for all American institutions, not merely some American institutions," asserting that his views on labor and capital "were exactly the views which T. R. held just before he died; and the views for which he would be fighting now if he were alive." Beveridge was probably right in the latter feeling.
[11] Garfield to Robins, Aug. 8, 1924, Robins Papers, Box 19.

Act, not because he lacked sympathy for labor's struggle against injunctions and its quest for the eight-hour day, but rather because he thought that these measures advanced the goals of a special interest group at the expense of the public interest. Class legislation, no matter how worthy its object, rubbed against the grain of American institutions. Consistent with these sentiments, he had voted against the antistrike provisions of the Esch-Cummins bill in 1920, for "I could not as a believer in our form of government . . . vote to enact a law that a man should not quit work." William Allen White shared Borah's view that labor, whatever its just demands, had to bend to the public interest as defined by men free from class and economic commitments. Although the Kansas editor had supported the Adamson Act and often defended labor against conservative criticism, he held that labor could not be allowed to impose its demands upon society. The public good, he declared, was of more importance "than the rights of any group to threaten revolution for a passing and temporary injustice." He initially supported the Kansas Court of Industrial Relations, for, despite organized labor's hostility to this innovation, he was convinced that the best repository for labor's claims was the public and its representatives. "If the injustice is grave," he insisted, "public sentiment may be depended upon the right this injustice."[12]

Progressives who occupied this difficult middle ground often had ambivalent attitudes toward labor. The sculptor Gutzon Borglum was a particularly good example of the Republican progressive who sympathized with unionists and even co-operated with them, but who could not envision laborites in anything more than a secondary role in progressive politics. A member of a labor union, Borglum had vigorously defended the labor movement's postwar militancy and developed

[12] Borah to W. A. Heiss, Jan. 9, 1920, Borah Papers, Box 198; Darrell LeRoy Ashby, "Senator William E. Borah and Progressivism in the 1920's" (unpublished Ph.D. dissertation, University of Maryland, 1966), 110-15; Emporia *Gazette*, Oct. 28, 1921.

important connections with labor publicists and leaders. In 1922 he rallied the railroad unions in support of Nebraskan Robert Howell in his successful progressive Republican campaign for election to the United States Senate. It was the sculptor-progressive who alerted the unions' newspaper *Labor* to the importance of Howell's bid for election and who helped circulate a pro-Howell edition of the journal in railroad centers. Indeed, Howell told him that his activities had undoubtedly helped to carry the labor vote in the GOP primary. Yet, as useful as Borglum found the votes and publications of union men, he felt that the labor movement was too collectivized and its members too dependent to be the vanguard of a progressive resurgence. Voicing the feelings of many progressives, Borglum declared that he had "no faith in the Labor Unions. . . . It is the farmer that [*sic*] makes the great political changes of the future. It is the man who walks and thinks for himself, who cannot be discharged."[13]

Equally revealing of ambivalent progressive attitudes toward labor was the stand of a group of eastern intellectuals and reformers, led by Amos R. E. Pinchot and George L. Record. Pinchot had been a Roosevelt Republican and Record had been an influential early supporter of Woodrow Wilson, but they became convinced that neither party would be a vehicle for reform in the 1920s and they concentrated upon building a reform platform and encouraging independent political action. The result of Record's and Pinchot's efforts was a program of nationalization of the railroads and important mineral resources, with the government to lease concessions

[13] In 1919 Borglum wrote a pamphlet defending labor against an attack by Nicholas Murray Butler. See Paul Murphy, "Sources and Nature of Intolerance in the 1920's," *Journal of American History*, LI (June 1964), 64. For Borglum's role in the 1922 Nebraska campaign, see Edward Keating to Borglum, July 10, Borglum to Keating, July 11, and Howell to Borglum, Aug. 12, 1922, John Gutzon Borglum Papers (Manuscript Division, Library of Congress), Box 60; hereafter cited as Borglum Papers. The sculptor's remark on the ineffectiveness of laborites in politics is in a letter to Dr. Delmer E. Croft, May 12, 1922, Borglum Papers, Box 60.

to private business in a manner consistent with the public interest. Pinchot, Record, Grenville MacFarland, Gilson Gardner, and others interested in this plan sought continually to interest progressive politicians in their formula, to form liberal clubs and movements, to publicize their views, and to play a part in progressive political action.[14] All these men were sympathetic to the plight of the worker and the tribulations of organized labor. They attacked the twelve-hour day, criticized the labor injunction, and encouraged embattled strikers in a number of industrial disputes. But their overriding interest in the labor movement derived from the fact that important labor elements supported various forms of nationalization. While the AFL leadership shied away from advocacy of public ownership, the railroad unions in the 1920s, and at times even the UMW, supported the Plumb plan and programs of nationalization of resources. The concern of the progressives was primarily for greater efficiency, resource conservation, and curbing monopoly, and the concern of the unionists was for fair labor standards, but these different emphases seemed complementary rather than antagonistic. Thus, public ownership reformers sought to recruit laborite support, and some important unionists showed a lively interest.[15]

Yet a gulf separated these public-minded reformers from the labor movement. Pinchot felt that organized labor, whatever its just grievances and whatever its political usefulness, represented a special interest. As such, its goals were not necessarily wrong; they were simply too limited. All too often, the single-minded insistence of such groups upon

<hr/>

14 For the Pinchot-Record program, see Amos Pinchot to Frederic C. Howe, May 29, 1922, Amos Pinchot Papers, Box 43, and Glad, "Progressives and the Business Culture," 82-83. There is an undated and untitled prospectus or summary of the Pinchot-Record program and strategy in the Amos Pinchot Papers, Box 148.

15 For labor's interest in the Pinchot-Record progressive program, see Edward Keating to Record, March 29, and July 14, 1922, Amos Pinchot Papers, Boxes 45 and 44 respectively. For the desire of public ownership supporters to effect a liaison with labor, see Robert Bruere to Amos Pinchot, May 22, 1923, Amos Pinchot Papers, Box 45.

their own narrow demands sabotaged general reform. At best, this myopia delayed meaningful, broad-based reform; at worst, of course, it could create "a huge new balance of power to be rolled up by labor until it overshadows capital's present balance of power." Pinchot and his friends appealed to labor to submerge its special interests in their more general and more public-minded (and hence more worthy) program.[16]

Illustrative of this view of labor was Record's 1922 campaign against conservative Senator Joseph Frelinghuysen in the New Jersey Republican primary. Pinchot and Record appealed for labor support, arguing that the labor movement was a natural ally in the fight of progressives against conservatives. Still, they refused to support specific labor reforms or legislation. If Record and people like him were elected, labor and other understandably dissatisfied groups would benefit, but, Record contended, "All class legislation, whether for farmers or for labor Unions or otherwise . . . , is politically inexpedient, even if it is economically sound." Programs based upon the public interest and opposition to monopoly, he declared, had a wider appeal to farmers and workers as well as to the general public than could a special interest appeal.[17] The reformers invited organized labor to contribute, but they would allow unionists no role in defining the terms of progressive action.

Indeed, some members of the Pinchot-Record group went even further. Far from encouraging unionists to help define progressivism, they envisioned intellectuals such as themselves

16 Pinchot's comments about the fragmentation of reform efforts are revealed in a speech before the Civic Club, Jan. 1923, Amos Pinchot Papers, Box 228. See also Glad, "Progressives and the Business Culture," 82-83. For the reformer's fear of possible labor arrogance and domination, see his unpublished article commenting on an Interchurch World Movement report on labor conditions in the steel industry, Jan. 1923, Amos Pinchot Papers, Box 144.

17 For the reformers' efforts to secure labor support, see Pinchot to Frederic C. Howe, May 29, 1922, Amos Pinchot Papers, Box 43. For their insistence upon public interest politics, see Record to Edward Keating, Dec. 18, 1922, Amos Pinchot Papers, Box 43, and Pinchot to Philip E. Ziegler, editor, The Railway Clerk, June 18, 1924, Amos Pinchot Papers, Box 46.

playing a major role in the future of the labor movement. In 1923 Grenville MacFarland, a Bostonian active in the public ownership movement, discussed the relationship of labor to progressivism with Pinchot. Samuel Gompers had outlived his usefulness, MacFarland declared, and when the AFL leader died or retired, "We [will] come to a great parting of the way. If labor puts at its head a man like Sidney Hillman [head of the Amalgamated Clothing Workers of America] and thus joins hands with the radical intellectuals, we shall make great progress." MacFarland predicted that the AFL craft unions and the mass-membership industrial unions such as Hillman's would engage in a great struggle for dominance. Reformers such as Pinchot and MacFarland "ought to be prepared to have a hand in this crisis because it means so much to the country," the Boston progressive asserted. Perhaps with an eye upon the intellectual-led labor parties of Europe, Mac-Farland contended that "the object of the intellectuals in politics is to be the general staff of the labor forces."[18]

Such sentiments were ironic, for even as progressives sought to define their relationship with labor, unionists were assuming the lead in independent political activity. Many groups and individuals were unhappy with the politics of normalcy. Farm groups, finding little hope for relief within the established parties, had for several years supported agrarian radicals, especially in the northern plains states. Many intellectuals and prewar progressives had long since repudiated the party of Harding and Coolidge. However, it was organized labor, led by the powerful and cohesive railroad brotherhoods, that instigated effective independent political action during 1922-1924.[19]

[18] MacFarland to Amos Pinchot, March 13, 1923, Amos Pinchot Papers, Box 45. Pinchot agreed with MacFarland in a letter dated March 19 in *ibid*.

[19] Kenneth Campbell MacKay, *The Progressive Movement of 1924*, Columbia University Studies in History, Economics and Public Law, No. 257 (New York, 1947), 28; Russel B. Nye, *Midwestern Progressive*

In the early 1920s the railroad unions still held hopes for the Plumb plan and saw in independent political activity a means of achieving their goal. After hopes dimmed for this program of public operation of the railroads, the unionists still sought drastic revision in the labor provisions of the Transportation Act. Although some of the sixteen standard railroad labor unions were declining in influence and numbers after the war, the operating brotherhoods remained strong and politically powerful. With approximately 1,500,000 members in the various railroad labor organizations, these unions formed a bloc that few politicians desired to antagonize, especially since the Plumb plan, and later the effort to revise existing railroad labor legislation, provided their leaders with specific and important issues.[20]

Early in 1922 the railroad unions joined with other reform groups to establish the Conference for Progressive Political Action (CPPA), issuing a call for progressives and reformers to meet in Chicago on February 20, 1922. The CPPA, whose leadership came largely from the ranks of organized labor, invited representatives of church and women's groups, independent progressives such as Pinchot and Record, socialists, and leaders of thirty-six farm organizations to attend. "The idea," declared one progressive, "is to begin to function politically. Not necessarily a new political party; perhaps something on the line of the Non-Partisan League," which supported reform candidates within the established parties.[21]

The Conference for Progressive Political Action appeared to be exactly what the progressive movement needed to revive

Politics: A Historical Study of Its Origins and Development, 1870-1950 (East Lansing, Mich., 1951), 325; and Nathan Fine, Labor and Farmer Parties in the United States, 1828-1928 (New York, 1928), 398-429.

[20] MacKay, The Progressive Movement of 1924, pp. 31-33.

[21] Nye, Midwestern Progressive Politics, 325; William H. Johnston, president of the International Association of Machinists, to Amos Pinchot, Feb. 4, 1922, Amos Pinchot Papers, Box 43; The words quoted are contained in Gilson Gardner to Amos Pinchot, Feb. 7, 1922, Amos Pinchot Papers, Box 43.

its influence. The announcement of the meeting declared that division and misunderstanding had too often plagued reform efforts in the past; it pledged "an effort to make use of those constructive forces already in existence and by cooperation to bring about political unity." Here, then, was to be a broad-based and aggressive liberal movement, designed to join workers, farmers, and their supporters. "Producers," headlined *Labor*, "Join Forces to Throw off Political Chains."[22]

But rhetoric could not insure unity. The labor unions, having led in the formation of the movement, quickly became the center of controversy. Organized labor itself was not unified. Many of its leaders, whatever their personal sympathy with the goals of the CPPA, opposed political involvement and maintained the economic focus of "pure-and-simple" unionism. More radical laborites wanted American workingmen to stand at the head of a new political party and felt that the CPPA was too opportunistic and too limited in outlook to contribute toward this end. Even among the brotherhoods' leaders differences of opinion developed. W. G. Lee, president of the Brotherhood of Railway Trainmen, was a Republican and proved unwilling to sanction an anti-GOP stand. Lucius E. Sheppard, president of the Order of Railway Conductors, Edward Keating, editor of *Labor*, and most others held to a nonpartisan approach, seeing in the CPPA a means of encouraging prolabor progressivism within the major parties, but avoiding third party adventures. William H. Johnston, president of the International Association of Machinists and chairman of the CPPA's political action body, the Committee of Fifteen, sought a new political movement, for he saw "no hope in the old parties." These divisions became even more open and harmful as the AFL began to consider the possibilities of independent political action.[23]

[22] The CPPA's announcement is quoted in Nye, *Midwestern Progressive Politics*, 325. *Labor's* headline is in its Feb. 25, 1922, issue.

[23] Keating's view is reflected in *Labor's* editorials throughout the 1920-1924 period. The nonpartisan versus third party controversy among

Internal quarrels aside, labor's presence in any liberal coalition met with suspicion and disfavor. Farmers often viewed their interests as separate and even in conflict with those of laborites, arguing, for example, that high railroad freight rates were partly the result of the high wages and short hours enjoyed by the operating railroad men. Socialists, attracted by the political rumblings and eager to join forces with progressive groups, had a longstanding antipathy toward unionists to whom political action often was a temporary expedient and not a fundamental commitment.[24]

Another element of potential disunity was the relationship between general reformers and laborites. Programs such as the Plumb plan drew public ownership advocates and the railroad unionists together, but suspicion lurked on both sides. To many intellectuals and progressives, organized labor was too timid and too selfish to provide impetus for political regeneration. "The curse of the labor movement," wrote Mercer Green Johnston, "has been and still is the little-mindedness—the hard and narrow and exclusive sectarianism—of those in positions of leadership." For their part, unionists frequently regarded intellectuals and reformers as theorists who could make sweeping proclamations but who did not

---

railroad labor leaders smoldered beneath the surface in the early days of the CPPA, but it became more open after La Follette's defeat in 1924. See "Report of the National Progressive Convention Held at Chicago, Feb. 21-22, 1925," mimeographed minutes, in Mercer Green Johnston Papers, Box 70. William H. Johnston's quoted remarks are drawn from this document. Mercer Green Johnston reported that unionists in Maryland would have nothing to do with the 1922 Chicago convention which established the CPPA and that "They fairly hissed at the names of Morris Hillquit and Sidney Hillman on the Committee of Fifteen," for these two men—one a socialist and the other an industrial unionist—were ardent supporters of a permanent third party.

[24] For a valuable discussion of farmer-worker antagonism and its effects on progressive politics in the 1920s, see Ashby, "Senator William E. Borah," 118-20. Hayes Robbins, *The Labor Movement and the Farmer* (New York, 1922), discusses the problem in a contemporary setting. For the skepticism of socialists regarding organized labor's political effectiveness, see Fine, *Labor and Farmer Parties*, 415, and David A. Shannon, *The Socialist Party of America: A History* (New York, 1955), 168-78.

have to face economic pressure, the antagonism of the major parties, or the demands of a vast constituency. In general, the leaders of the major railroad labor organizations were most ardently in favor of independent political action when hopes for the Plumb plan were still alive. Later, as abolition of the Railroad Labor Board and creation of different federal dispute-handling machinery became more realistic goals, they realized that independent political action was useful mainly as a prod to the existing parties. As the Democrats and Republicans began to support new railroad labor legislation, the unionists' enthusiasm for progressive politics waned sharply.[25]

Still, in February 1922 these doubts were in the future. The Chicago conference was a huge success, with farmers, laborites, churchmen, intellectuals, and middle-class reformers achieving a rare, if momentary, unity. After deferring the question of forming a third party and agreeing to work for the election of progressive candidates in the approaching 1922 primaries and general elections, they dispersed to begin their attacks upon the Old Guard.[26]

The CPPA's Committee of Fifteen, which directed the progressive forces in the 1922 elections, found fertile ground. Dissatisfaction with the Harding administration grew, especially after its inept handling of the strikes during the summer. The Daugherty injunction triggered renewed labor antagonism, and farmer dissatisfaction kept the political prairie fire burning. Administration Republicans lost heavily in the primaries and in the fall elections. Western agrarians unseated a number of standpat senators and congressmen, and twelve of the

[25] The quotation is from Johnston to Keating, March 16, 1922, Johnston Papers, Box 47. For discussions of the relationship among laborites, reformers, and politicians in railroad labor legislation, see Robert H. Zieger, "From Antagonism to Accord: Railroad Labor Policy in the 1920s," *Labor History*, IX (Winter 1968), 23-38.
[26] The CPPA convention is described in MacKay, *The Progressive Movement of 1924*, pp. 60-66. See also mimeographed sheet from the CPPA on the "North Dakota and Minnesota Senatorial Elections," n.d., Borglum Papers, Box 61.

sixteen gubernatorial candidates whom the CPPA had endorsed triumphed. Critics of organized labor such as Senators Miles Poindexter of Washington and Frank Kellogg of Minnesota, and senatorial candidate Albert J. Beveridge of Indiana also met defeat. *Labor* declared that the outcome "wasn't a 'Democratic landslide,' but it was a Progressive triumph, such a victory as the Progressives have not won in this country in many a day." Hopefully, commented Amos Pinchot, when he learned of his brother's victory in the Pennsylvania gubernatorial primary, there seemed "to be real signs of a revolt against the old order."[27]

With their 1922 success buoying them, the members of the CPPA struggled for the next year and a half to hold the diverse coalition together. Socialists advocated the formation of a third party, while communists attempted to infiltrate the movement through some of the farmer-labor movements of the northern plains states. At meetings in December 1922, December 1923, and February 1924, however, the railroad unions held the balance of power, resisting third party demands, rejecting the communists, and, their critics charged, marking time until one of the major parties became more accommodating. But it became increasingly evident that neither party would reembrace progressivism, and sentiment began to mount for an independent presidential nomination, with Wisconsin Senator Robert M. La Follette the obvious choice of virtually everyone in the CPPA.

At its February 1924 meeting, the CPPA issued a call for a national progressive convention to be held in Cleveland on July 4. After the dreary Republican convention in June, which nominated Coolidge and Charles G. Dawes, over 600 delegates descended upon the Ohio city. Present were farm leaders,

[27] Progressive election victories are summarized in Nye, *Midwestern Progressive Politics*, 326. *Labor*'s joy is reflected in its Nov. 11, 1922, issue, while Pinchot's enthusiasm is contained in a letter to Charles R. Crane, June 10, 1922, Amos Pinchot Papers, Box 43.

members of the Committee of 48, a progressive group with national aspirations, and socialists, together with the leaders of the railroad labor unions and other laborites. Here, as at other CPPA meetings, communists sought entry, but La Follette led the way in excluding them.[28]

Amid great enthusiasm, the Cleveland convention nominated La Follette and Democratic Senator Burton K. Wheeler of Montana. Some delegates wanted to create a formal third party, replete with congressional candidates and local organizations, but neither La Follette nor the unionists welcomed the idea. The candidate felt that the progressives should confine their limited resources to the presidential election, and the unionists were more interested in a revolt that would force concessions from the major parties than they were in an expensive and uncomfortable permanent political movement. The brief platform, which La Follette had written, voiced many of the slogans of the prewar populist and progressive movements, declaring, "The great issue is the control of government and industry by private monopoly." The cure for monopoly, however, was not government ownership, but rather, except in the case of water power and eventually railroads, trust-busting. For labor, the platform and the recommendations of the committee on resolutions endorsed the right of collective bargaining, urged the abolition of the labor injunction, and supported limitation upon the judicial review activities of the courts. More specifically, the committee on resolutions called for "Repeal of the Cummins-Esch law, [and] Public ownership of railroads, with democratic operation, with

[28] The standard account of the CPPA's activities and the 1924 convention is MacKay, *The Progressive Movement of 1924*, pp. 66-116. James Weinstein, "Radicalism in the Midst of Normalcy," *Journal of American History*, LII (March 1966), 773-90, contends that La Follette and the unionists in the CPPA used the communist issue to discredit the Minnesota Farmer-Labor party's efforts to forge a permanent third party. For the participation of the socialists in the CPPA and in the 1924 Progressive movement, see Shannon, *The Socialist Party of America*, 168-81.

definite safeguards against bureaucratic control."[29]   Laborites were content with the platform and the La Follette candidacy. Most brotherhood leaders supported the Wisconsin progressive, and Gompers declared that the Republican party was "beyond hope" and that the Democratic party was better only in comparison with the GOP. On August 2 the AFL executive council followed the lead of the railroad unions and endorsed La Follette and Wheeler, the only time in its history that the Federation endorsed a presidential candidate not nominated by either major party.[30]

Despite the support of the AFL and the brotherhoods for La Follette, the Republican party did not concede the labor vote to the insurgents. With Coolidge men firmly in control, it quickly mobilized to combat the Wisconsin senator's appeal among workers. Even before the July 4 Cleveland meeting, Republicans were concerned about progressive attempts within the party to capture the allegiance of workers. In April, when Hiram Johnson challenged Coolidge in the New Jersey presidential primary, local Republican leaders called upon the national committee to supply speakers to counter the California maverick's attempt "to upset workmen."[31]

The Republican platform reflected the party's concern for the labor vote. It advocated a child labor amendment and minimum wage standards in cases coming under the jurisdiction of the government. Emphasizing the GOP's role in eliminating the twelve-hour day in the steel mills, the platform proclaimed,

[29] The Progressive platform is contained in Kirk H. Porter and Donald B. Johnson, comps., *National Party Platforms*, 3d ed. (Urbana, Ill., 1966), 252-56. See also "Report of Committee on Resolutions of the Conference for Progressive Political Action, July 5, 1924," in MacKay, *The Progressive Movement of 1924*, pp. 270-73.

[30] Gompers to Frank Morison, Aug. 19, 1924, Gompers-AFL Papers, Box 44; MacKay, *The Progressive Movement of 1924*, 270-73.

[31] E. C. Stokes (Republican National Committeeman for New Jersey) to George B. Lockwood, secretary of the Republican National Committee, April 1, 1924, Edward T. Clark Papers (Manuscript Division, Library of Congress), Box 9; hereafter cited as Clark Papers.

"We declare our faith in the principle of the eight-hour day and the six-day week in all industry." It also supported a law to regulate the interstate shipment of the products of prison labor, a reform that the AFL had urged for forty years.[32]

Republicans pictured Coolidge as a friend of the toiling masses during his service in the Massachusetts legislature, as governor of that state, and as president. While in Bay State politics, he had supported bills for everything from the licensing of barbers to the eight-hour day for women, all of which the Republicans described as prolabor measures. Declaring the Republican party to be the traditional friend of the laboring man, the National Committee reviewed forty years of Republican-sponsored prolabor legislation. This benevolent trend had culminated in the Harding and Coolidge administrations when the Republicans tackled the problem of unemployment by increasing the tariff and restricting immigration. Republicans pictured these policies as explicitly prolabor in intent. Thus, under the low tariff of the Wilson administration, cheap foreign goods had allegedly flooded the American market, lowering wages. The Democrats had also thwarted meaningful limitation of immigration, and as a consequence, went the Republican argument, "millions of Europeans were preparing to emigrate to the United States, fleeing war-devastated Europe." Again the GOP had rallied to the defense of the worker, for "American labor was entitled to protection from such destructive competition," and the Republicans were willing and able to supply that protection.[33]

The Republican effort to attract labor support was more systematic than in 1920. Davis traveled widely as the administration's emissary to labor. With an eye on the railroad

[32] Draft of the 1924 platform by Ogden L. Mills, ca. June 1924, Coolidge Papers, File 219B; Porter and Johnson, *National Party Platforms*, 258, 262-63.
[33] "Labor Record of the President," in *Republican Campaign Textbook* (n.p., 1924), 269-74; *Labor Record of the Republican Party and the President* (Republican National Committee pamphlet, 1924).

workers' votes, Coolidge indicated his support for revision of the labor sections of the 1920 Transportation Act. Meanwhile, the Republican National Committee established a labor bureau within the party structure, headed by J. P. MacArdle.

MacArdle and other Republicans were skeptical about the extent of rank-and-file support for La Follette among workers and about the impact of the nebulous labor vote.[34] Nonetheless, the labor bureau director felt that the party should work to reduce the pro-La Follette influence that labor leaders such as D. B. Robertson and Warren S. Stone were exerting among railworkers. Younger employees on the railroads, he asserted, would be particularly susceptible to GOP appeals: MacArdle advised that "missionary work be done among this [younger] element" along the railroads. One Republican campaign aide suggested that the party emphasize to workers "the simple American life of the President," and MacArdle adopted this approach in much of the campaign literature. Throughout the campaign, Republican literature stressed Coolidge's prolabor achievements throughout his career, as well as his homespun, simple life.[35]

In addition to emphasizing the achievements of their party and candidate, Republicans lashed out at La Follette, branding him as a socialist or a communist. Underscoring the endorsement of socialists such as Morris Hillquit and Victor Berger

[34] A variety of people speculated about the size and even the existence of the labor vote in the 1920s. The most common conclusion was that labor rarely, if ever, voted in a bloc, but that its potential power was so vast that such a possibility could not be ignored. See MacArdle memorandum, July 25, 1924, Clark Papers, Box 15, and unidentified memorandum entitled "Membership of organizations affiliated with the American Federation of Labor," ca. Aug. 1924, Coolidge Papers, File 1917. For an astute contemporary assessment of the labor vote, see H. L. Mencken, "Labor in Politics," Aug. 11, 1924, in *H. L. Mencken on Politics: A Carnival of Buncombe,* ed. Malcolm Moos (New York, 1960). 87-91.

[35] MacArdle memorandum, July 25, 1924, Clark Papers, Box 15; unsigned memorandum to C. Bascom Slemp, n.d., Coolidge Papers, File 1917; MacArdle to Ogden Mills, Oct. 10, 1924, Mills Papers, Box 2; *Labor Record of the Republican Party and the President.*

for the Wisconsin senator, Republican orators concentrated upon discrediting the progressives, at times virtually ignoring the able but bland Democratic nominee, John W. Davis. One Republican campaign appeal declared that "If you want to bring to America class cleavage . . . if you want to bring in class hatred . . . then lend your power to this movement which offers the only real alibi for the socialist to get a foothold." Another Republican charged that La Follette was a front for every discredited radical group in the country. "Publicly he states he does not wish the support of the IWW . . . ," wrote James R. Garfield, "but practically he appeals to them." Secretary of Labor Davis was particularly active in working-class areas, seeking to persuade "The workers of this country . . . to follow the American flag no matter who may wave the red banner of discontent."[36]

The GOP sought to dispel the impression that labor had turned overwhelmingly to La Follette and Wheeler. The party captured its usual assortment of labor leaders who announced for the Republican ticket. A group of pro-Coolidge unionists, with John L. Lewis in the vanguard, called upon the president at his Plymouth, Vermont, home to demonstrate labor's support for him. The legislative representative of the United Mine Workers, Walter J. James, assured the president of his active support. W. G. Lee, president of the Brotherhood of Railroad Trainmen, assured the White House that despite news reports to the contrary, his organization was neutral and regarded Coolidge as having a nearly perfect labor record. Toward the end of the campaign, John H. Donlin, president of the AFL Building Trades Department, announced for

[36] Speech of Raymond Robins, Oct. 1924, quoted in telegram from Walter H. Newton, assistant director of the Republican National Committee, to Robins, Oct. 9, 1924, Robins Papers, Box 20; James R. Garfield to Robins, Aug. 8, 1924, Robins Papers, Box 19; James J. Davis, "The Man Who Works in America," typescript, June 23, 1924, and Davis, "Statement Re La Follette Socialist Party," Aug. 31, 1924; Davis Papers, Box 40. There is a vivid account of the attack upon La Follette in Nye, *Midwestern Progressive Politics*, 336-40.

Coolidge, declaring that "he has shown himself to be a sincere friend of union labor." Even Mother Jones, the aged firebrand of the Industrial Workers of the World, endorsed the president.[37]

The party, however, found two major obstacles in its efforts to capture labor support. One was the 1922 injunction, which remained fresh in the minds of railroad workers, and the other was the presence of Charles G. Dawes on the ticket with Coolidge. In the railroad matter, however, the administration took steps that at least partially redeemed the party from the stigma of Daugherty's action. In the spring of 1924, with the breaking of the Teapot Dome scandal, Coolidge had demanded and received the resignation of the controversial attorney general. Moreover, in a Labor Day speech the president showed himself amenable to significant changes in the Railroad Labor Board, thus blunting the brotherhoods' attack.[38]

Dawes' presence on the ticket proved more difficult. Curiously, the party had selected him not because of his antilabor bent but in spite of it. Coolidge had wanted Senator Borah for his running mate, and when the Idaho progressive declined, the convention nominated Frank O. Lowden, the governor of Illinois, who promptly refused. Although many Republicans were delighted to have as the nominee such an ardent open shop advocate as Dawes, the prolabor records of the other two men indicated that the GOP was not particularly interested in labor baiting. Still, labor leaders remembered his Minutemen of the Constitution and his role in smashing the Chicago building trade unions. To one prominent brotherhood official, Dawes' nomination revealed "how little the working men and women of America may expect from the Republican party,"

[37] New York *Times*, Sept. 1, 26, Oct. 28, 1924; Walter J. James to Coolidge, Sept. 15; and W. G. Lee to a Coolidge aide, Aug. 18, 1924, Coolidge Papers, File 1917.

[38] Coolidge Labor Day speech, Sept. 1, 1924, in New York *Times*, Sept. 2, 1924; William L. Chenery, "Railroad Labor Board Under Campaign Fire," New York *Times*, Oct. 26, 1924.

for Dawes was "the most notorious open shopper and active enemy of organized labor in this country."[39] Dawes' nomination indicated that the GOP, while not embarking upon an avowedly antilabor course, felt that Coolidge's popularity and Republican prosperity would offset the Chicago banker's candidacy. To be more certain of this, Republican orators and party spokesmen tried to present the reparations expert as a friend of labor and as a great international statesman. They depicted those who criticized Dawes as desperate and irresponsible. "Recent attacks on General Charles G. Dawes," declared Davis, "are a part of a program of vilification and abuse designed to mislead . . . the American people." Davis emphasized the high esteem in which Ramsay MacDonald, head of the British Labour party, held the former director of the Bureau of the Budget, and he termed the Dawes' plan for war debt reparations as a great step toward peace.[40] Early in the campaign, John R. Alpine, a former AFL vice president and once leader of the Plumbers and Steamfitters International Union, told Republican leaders of the help that Dawes had given his union in 1913. Alpine, who was now in private business, had many friends among labor leaders and worked to counteract the anti-Dawes expressions emanating from the AFL, La Follette's supporters, and the Democrats. The Republican National Committee reprinted Alpine's testimony and circulated it to speakers bureaus and publicity managers. Judson Welliver, one of Coolidge's aides, commented optimistically, "This should answer those who are hostile to Dawes on the theory that he is an enemy of labor."[41]

[39] There is a good account of the vice-presidential nomination in Ashby, "Senator William E. Borah," 184-92. See also Donald E. Williams, "Dawes and the 1924 Republican Vice Presidential Nomination," Mid-America, XLIV (Jan. 1962), 3-18. The quoted words are D. B. Robertson's in the New York Times, Sept. 9, 1924, while the AFL position is outlined in "Why Labor Should Support La Follette and Wheeler," American Federationist, XXXI (Oct. 1924), 811.

[40] Davis statement, "Re: Attacks on Charles Dawes," Oct. 8, 1924, Davis Papers, Box 40.

[41] Meyer Bloomfield to C. Bascom Slemp, July 17, 1924, with

No amount of apologetics could counteract labor's distrust of Dawes if the candidate refused to cooperate and continued to proclaim his provocative views. Early in the campaign, the nominee was determined not to allow political expediency to interfere with his patriotic duty to expose the machinations of selfish labor leaders. Early in August at Augusta, Maine, Dawes delivered an antilabor speech that revealed the sort of campaign that he wanted to conduct. Launching a full-scale attack on labor union leadership, he asked, "Why do so many politicians of both parties continue to regard the great, intelligent, honest, and conservative body of trade unionism as if it were a puppet in the hands of a few radical labor leaders and political demagogues?" Dawes did not identify these "few radical labor leaders," but past utterances of his had included such prominent unionists as Illinois AFL official Victor Olander and Samuel Gompers in this category. This assault created consternation in the Republican hierarchy. National chairman William M. Butler warned the candidate that the speech was ill-advised and harmful to the Republican cause. "An attack on labor leaders, good or bad," he informed Dawes, "always consolidates Union members and their sympathizers. I know this from 25 years experience in manufacturing and politics. It is not a new situation. This speech will solidify labor against our candidates." Indignantly the patriot-politician replied that he would stand firm on his principles regardless of the political consequences,[42] but Dawes' remaining campaign speeches dealt largely with international affairs and farm problems.

Despite the liability of Dawes' name on the ticket, the Republican party successfully avoided identification as rigidly

---

enclosed letter from John Alpine to Bloomfield, July 16, 1924; William M. Butler, chairman of the Republican National Committee, to Slemp, July 25, 1924; Welliver memorandum, ca. Aug. 1924, all in Coolidge Papers, Files 1917 and 2000.

[42] Dawes speech, ca. Aug. 9, 1924; Butler to Dawes, Aug. 18, and Dawes' reply, Aug. 19, Dawes Papers, Box labeled "Campaign, 1924."

antilabor. The Coolidge-Dawes slate won an overwhelming victory, which would have been impossible without the votes of working people. Neither Teapot Dome nor farm unrest nor labor dissatisfaction could deter almost sixteen million Americans from endorsing Silent Cal. With 54.1 percent of the vote, the president easily outdistanced both La Follette and Davis.[43]

In the latter stages of the campaign, organized labor, which had played such a vital part in initiating the La Follette coalition, all but deserted the insurgent movement. While some of the actions of the Harding administration had incensed laborites, Coolidge had done nothing to add to this antagonism. Indeed, by dimissing Daugherty and proclaiming himself favorable to change in the Esch-Cummins Act, the president had blunted the most significant specific labor issues. Unionists might have felt that a La Follette victory would give them great influence in government, but as the Wisconsinite's chances dwindled, the adventure became too risky for America's labor leaders. Many of them, even while personally favorable to La Follette, had opposed formal endorsement, feeling it unwise to sacrifice the status that they enjoyed with the established parties for a lost cause, no matter how noble. Labor leaders had never been committed to third party action; as the campaign progressed it became ever more apparent that they cared far more for immediate accommodation with the party in power than for risking present standing for long-range progressive goals. While instrumental in originating the CPPA, laborites defaulted in their support for the Progressive candidates.[44]

[43] David Burner, *The Politics of Provincialism: The Democratic Party in Transition, 1918-1932* (New York, 1968), 137, however, credits La Follette with an impressive showing among workers; "it was La Follette . . . ," Burner declares, "who first won the workingmen from the Republican party in great numbers."
[44] For a pro-La Follette, antiendorsement view, see John Philip Frey to W. A. Appleton, Sept. 23, 1924, Frey Papers, Box 1. For labor's declining support of the Progressive ticket, see MacKay, *The Progressive*

Labor's hesitancy hurt the Progressive challenge. Damaging also was the adverse reaction of some Republican progressives to labor's role in the La Follette movement. To some, the issue was one of class domination and labor arrogance. Thus, one progressive feared that "There will develop around La Follette . . . a radical Farmer-Labor group associated with trade union leaders, aided by the still more radical and communistic and socialistic thought." Gutzon Borglum, while sympathetic to La Follette himself, had no sympathy "for imported isms," and concluded, "I don't think a sane, clean Anglo-Saxon progressivism is before the voters." He even chided La Follette for running on a platform shaped so obviously by laborites; in an effort to get labor support, La Follette, Borglum contended, had abandoned his oldtime progressivism.[45]

The eastern intellectuals also became disenchanted with their association with labor as well as with the La Follette effort. The Pinchot group was among the most persistent in advocating a permanent third party, while the unionists were among the most determined in resisting this movement. As the railroad brotherhoods became more and more willing to put aside the Plumb plan and increasingly ready to accept Coolidge's invitation to revise the Railroad Labor Board, the split between these progressives and their laborite cohorts widened. As early as Record's 1922 campaign against Frelinghuysen, the Pinchot group's attitude had been spelled out. "Distinctly labor planks are politically a failure," the Record political prospectus had argued then, for labor's legitimate demands "can be secured without any discussion

---

Movement of 1924, pp. 199-204. Oswald Garrison Villard even declared, "Many of the New York unions deliberately sold us out in the last week of the campaign, presumably for cash." (Quoted in D. Joy Humes, *Oswald Garrison Villard: Liberal of the 1920s* [Syracuse, N.Y., 1960], 145).

45 "E.A.R." to Borglum, Feb. 14; Borglum to Oswald Garrison Villard, Sept. 16; Borglum to La Follette, July 4, 1924, all in Borglum Papers, Box 61.

before the public in a campaign." Once the prospect of the
Plumb plan had vanished and revision in the existing statute
had become the only realistic goal, unionists no longer felt
a community of interests with these progressives, who in turn
saw vindicated their fears that interest-group politics could
not sustain general reform.[46]

Labor's disaffection and progressives' timidity indicated the
transitory nature of the 1924 progressive movement. The
progressives hoped that general progressive action would
destroy the political power of the special interests which
dominated the GOP and would eventually bring about
enlightened government in the name of the public interest.
Since many Republican actions had been inimical to labor,
workers would be among the first to benefit from the ensuing
general reformation. Such progressives as Record and Pinchot
could wait and could accept momentary defeat as part of the
price that they would pay for eventual triumph. Unionists,
however, felt that they could not suffer setbacks and wait
patiently for changes in the political climate. Labor leaders
had to produce results for their members, and if labor joined
in an aggressive campaign against the major parties it would
necessarily face the consequence of powerful political
antagonism. Moreover, many labor leaders, including Gompers,
were fundamentally skeptical of political action of any kind,
fearing that involvement in politics would divert the labor
movement from its basic economic goals.

Despite the closeness of their views and frequent community
of interests, laborites and progressives were incompatible in the

[46] The quotes are from a typescript document relating to Record's
1922 campaign, ca. 1922-1923, Amos Pinchot Papers, Box 148. For
Pinchot's unhappiness with the La Follette effort in 1924, see Glad,
"Progressives and the Business Culture," 84-85. The third party debate
came to a head after the election as progressives sought to continue the
politics of protest. See James H. Shideler, "The Disintegration of the
Progressive Party Movement of 1924," *The Historian*, XIII (Spring 1951),
189-201, and "Report of the National Progressive Convention . . . 1925,"
in Johnston Papers, Box 70.

1920s. Both groups were at once too advanced and too hide-bound to form an effective coalition. Progressives were willing to lay patient groundwork for an eventual liberal renaissance, but were unwilling to champion labor's interests explicitly or to share with labor leaders the direction of the movement. Labor leaders, especially among the railroad unions, saw very clearly the need for a political alliance that was interest-group centered, but they were, in the final analysis, unable to reconcile themselves to the permanent loss of status among the conservative, older parties which real and lasting progressive political action would have entailed. The 1924 election demonstrated this double paradox: Labor led in forming independent political action, but retreated to the rear when the battle reached its height. Meanwhile, progressives welcomed the financial and voting support of the unions, but even those who did not openly repudiate the La Follette movement because of its labor orientation sought to mute the labor aspect of progressive political activity.

Republican progressives failed in the 1920s. They failed to defeat the Old Guard in the 1920 campaign, they failed to assume control of the party in the vacuum of 1923, and they failed in independent action in 1924. Their failure was due to a lack of leadership, their inability to agree upon a program, and their unwillingness to shift the base of progressive activity. Labor, unhappy with Republican rule, seemed a partner in progressive action, but the GOP was able to divert from the La Follette movement the votes of millions of workers. Labor, because of its reluctance to alienate the GOP, and the progressives, because of their reluctance to change the focus of reform activity from the nebulous public interest to specific interest groups, could not forge the permanent coalition necessary for political success. The movement that brought them together temporarily in 1924 evinced this clearly: Betrothed, labor and the progressives could not wed.

9 The Railway Labor Act of 1926

IN THE GENERAL debate during the 1920s over the relationship between government and labor, no issue was more significant than that of railroad labor. The railroads had long been the subject of federal interest, and since the 1870s the problem of peaceful settlement of railroad labor disputes had often demanded the attention of Congress. More recently, the Adamson Act, federal operation of the railroads, the 1920 Transportation Act, and the 1922 strike had made this issue among the liveliest in American politics. The political and economic power of the major railroad unions, their gains during the Wilson administration, and their leadership in progressive politics made them primary targets of conservative criticism. Simultaneously, these same factors convinced many public figures of the need to placate these unionists and of the desirability of avoiding their wrath, not only in the interest of political expediency but also in the interest of labor peace and efficient transportation.[1]

The Republican response to railroad labor reflected this division of opinion. Opponents of the railroad laborites found powerful friends within the GOP, most notably Attorney General Daugherty and Ben W. Hooper, chairman of the Railroad Labor Board (RLB), as well as a number of legislators. Initially Republican policies followed the views of such men. Affronted by the Adamson Act and spurred by the postwar turbulence of organized labor, Republicans played the major roles in such legislation and action as antistrike proposals, the creation of the RLB, the repudiation of the Plumb plan, the 1922 "outlaw" resolution, the 1922 injunction, and the thwarting of the unions' efforts to revise the labor sections of the Transportation Act. But hostility toward labor yielded few benefits and created many problems. The 1922 strike marked the climax of this hostile approach, for after the injunction the railroad laborites seethed with dissatisfaction, refused to cooperate with the Railroad Labor Board, and intensified their efforts to abolish it. The progressive activities of the brotherhoods also testified to the political danger of continued antagonism. Gradually, more moderate opinions began to shape the policy of the Republican party in railroad labor affairs. Led by Hoover, who deplored the bitterness and discord that accompanied early Republican actions, and by Davis, the party adjusted to an accommodation with the unionists. Just as the antistrike proposals of 1919 and 1920 and the Daugherty injunction of 1922 were monuments to the aggressive Republican opposition to the railroad unions, the 1926 Railway Labor Act was a result of the emerging accommodationist influence in the GOP.

In 1923, when Calvin Coolidge became president, railroad labor matters demanded his attention. The 1922 strike had left a trail of bitterness and dissatisfaction, and on several railroads the strike remained unsettled. Refusing to cooperate with the Railroad Labor Board, the unions increased their attacks upon the federal agency. As militant unionists began their involvement in independent politics, Republicans joined them in their opposition to the RLB. Increasingly, the question for many members of the GOP was not how to salvage the controversial agency, but how to get rid of it gracefully.

The unionists had many grievances against the Railroad Labor Board and its nine members. At the heart of their hostility was the feeling that it represented a compulsory and coercive approach to labor disputes. Established at the height

[1] For a background concerning railroad labor legislation, see Elwin W. Sigmund, "Federal Laws Concerning Railroad Labor Disputes: A Legislative and Legal History, 1877-1934" (unpublished Ph.D. dissertation, University of Illinois, 1961), esp. chapts. 4-7, and Gerald G. Eggert, *Railroad Labor Disputes: The Beginnings of Federal Strike Policy* (Ann Arbor, Mich., 1967), chapt. 1.

of postwar antagonism toward labor, it had been granted authority to "establish rates of wages, salaries and standards of working conditions [for every class of employee] which in the opinion of the Board are just and reasonable." Although its decisions were not enforceable in the courts, laborites regarded it suspiciously as a preliminary step toward compulsory arbitration or an industrial court. The efforts of the unions in 1919 and 1920 had helped to prevent an antistrike provision from becoming law, but laborites felt that in creating the RLB, Congress had ignored their wishes by establishing this semijudicial, decisionmaking body.[2]

The unionists charged that the board had assumed an antilabor bias. The pattern of board decisions supported this contention, for even though it voted for the unions more often than against them, it had opposed their position in crucial questions involving wages and work rules, ordering several wage slashes and the abandonment of concessions gained during federal operation. In addition, the unions contended that the board had been extremely unfair in implementing its decisions. Even though the unions had reluctantly been quite faithful in abiding by even unfavorable decisions, the board had branded the 1922 strikers as virtual outlaws. On the other hand, the body seemed extremely tolerant of major carriers such as the Pennsylvania Railroad which had ignored and even flouted RLB decisions in key cases involving union-smashing practices and union recognition. It was with a good deal of justice that one brotherhood official declared that the RLB "is clearly not a two-edged sword. . . . It has a blunt edge when used against the employers . . . but when . . . turned against the employees it is sharp and cuts deep."[3]

[2] For the unions' opposition to the RLB, see Sigmund, "Federal Laws," chapt. 6; Edwin E. Witte, *The Government in Labor Disputes* (New York, 1932), 241-43; and Donald Richberg, *Tents of the Mighty* (New York, 1930), 187. For the texts of the labor sections (Title III) of the Transportation Act, see U.S. *Statutes at Large*, XLI, 1, 469-74.

[3] The unions' opposition to the board's decisions and its implementation of them is described in Sigmund, "Federal Laws," chapt. 7, and in

The laborites reserved their bitterest hostility for the members of the board, and especially for its chairman, Ben W. Hooper. Edward Keating, editor of *Labor*, admitted that Wilson's appointees had been an excellent group, but he and other railroad labor men regarded the Harding appointees as decidedly inferior. Two of the Ohioan's appointees to the three-man labor section of the board, E. F. Grable and Walter McMenimen, had little backing from the standard unions. But it was Hooper, a ruggedly individualistic Republican and former governor of Tennessee, whom the unionists most deeply disliked. Unable to restrain his language or to separate his personal antagonism toward certain of the major leaders from his role as an impartial arbiter, Hooper became involved in endless controversy. The chairman himself openly admitted his hostility toward the goals of the rail unionists. The political activities of brotherhood leaders and their support for the Plumb plan, he declared, "were so repugnant to the way of thinking of the ordinary East Tennessee mountain man that I made no effort to suppress my indignant disapproval." In retaliation, the executive council of the AFL accused him of seeking dictatorial powers, while brotherhood leaders argued that Hooper's prejudice against them as individuals found expression in his official decisions.[4]

Robert H. Zieger, "From Antagonism to Accord: Railroad Labor Policy in the 1920s," *Labor History,* IX (Winter 1968), 27-28. For a contemporary assessment, see William L. Chenery, "Railroad Labor Board Under Campaign Fire," *New York Times,* Oct. 26, 1924. The labor official quoted is D. B. Robertson of the Locomotive Firemen and Enginemen, cited in Philip Locklin, *Railroad Regulation Since 1920, 1931 Supplement* (New York, 1931), 140-41.

[4] Edward Keating, *The Gentleman from Colorado: A Memoir* (Denver, 1964), 480. For the unionists' dislike for Grable and McMenimen, see Harry D. Wolf, *The Railroad Labor Board* (Chicago, 1927), 392. For Hooper's remarks, see Ben W. Hooper, *Unwanted Boy: The Autobiography of Governor Ben W. Hooper,* ed. Everett Robert Boyce (Knoxville, Tenn., 1963), 182-83. For the unionists' hostility toward Hooper, see Report of the AFL Executive Council, in *Proceedings of the 43d Annual Convention* (1923), 274, and Locklin, *Railroad Regulation Since 1920,* p. 142. See also Chenery, "Railroad Labor Board Under Campaign Fire."

Republicans also voiced criticism. Davis, for example, found Hooper utterly inflexible when the secretary sought the chairman's cooperation in mediating the remnants of the shopmen's strike. Davis called the board a "quasi-Governmental, partisan institution," and in 1923 he called publicly for the scrapping of the board. He began working to eliminate the RLB and to have railroad labor matters handled with more traditional methods.[5]

In Congress, regular Republicans joined a number of Democrats and progressives in criticism of the board and its methods. Early in 1923, Representative John G. Cooper of Ohio, a member of the Brotherhood of Locomotive Engineers, attacked the agency as an authoritarian and meddlesome institution. Senator Arthur Capper of Kansas noted with concern that railroad workers in his state were calling for its abolition. Said Representative Joseph N. Tincher of the same state, "No one wants the Labor Board now."[6]

While Harding was president these criticisms impelled no change in policy. Harding had committed himself to support of the RLB and its members. Throughout the strike of 1922 the president had based all settlement proposals upon this stand. The controversial ending of the strike, while it convinced some people of the uselessness of the board, even further committed Harding to it, for to sanction its dismemberment now would constitute a repudiation of his attorney general and an admission that his whole approach

[5] There is a revealing exchange of letters between Hooper and Davis in Feb. and March 1923. See esp. Hooper to Davis, March 3, and Davis to Hooper, March 5, 1923, USCSR, File 165/277B. For Davis' various assaults upon the board, see New York Times, Oct. 15, 1922; Davis to D. B. Robertson, Dec. 8, 1922, USCSR, File 165/277B, and to Sen. Arthur Capper, Nov. 7, 1923, USCSR, File 165/277C; and U.S., Department of Labor, Eleventh Annual Report (Washington, D.C., 1923), 115. The quotes are from the Times article and the letter to Capper, respectively.

[6] Cooper speech, Jan. 10, 1923, Congressional Record, 67th Cong., 4th sess., 1923, 64:1549-50; Capper to James J. Davis, Nov. 2, 1923, USCSR, File 165/277C; Tincher speech, Dec. 11, 1922, Congressional Record, 67th Cong., 4th sess., 1922, 64:306.

to the strike had been wrong. In some of his last statements on the subject late in 1922 he acknowledged that the board was "not so constituted as best to serve the public interest," but his vague recommendations for change were in the direction of a stronger board, whose decisions would be enforceable in the courts. Railroad workers, he declared in September 1922, must "surrender their right to strike," relying upon the government to protect their interests.[7]

Throughout most of 1923 opponents and supporters of the RLB marked time. Congressional and cabinet criticism grew but did not coalesce into specific proposals. In June, Ralph M. Easley of the National Civic Federation (NCF) reported that the railroad unionists were "determined to smash [the board] . . . if they have sufficient political strength." During the year the laborites remained active in the Conference for Progressive Political Action while at the same time they worked to eliminate the board, at first by seeking the co-operation of the railroads and eventually by drafting their own legislation. Railroad executives were divided. Some favored strengthening the board, while others, such as W. W. Atterbury, an influential Pennsylvania Railroad executive, urged virtual termination of all federal machinery. Still others, including Daniel Willard, the perceptive head of the Baltimore and Ohio, stood in the middle. According to Easley, most railroad managers felt that while they "had no special love for the Labor Board," they "were afraid that if they started to amend the [Esch-Cummins] act, they would lose the whole measure."[8]

[7] U.S., *Annual Message of the President to the Congress of the United States* (Dec. 8, 1922); Harding to Homer Hoch, Sept. 27, 1922, Harding Papers, Box 62.
[8] Easley described a conference held under the NCF's auspices between the brotherhood leaders and important carriers in Easley to Hoover, June 5, 1923, Hoover Papers, Box 120. The maneuvers of the unionists are described in D. B. Robertson to Easley, July 30, 1924, NCF Papers, Box 64. For Atterbury's view, see his letter to Davis, Nov. 18, 1922, USCSR, File 165/277B.

By late 1923 it became clear to most observers that the Railroad Labor Board could not long survive in its present form. Harding's death had removed one major obstacle to revision, and the new president, while noncommittal, shared none of the responsibility for the events of 1922. In November 1923 perhaps fearing that revisionist sentiment was gaining ground, Hooper, a jealous guardian of the board's prerogatives, attempted to persuade Coolidge that the RLB was stronger than ever before. Far from harming the body, he contended, the 1922 strike "has really served a useful public purpose." By demonstrating that a strike against the public interest and sentiment could not work, the Railroad Labor Board deserved a vote of confidence. "It required one good-sized strike to make manifest the power of public sentiment behind the decisions of the Labor Board," he argued. With the board firmly in control, he predicted a period of peace on the nation's railroads.[9] The chairman's enthusiasm apparently had little effect, for two weeks later in his first Annual Message to Congress, the president commented upon the board's limitations and hinted that if the carriers and the unions would cooperate to write substitute legislation, Congress should give it careful consideration.[10]

No conferences took place in 1924, for the executives were reluctant to tamper with the Transportation Act and the unionists initiated their own action. Impatient with the carriers and prodded by their restive membership, in February the labor leaders unilaterally introduced legislation to abolish the RLB and to establish other means of settling labor disputes along the railroads.[11] Known as the Howell-Barkley bill

[9] Hooper to Coolidge, Nov. 26, 1923, Coolidge Papers, File 58.
[10] U.S., "Annual Message of the President of the United States to a Joint Session of the Senate and House of Representatives, Dec. 6, 1923," in U.S., Congress, House, 68th Cong., 1st sess., *House Miscellaneous Documents* (Washington, D.C., 1924), I, p. 6.
[11] The activities of the railroad labor leaders and the impatience of their members are revealed in several letters from D. B. Robertson to

because of its sponsorship by progressive Republican Senator Robert Howell of Nebraska and Democratic Congressman Alben W. Barkley of Kentucky, this measure was authored by attorney Donald Richberg and his assistant David Lilienthal, counsels for the brotherhoods. The proposal envisioned the abandonment of the Railroad Labor Board and its replacement by a five-member Board of Mediation, whose functions would be mediatory and not decisionmaking. It named the sixteen standard railroad labor organizations as bargaining agents, thus seeking not only the recognition of the general right of collective bargaining and the formal acknowledgment of the operating brotherhoods but also the recognition of the weakened AFL shopcrafts organizations. To lend further support to these unions, it called for the formation of four national adjustment boards, one each for disputes arising in connection with train-service (operating) employees, machinists and shopmen, clerks and freight handlers, and inland waterway transportation employees. Through the device of these four national adjustment boards, its authors hoped to lend encouragement to the traditionally weaker nonoperating employees' organizations and to prevent individual railroads from forcing their wills upon these unions. The unionists hoped to preserve the status of the operating brotherhoods, to give needed support to their less secure AFL colleagues, and to halt the inroads of company unionism among the nonoperating railroad workers. Thus, the Howell-Barkley bill sought at once a return to previous methods and new support for organized labor. In seeking the replacement of RLB with a national Board of Mediation without decision-rendering functions, it returned to the voluntaristic methods of handling railroad labor disputes created by the Erdman and Newlands Acts. However, by naming the standard organizations and

---

Ralph M. Easley, in the NCF Papers, Box 64. See particularly the letters dated July 7, Sept. 5, and Nov. 6, 1924.

by seeking so boldly to shore up the sagging nonoperating unions and to afford them the kind of status and recognition which the operating unions already enjoyed, the bill represented a significant change in labor legislation. If passed, it would not only dismantle the RLB but also provide a degree of federal support for organized labor never before seen.[12]

Chances of passage seemed excellent. Here was a definite proposal to eliminate the heavily criticized RLB and to return to popular prewar methods of settling disputes. Barkley, in his introduction of the measure in the House, carefully cited the frequent criticisms of the Railroad Labor Board emanating from the Harding and Coolidge administrations. The Kentuckian especially noted Coolidge's remarks the previous December that the board was "not altogether satisfactory." With the brotherhoods' political militancy increasing, the measure had the support of a majority in the House, and perhaps in the Senate as well.[13]

But the opposition was strong also. Most railroad executives were unwilling to scrap the RLB and were certainly unwilling to see their company union programs jeopardized. Carrier representatives denounced the bill as a means of insuring the closed shop. One executive proclaimed it the most "serious anti-railroad legislation . . . since the Adamson bill." Railroads printed petition forms, circulated them to their company union employees, collected them, and sent them to congressmen and senators. In speaking so glowingly of the RLB and in

[12] See Leonard A. Lecht, *Experience Under Railway Labor Legislation* (New York, 1955), 48-50, and Leo Troy, "Labor Representation on American Railways," *Labor History*, IX (Winter 1968), 297-308. For the text of the bill (H.R. 7358; S. 2646), see *Congressional Record*, 68th Cong., 1st sess., 1924, 65:7880-85. The importance of the adjustment boards to the unions is indicated in Robertson to Easley, Sept. 5, 1924, NCF Papers, Box 64.

[13] Barkley's speech of April 15, 1924, quoting Harding, Coolidge, Hoover, and Davis is in *Congressional Record*, 68th Cong., 1st sess., 1924, 65:6385-86. Votes on procedural matters associated with the bill in the House indicated that it would have passed if it had come to a vote. It cleared the Senate Commerce Committee by a 10-3 vote.

criticizing so severely the Howell-Barkley bill, these petitions supposedly represented those railroad workers happily untouched by the arrogance and politicking of the standard unions. Thus, officers of the Atchison, Topeka, and Sante Fe Railroad told Senator William McKinley of Illinois, "We are sending you the signatures as they were handed to us by the employees and you will note they are sealed with the finger marks of honest toil."[14]

More serious was the opposition of members of the Coolidge administration. Predictably, Hooper lashed out at the Howell-Barkley bill, calling it "an iniquitous measure drafted by certain labor organizations and introduced without the crossing of a t or the dotting of an i." Secretary of Labor Davis cautiously rejected the legislation on the grounds that its machinery would be too complex and too expensive to secure public support. Hoover, although he had often attacked the RLB, held the substitute legislation to be inadequate. He attempted, even while debate over it progressed, to arrange meetings between carriers and unionists to forge alternative legislation, but he had to report that his early efforts were unsuccessful. It was this cooperative method of revision that President Coolidge had suggested in December 1923 and the one to which the administration was committed. Thus, Barkley's attempt to link the president to the pending legislation could not be successful.[15]

[14] Excerpts from the hearings revealing the carrier's opposition can be found in New York *Times*, March 29, 30, and April 23, 1924. The Adamson Act quote is in the latter and is a remark of Alfred P. Thom, general counsel of the Association of Railway Executives. The citation for the difficult-to-obtain hearings is U.S., Congress, Senate, Subcommittee of the Committee on Interstate Commerce, *Hearings on S 2646; . . .,* 68th Cong., 1st sess., 1924 (Washington, D.C., 1924). The petitions and memorials against the bill from the carriers and the company union employees are in U.S. Senate Records, File 68A-J31, Drawers 216-18. The one cited is from officials of the Atchison, Topeka, and Sante Fe Railroad to Sen. McKinley, Feb. 13, 1924, Drawer 217.

[15] Hooper to Coolidge, April 17, 1924, Coolidge Papers, File 58; Davis to Coolidge, ca. Feb. 1924, Coolidge Papers, File 15; Hoover to Samuel Winslow, May 1, 1924, Hoover Papers, Box 250.

Regular Republicans in Congress voiced the administration's hostility toward the bill. While a number of progressive Republicans joined the Democrats in its support, such powerful administration spokesmen as Speaker of the House Frederick Gillett, floor leader Nicholas Longworth, chairman of the House Committee on Interstate and Foreign Commerce Samuel Winslow, Everett Sanders, soon to be appointed Coolidge's private secretary, and Ogden L. Mills, an influential New York congressman attacked the measure and the methods of its supporters. To Sanders, who claimed that he had often defended the interests of railroad workers, the proposal was too far reaching. He, along with Longworth and other Republicans, urged careful revision of the RLB, not abandonment of it. Winslow sought to bottle it up in his committee, while several Republicans charged that the railroad unions were unfairly bringing political pressure to bear upon the House. Despite all the opposition, Mills feared that "the House will adopt the bill unless the hardest kind of work and aroused public opinion can prevent it." The New York Republican declared that his colleagues were prepared for "another Adamson Law surrender and compared to the Barkley Bill the Adamson Law was a trifling matter." He directed an urgent plea to New York publishers Frank Munsey and Ogden Reid to speak out against it soon.[16]

During April and May, the House debated the Howell-Barkley bill. With about 40 Republicans joining the Democrats in support of the measure, the slim Republican majority vanished. Longworth, Gillett, and Winslow were hard pressed to prevent a vote. Winslow refused to schedule hearings before the House Committee on Interstate and Foreign Commerce, but on April 21, the friends of the measure circulated a

---

[16] For Longworth's remarks of May 5, 1924, see *Congressional Record*, 68th Cong., 1st sess., 1924, 65:7872-73. For Sanders' remarks of May 2, see *ibid.*, 7702-7703, and for Winslow's, see *ibid.*, 6655. Mills' alarm is revealed in Mills to Frank Munsey and to Ogden Reid (identical letters), April 28, 1924, Mills Papers, Box 79.

discharge petition, freeing it from committee control. Two weeks later, amid great tension the House formally relieved the committee of its jurisdiction over the measure by a vote of 194 to 181. But the Republican leadership fought back from this early setback and eventually stalled the bill. Longworth, Gillett, and Sanders filibustered and succeeded in making it pending business, thus limiting discussion of it to two days a month and effectively preventing a final vote. Through all this maneuvering, legislative representatives of the railroad unions sat in the House gallery, carefully checking names and votes. Clearly, the New York *Times* correspondent remarked, the railroad labor issue promised "to play an important part in the campaign for the election of a party majority in the House next November."[17]

Indeed, with the unionists becoming ever more firmly committed to independent political action, the victory of Republican leadership in the Howell-Barkley battle threatened to be a costly one. Even Hooper, who fervently defended his board from criticism, grew apprehensive over the political consequences of the railroad labor situation. Toward the end of the battle in the House he candidly revealed his thinking to Coolidge. Still holding the Howell-Barkley bill to be "a vicious, partizan [*sic*], socialistic measure," he now felt that political expediency called for a more positive response from the GOP. So far, he complained, Republicans had simply opposed the Howell-Barkley measure. He suggested that Republicans introduce a congressional resolution asking the president to appoint a commission representing the public, the unions, and the carriers to study railroad labor matters. While Congress would almost certainly not pass such a resolution it "would give Republicans a definite, sensible,

[17] In addition to the items cited above, the New York *Times*, April 22, 23, May 6, 7, 1924, provides a vivid and accurate description of the debate and legislative maneuvering. See also Sigmund, "Federal Laws," 170-73. In the Senate, the bill cleared the Commerce Committee by a 10-3 vote, but no floor vote was held. New York *Times*, June 1, 1924.

practical position upon which to stand." Hooper contended that such a move would cut the ground out from under the Howell-Barkley forces without committing the administration to any particular action. It would greatly help the president and party politically as well. Most of the leaders of the rail unions were strongly against Coolidge, he admitted, but the maneuver that he suggested would show that the party was sympathetic to reform and would provide a powerful incentive for railroad workers (in distinction to their "leaders") to support the GOP. The problem of the GOP, Hooper concluded, "is to make [an] appeal to the rank and file of the . . . employees." Such an appeal as he outlined would have a good chance of success, he suggested, because "There is very considerable factionalism among them."[18]

Coolidge did not respond directly to the chairman's suggestion, but after the Howell-Barkley debate he issued a strong statement on the need for revision of existing legislation. On Labor Day, 1924, the president told unionists that he acknowledged the need for some change in the existing arrangement. In his December 1923 statement he had emphasized the contributions of the board, but now he dismissed it as unwieldy and controversial, declaring it "could probably be modified, through mutual agreement [between the carriers and the unions], to the benefit of all concerned." Thus, the board, once a bulwark against the postwar pretensions of organized labor, had become an unsuccessful experiment.[19].

Coolidge and Hoover had already been seeking to bring about carrier-union discussions. In a number of utterances the secretary of commerce had criticized the board. Moreover, he remained in close touch with Easley, who in turn knew the thinking of the labor leaders and many of the carriers. As early as December 1923 Hoover had met with D. B. Robertson,

[18] Hooper to C. Bascom Slemp (Coolidge's secretary), May 31, 1924, Coolidge Papers, File 58.
[19] Coolidge speech, Sept. 1, quoted in New York *Times*, Sept. 2, 1924.

president of the Locomotive Firemen and Enginemen, to discuss legislative possibilities.[20]

Meanwhile, Coolidge's Labor Day remarks evoked quick responses from leading railroad representatives. Replies to his suggestions revealed that management opinion was still split. Alfred P. Thom, general counsel for the American Railway Association and the Association of Railway Executives, reflected the views still held by most carriers belonging to these influential bodies. He informed the president that the railroads he spoke for sought the strengthening of the board, not its abolition. However, some carriers reacted more favorably to Coolidge's remarks. By September 1924 Daniel Willard, whose Baltimore and Ohio Railroad enjoyed the confidence of the employees and unions, had become convinced that the RLB could not function. While he still favored the Esch-Cummins machinery, he told Coolidge that the railroad unions had no confidence in the board and were committed to its abolition. Willard had come reluctantly to Coolidge's conclusion that the railroads and the unions should meet together to write a new railroad labor measure.[21]

Thus, the Republican party, having helped to create the Railroad Labor Board in 1920 and having recently thwarted the Howell-Barkley bill, was now committed to a definite method of rewriting railroad labor legislation. For the present, it was enough to promise this revision; a presidential campaign was no time for careful negotiation and legislative drafting. So Coolidge asked Willard to bring the subject to his attention in November, while Easley told Hoover that it would be up

20 For an example of Hoover's public criticism of the board, see U.S., Department of Commerce, *Annual Report: 1922* (Washington, D. C., 1922), 25. For references to Hoover's conversations with unionists in late 1923, see L. G. Griffing and D. B. Robertson to Hoover, Nov. 14, 1924, Hoover Papers, Box 261; Hoover to William N. Doak, Oct. 30, 1925, Hoover Papers, Box 116; and Robertson to Easley, July 30, 1924, NCF Papers, Box 64.

21 Thom to Coolidge, Sept. 3, and Willard to Coolidge, Sept. 2, 1924, Coolidge Papers, File 1495.

to him, after the election, to get the carriers and the unions together and to straighten out the Howell-Barkley bill.[22]

Actually, when the two groups began their meetings in 1925, Hoover and other government officials tried to remain as aloof as possible. Although the secretary of commerce kept in close touch with the deliberations, neither he nor the president thought it desirable for the administration to identify itself with the arrangements the two parties were making. Just as in the drafting of the Newlands Act thirteen years earlier, the government largely allowed the interested parties to formulate the legislation to which they would be subjected. In October 1925 Hoover lent his tentative support to the proposal that was being hammered out by the unionists and the managers, remarking to one brotherhood official that it was almost entirely along the lines of the memorandum that he had written on the subject two or three years earlier. A few days later he felt encouraged by the progress of the conferences. Toward the end of the year in his annual message, Coolidge noted with approval the apparently successful meetings and appeared to give further administration support to the emerging legislation. But Hoover made it clear to Everett Sanders, Coolidge's secretary, that the administration should not become too closely identified with the proceedings. In mid-December he noted approvingly that the drafting of the railroad labor legislation was virtually completed, but he declared it "much better if it is introduced . . . by them—not by the Administration. I believe also that it would be better if we take no part in the question."[23]

[22] Coolidge to Willard, Sept. 5, 1924, Coolidge Papers, File 1495; Easley to Hoover, Sept. 30, 1924, Hoover Papers, Box 120. At first the unions opposed the holding of these conferences on the grounds that they would "mean further delay and perhaps unsurmountable complications in handling the Howell-Barkley Bill," for which they still held hopes. Robertson to Easley, Nov. 6, 1924, NCF Papers, Box 64.

[23] Hoover's remarks are contained, respectively, in Hoover to William Doak, Oct. 30, 1925, Hoover Papers, Box 116; to Everett Sanders, Nov. 6, 1925, Coolidge Papers, File 358; and to Sanders, Dec. 12, 1925, Hoover

Drafted by Thom and Richberg in accordance with the agreements reached by the officials of the unions and railroads, the new legislation was quite similar in important respects to the defunct Howell-Barkley measure. It too abolished the RLB and erected a five-member United States Board of Mediation. This agency would use its good offices and mediatory services to attempt to settle disputes, but it would have no power to render decisions, to enforce its recommendations, or to publicize negotiations. If its efforts failed, it could propose, but not require, arbitration. If all its processes failed, the president could appoint an emergency or factfinding board and could impose a cooling off period during which neither party could change the terms of employment.

With the exception of the emergency board, this machinery was virtually identical to that of the Howell-Barkley bill. It was in the areas of union recognition and boards of adjustment that it differed most from its precursor. The new measure explicitly endorsed the right of employees to bargain collectively through agents of their own choosing, a milestone in federal labor law. But it did not name the standard organizations, as had the former proposal. Moreover, whereas the Howell-Barkley bill had envisioned national boards of adjustment, through which carriers and workers would adjust grievances before they erupted into full-scale labor disputes, the new measure created only systemwide boards of adjustment, through which workers and carriers could reach preliminary settlements through representation that varied with each railroad system. The ultimate result of this would be to sustain the company unions among the nonoperating employees which the Howell-Barkley bill had sought to undermine, for carriers could more easily maneuver their employees out of the relatively weak AFL unions and into local or company unions if they were not subject to scrutiny and criticism of national boards of adjustment.[24]

From the unions' point of view the legislation was a mixed bag. It destroyed the RLB, created more acceptable machinery, removed the compulsory features of previous legislation, and proclaimed the right of collective bargaining. But it failed to give strength to the nonoperating unions, to halt the company union drive, or to provide adequate machinery for grievance adjustment. The carriers preserved for the time being their company union programs and forestalled the formal recognition of the standard railroad labor organizations, but they had to acknowledge the rights of their employees to bargain collectively. Many railroad managers viewed with equanimity the demise of the RLB, for it had been a troublesome and controversial agency. But others in the railroad industry considered the new legislation to be a defeat for them, for only six years previously they had been on the verge of having Congress pass an antistrike enactment. To them, the new bill demolished hopes that the operating brotherhoods could be rendered less arrogant and powerful. Most interested parties, however, regarded the bill as a compromise. Some railroads and some minor railroad unions opposed it, but generally unionists were content with the destruction of the RLB and the compulsory, antistrike movement, while most carriers were willing to abandon these features so long as they could continue their company union programs unhindered.[25]

[24] Sigmund, "Federal Laws," 186-91; A. R. Ellingwood, "The Railway Labor Act of 1926," *The Journal of Political Economy*, XXXVI (Feb. 1928), 63-82; *U.S. Statutes at Large*, XLIV, 577-87. For a discussion of the adjustment board issue and its significance, see Troy, "Representation on American Railroads."

[25] Although many railroad executives regarded the bill as somewhat prolabor, Ralph M. Easley, executive director of the National Civic Federation and a link between unionists, carriers, and the government on the issue, claimed, "It is not the labor organizations but the railroads that need the protection of this measure." Easley to Elliott H. Goodwin, vice president of the United States Chamber of Commerce, Feb. 13, 1926, NCF Papers, Box 65.

Whether this compromise would become law depended in good part upon the GOP. Between 1919 and 1922 resentment against the railroad unions and eagerness to chasten them had centered in the party. During this period Republicans had proposed and supported legislation and policies designed to check the railroad laborites. The new measure in effect proclaimed the end of this movement and the failure of the policy. Antistrike legislation, semijudicial boards, and far-reaching injunctions had not worked. The turmoil, controversy, and political agitation that these approaches had created were neither efficient nor politic. Thus, despite the postwar policies of the GOP it was not difficult for most Republicans to accept the new measure, especially since Davis, Hoover, and Coolidge had encouraged its formulation.

Emphasizing this reversal of Republican policy and seemingly insuring the passage of the bill, on January 7, 1926, Senator James E. Watson of Indiana and Congressman James Parker of New York, Republican chairmen of the commerce committees of both houses, introduced it. On January 6 and 7, Coolidge met with union and carriers officials and hinted strongly that he approved of their efforts. Thom and Richberg, speaking jointly for the carriers and unions, issued a press release which placed their legislation squarely in the context of Coolidge's oft-repeated suggestions for revision of the labor sections of the Transportation Act. With such massive support, the Republican congressional leadership looked forward to quick passage.[26]

Significant opposition soon developed, however. It centered upon two aspects of the Watson-Parker bill: the removal of the public's representatives from railroad labor settlements and the possibility of higher railroad freight rates because carriers would be willing to grant higher wages if unsupervised by

[26] New York *Times*, Jan. 7, 8, 1926; press release by Thom and Richberg, Jan. 7-8, 1926, United States Senate Records, papers relating to Senate Bill 2306, 69th Cong., 1st sess.

public representatives. Hooper charged that public representatives such as himself had not been consulted and that the legislation would remove federal presence from settling disputes. In hearings before the Senate commerce committee, carriers representing about 20 percent of the nation's railroad mileage, and officers of the National Association of Manufacturers (NAM), attacked it on similar grounds. Petitions and memorials from the NAM and businessmen deluged the White House, reflecting these criticisms of the legislation, and giving Coolidge and his aides extra reasons for caution.[27]

On the floor of Congress, western Republicans joined some southern Democrats in opposition. Here the chief concern was that the removal of a strong federal presence would encourage railroads to grant union wage demands and that the increased costs would in turn cause the carriers to press for higher freight rates. Congressman Homer Hoch of Kansas proposed an amendment that would allow the Interstate Commerce Commission (ICC) to deny carrier rate increases if it felt that these demands resulted from an unwise granting of wage increases. Hoch, who had no objection to the general intent of the Watson-Parker bill, wanted to empower the ICC to say to carriers who bowed to union demands, "If you have made an unwarranted contract, the burden . . . shall not be passed on to the public." Republican Senators Charles Curtis of Kansas and Peter Norbeck of South Dakota voiced similar sentiments in the Senate. Curtis inserted in the *Congressional Record* a letter from the National Grange and the American Farm Bureau Federation, jointly representing two million farmers,

[27] Hooper to Rep. James S. Parker, Feb. 18, 1926, Railroad Labor Board Records (Record Group 13, National Archives), Box 167; James Emery, general counsel for the NAM, to Coolidge, Feb. 15, 1926, Coolidge Papers, File 3393; Everett Sanders to William Doak, Feb. 16, 1926, Coolidge Papers, File 3393. The NAM-inspired petitions are in Coolidge Papers, File 3393. Objections to the proposed legislation can also be found in U.S., Congress, House, Committee on Interstate and Foreign Commerce, *Hearings on H. R. 7180; Railway Labor Disputes*, 69th Cong., 1st sess., 1926.

opposing the measure. Norbeck attacked the bill repeatedly, arguing that the farmer would ultimately have to pay the price for the higher railroad wages that would surely result. After failing to have the measure recommitted to the Senate commerce committee, he proposed an amendment that would change the bill's title to "A bill to increase the farmer's working day from 14 to 16 hours, and to reduce the railroad man's working day from 8 to 7 hours." In view of the lopsided votes against his efforts, he concluded that Congress was bowing before the threat of the railroad labor vote. After Congress had passed the bill, he took his case to Coolidge, urging a presidential veto. Overwhelming labor pressure, he argued, had victimized the Senate. The result of the Watson-Parker bill would be to raise wages, to increase railroad rates, and to reduce the farmers' real income. "If large increases are granted [as seems certain], the effect will be enormous and it will take two [McNary-]Haugen bills instead of one to get the American farmer's dollar back to par," he warned Coolidge.[28]

In the face of such opposition, Coolidge neither asserted nor denied his administration's support. Friends of the measure felt confident that they were simply endorsing the result of carrier-union negotiations, which enjoyed the blessing of the president, but they could point to little tangible evidence in the debates. Senator Watson urged a favorable vote because the legislation had been drafted in accordance with the method suggested by the president on a number of occasions. "Can the Senator produce to the Senate any evidence that the President has sponsored this bill?" Curtis asked. Watson replied simply that everyone knew that Coolidge had given it his approval. Curtis insisted that he knew no such thing. Vexed, Watson remarked, "Well, I know it," but he could produce no direct proof of the president's endorsement of

[28] Hoch's remarks are in *Congressional Record*, 69th Cong., 1st sess., 1926, 67:4571. The farm organizations' letter is reprinted in *ibid.*, 8887. For Norbeck's maneuvers and remarks, see *ibid.*, 9054, 9058, 9189, and 9207, and his letter to Coolidge, May 14, 1926, Coolidge Papers, File 3393.

this particular measure.[29] At the beginning of the debate, the New York *Times* reported that observers generally viewed the measure as administration legislation, but Coolidge stated that he did not consider it as such, although he was not opposed to it as an experiment.[30]

On May 20, 1926, despite the hopes of farm organizations, the NAM, some railroad leaders, and various congressmen and senators, Coolidge signed the Watson-Parker bill. The enactment represented a partial victory for the operating brotherhoods and for a majority of the railroads, a defeat for critics of the brotherhoods, a setback for the nonoperating rail unions, and an impressive political achievement for the Republican party. In securing a return to the prewar methods of handling disputes and in having Congress endorse the right of collective bargaining, the operating unions had thwarted the earlier efforts to cripple them. The carriers, unable to hobble these organizations, could at least maintain their company unions for nonoperating employees, thus continuing their efforts to eliminate the gains that the AFL bodies had made during the war. As for the GOP, it had executed a skillful retreat from the dangerous position it had assumed after the war and could now lay claim to sponsorship of this important and enlightened legislation.[31] Eventually finding a middle way between ardent

[29] The Watson-Curtis exchange is in *Congressional Record*, 69th Cong., 1st sess., 1926, 67:8973.

[30] For the *Times*' comment on the bill, see its Feb. 28, 1926, issue, while Coolidge's disclaimer is in the paper's March 6 issue. See also Howard Quint and Robert Ferrell, eds., *The Talkative President: The Off-the-Record Press Conferences of Calvin Coolidge* (Amherst, Mass., 1964), excerpts from Coolidge's press conferences of Feb. 12 and July 6, pp. 130 and 99 respectively.

[31] At least two prominent Republicans—Hoover and Watson—claimed credit for the legislation. See Herbert Hoover, *The Memoirs of Herbert Hoover. II: The Cabinet and the Presidency, 1921-1933* (New York, 1952), 107-108, and James E. Watson, *As I Knew Them: Memoirs of James E. Watson* (Indianapolis, Ind., 1936), 212-13. Hoover's claim was by far the more justified, although the primary impetus came from the unions and, to a lesser extent, from the carriers. For a discussion of the implications of the measure for the unions, see Irving Bernstein, *The Lean Years: . . . , 1920-1933* (Boston, 1960), 215-20.

hostility toward labor and support for the prolabor innovations embodied in the Howell-Barkley bill, the Coolidge administration had disposed of the vexatious problem of railroad labor legislation.

Both critics and supporters of the Watson-Parker Act predicted a perilous time for the new Board of Mediation. Congressman Carroll Beedy of Maine, a vigorous opponent, declared that "This legislation will rise up to vex us in the future," while the New York *Times*, which supported it, warned that the new board "will face one of the most difficult situations in the history of the relations between labor and capital."[32] Despite such forebodings and the threats of a few dissident railroads and unions to boycott the new agency, it found a few major disputes. Establishing and maintaining a flexible and permissive administrative policy, the Board of Mediation operated amid an atmosphere of relative tranquility. Throughout the rest of the 1920s its moderation contrasted sharply with the abrasive statements and unfortunate actions of the board which it supplanted.

Aware of the controversy that some of the RLB's members had provoked, Coolidge named moderates to the new board. Actually, most suggestions for appointments passed through the hands of Hoover, who also picked the board's secretary, John Marrinan. To the chairmanship Coolidge appointed Samuel E. Winslow of Massachusetts, the former chairman of the House Committee on Interstate and Foreign Commerce. Other members were G. W. W. Hanger and Edwin Morrow, former governor of Kentucky, both of whom had served on the Railroad Labor Board, Hywel Davies, who had served in the United States Conciliation Service, and Carl Williams, editor of the *Oklahoma Farmer-Stockman*. Early in 1927 when Davies died and Williams retired, Coolidge selected Pat M. Neff, former governor of Texas, and John Williams, a

<hr>

[32] Carroll Beedy to Coolidge, March 8, 1926, Coolidge Papers, File 3393; New York *Times*, June 20, 1926.

California industrialist and former labor official, to fill their places. Hanger had voted consistently in favor of the unions while on the RLB and the carriers threatened for a time to contest his nomination on the Senate floor, but the opposition to him quickly collapsed.[33]

In its operations the new board took advantage of the relative peace and stability that now characterized railroad labor relations. It kept itself free of the turmoil and disputation that had ruined its predecessor. Deeply aware of the extent to which the carriers and unions had influenced the legislative process, its members and field mediators early inaugurated a policy of accommodation to the wishes of the parties involved in disputes.[34] For example in July 1926 Marrinan noted that the Act was poorly drafted and extremely vague in its language and definitions. "This," he informed Winslow, who relied heavily upon him, "resulted from strong representations expressed many times before the Committees of Congress that any change in the language of the Bill, as jointly prepared by the railroads and employees, would have the effect of throwing it back into further conferences . . . with a good chance of serious differences between them." Marrinan suggested that the Act left the new board a great deal of leeway; the ambiguity of the language, he felt, would make it necessary for the board to minimize formalized and legalistic procedures. The secretary advised Winslow to ask the unions' counsel, Donald Richberg, and the Association of Railway Executives' counsel, Alfred Thom, to act as an informal committee to

[33] There are various communications reflecting Hoover's influence in appointments, in Hoover Papers, Box 250. For the appointment of Marrinan, see Hoover to Winslow, June 19, 1926, *ibid.* For the opposition to Hanger, see the New York *Times,* June 15, 1926.

[34] Memorandum entitled "Notes on Mediation as Practiced under Erdman and Newlands Acts," n.d. (ca. Sept. 1926); memorandum (apparently prepared by Marrinan and field mediator George Cook), ca. Sept. 1926; memorandum from George Cook to Marrinan, Sept. 18, 1926, all in United States Board of Mediation Records (Record Group 13, National Archives), Box 1726; hereafter cited as USBMR.

clarify ambiguities in the law. And, though the chairman did not adopt this particular suggestion, he shared Marrinan's view of the board's mission and limitations.[35]

Winslow and others associated with the board continually proclaimed that their basic function was mediative. Arbitration was a last resort, which field representatives would suggest only when all other measures had failed. The board's mediators were to meet both sides upon their request, to listen patiently, to shun absolutely all signs of partiality, and to emphasize the peaceful nature of their mission. The board's function was to render its good offices, not to arbitrate, and the field mediators were to act flexibly, in response to varying local conditions. Winslow even sought to change the vocabulary of railroad labor negotiations, bringing it in line with his policy of harmony and accommodation. "In the early days of our mediation work," he reflected, "the words 'fight' and 'dispute' were freely used." Since then the board had "adopted in our vocabulary as substitute words 'problem' and 'discussion.' "[36]

Winslow worked hard to present the board as tolerant, reasonable, and noncompulsory. He felt that it should avoid any hint of partiality or favoritism. For example, it seemed obvious that the board should deal with the majority-supported bargaining agents in its mediation work, but he worried lest this attitude force minority organizations out of existence. Feeling that it was impossible "to interpret liberally the Railway Labor Act without giving some heed to the rights of minorities," Winslow wanted to guard against having the board appear "in a position of a voluntary coercive agent in behalf of the majority." Unfortunately, the Watson-Parker Act did not specify what the board should do in such cases,

[35] Marrinan to Winslow, July 28, 1926, usbmr, Box 1695; typescript copy of Winslow speech of Sept. 16, 1926, usbmr, Box 1690.

[36] Board of Mediation administrative and policy memoranda, prepared by Cook and Marrinan, Sept. 1926, usbmr, Box 1726; Winslow speech quoted in typescript copy of Associated Press dispatch, April 25, 1927, usbmr, Box 1689.

and the new agency would have to adopt a tentative policy and adjust its application to particular circumstances.[37]

In another situation, Marrinan indicated that the board should reassure unionists that it would not become involved in labor injunctions. He conceded that local conditions precluded the board, sitting in Washington, from issuing detailed instructions to cover every contingency. Still, he warned board member John Williams about the hostility "of the standard [railroad labor] organizations towards injunction proceedings." It would require "a very dire situation" indeed before the board would even consider resorting to them.[38]

This approach, with the support of labor and management, succeeded from the start. From the board's inception until the end of the Coolidge administration, there were no major strikes on the nation's railroads. Where mediation and arbitration failed, the Watson-Parker Act's time-consuming cooling-off procedures forestalled work stoppages. A threatened strike on western railroads in the late summer of 1928 exemplified this. The employees voted in favor of the strike on August 8, and the emergency board, which Coolidge did not appoint until the last possible moment, did not conclude its hearings until October 24. In November the unions were still negotiating on the basis of the emergency board's findings and the strike never took place.[39] Working through mediation, conciliation, and even through sheer delay, but rarely through arbitration, the Board of Mediation functioned in a manner that contrasted with the always-embroiled Railroad Labor Board and with the spirit of Harry Daugherty's 1922 injunction.

The Board of Mediation was not completely successful. Its provisions for grievance adjustment were highly unsatisfactory, for some carriers refused even to cooperate in the formation

[37] Winslow to Carl Williams, Dec. 7, 1926, USBMR, Box 1729.

[38] Marrinan to John Williams, May 7, 1927, ibid.

[39] Various communications between Winslow, Sanders, Clark, and Coolidge, Aug. 8 through Nov. 20, 1928, Coolidge Papers, File 3393.

of system boards, thus helping to create a backlog of thousands of unresolved, if sometimes petty, grievances. Moreover, the company union problem remained, for thousands of railroad workers found it impossible to resist the carrier-controlled organizations and join the standard unions. No doubt much of the modest success that the board enjoyed was due primarily to the general, if uneasy, peace on the railroads which had begun after the 1922 strikes.[40]

Still, the board did nothing to exacerbate relations. It allowed circumstances to heal, at least temporarily, old wounds. While its personnel was of only mediocre ability, they were largely free of the conflict-provoking attitudes and rhetoric in which Hooper had indulged. The Board of Mediation's establishment and operation testified to the eclipse of the harshly antilabor movement that had characterized railroad labor legislation and activity during the immediate postwar period. With the passage of the Watson-Parker Act and the tranquility of the next several years, the Republican party demonstrated that it had repudiated the strident extremism that had so strongly influenced the party from the passage of the Adamson Act to the Daugherty injunction. Capping ten years of intense public concern with railroad labor matters, the 1926 Railway Labor Act and its creature, the Board of Mediation, gave evidence of the GOP's eventual preference for political expediency and efficiency of railroad operation in place of antilabor rhetoric and political controversy.

[40] Bernstein, *The Lean Years*, 219-20; Sigmund, "Federal Laws," 193-94. Amendments to the Act in 1934 removed some of these problems and helped to check the company union movement. See Sigmund, "Federal Laws," chapt. 11. For an account sympathetic to the nonstandard unions, see Troy, "Representation on American Railroads."

10 Labor Policies in the Soft Coal Industry

No LABOR PROBLEMS throughout the 1920s so sharply challenged the nation as those arising in the soft coal mining areas. Chronic overdevelopment, intermittency of operations, unemployment, fluctuating markets and prices, incomplete unionization, and technological change joined to make bituminous coal mining the most distressed major industry in America. Strikes erupted in 1919, 1922, and 1927-1928. Violence exploded in southern Illinois in 1922, and labor warfare raged throughout the fields of the upper south as the United Mine Workers of America attempted to organize the miners there. Essential to the economy and available in abundance throughout the country, soft coal intruded constantly into the consciousness of the Republican party and its administrations, which otherwise enjoyed great success in their efforts to promote prosperity and to quiet social conflict.

Republicans sought repeatedly to solve the problems of the soft coal industry. Some urged price fixing, while others emphasized aid for consumers. For a time the idea of a federally sponsored and enforced code for the industry attracted much attention. Progressives urged various public ownership programs, while some conservatives advocated complete laissez faire. Just as the repeated soft coal crises affected various sections and interests differently, so the diverse proposals reflected the interests of sections, stockholders, managers, consumers, workers, reformers, and politicians.

Most programs for soft coal attracted little support, but the GOP administrations sanctioned and promoted two major public efforts to alleviate the nation's bituminous coal ills: the United States Coal Commission, which functioned between 1922 and 1923, and the Jacksonville Agreement, which went into effect in 1924. Both endeavors exposed the tangled roots of coal's problems and demonstrated the limited means of dealing with them available to government and its leaders. The Jacksonville Agreement and its collapse was particularly revealing, for it represented the major effort of Herbert Hoover to apply his views of labor relations to the coal situation. The ineffectiveness of the Coal Commission, the failure of the Jacksonville Agreement, and the misery and disorganization that continued to bedevil the industry represented the greatest failure of Republican labor policies and revealed the sharp limitations of Hoover's approach to labor problems.

The 1922 strikes provided the stimulus for the major efforts to cure coal's sickness, but even before 1922, public men, reformers, and laborites had sought to deal with the industry's problems. In 1919 the UMW convention had been receptive to the principle of nationalization of mineral lands, and the Pinchot-Record progressive program had as its key provision public ownership of these areas. In 1921 Republican Senator William Kenyon of Iowa, then chairman of the Senate Committee on Education and Labor, conducted hearings in the West Virginia coal regions. Appalled by working and living conditions and outraged by the violence that attended the union's efforts to organize the miners, Kenyon urged a federally sponsored code for the industry. It would specify the rights of employers, employees, and the public and would be administered by a nine-member board, patterned after, but with greater powers than, the Railroad Labor Board.[1]

Nationalization and industrial codes found few supporters,

---

[1] John Brophy, A Miner's Life, ed. John O. P. Hall (Madison, Wis., 1964), 152; U.S., Congress, Senate, Committee on Education and Labor, 67th Cong., 2d sess., West Virginia Coal Fields: Personal Views of Senator Kenyon and Views of Senators Sterling, Phipps, and Warren (Washington, D. C., 1922); Baltimore Sun, Jan. 28, 1922.

but the 1922 strikes created a demand for federal action. Senator Borah, who succeeded Kenyon as chairman of the Committee on Education and Labor, indicated early in 1922 that he favored some form of public ownership, and progressives sent suggestions and draft legislation to him for committee study. During the summer crisis Borah lashed out at the administration for its failure to end the strikes and protect consumers, and he threatened to introduce legislation that would provide for public ownership. Although he eventually honored Harding's request not to pursue this goal, the Idahoan did sponsor a bill late in June to initiate a thorough investigation of the coal industry. Since the operators and the UMW asked for the establishment of such a study, when the strike ground to a halt in August the Harding administration announced its support for the creation of a special coal investigating body.[2]

As it finally passed, the legislation provided for a seven-member United States Coal Commission (USCC). The members were charged with gathering and interpreting data regarding the various problems that beset the coal industry. When its investigations were completed, the commission was to issue a report and to submit recommendations for future action on the part of mineowners, miners, consumers, and the government. While its mandate was to study the entire coal industry, the circumstances surrounding its creation insured that it would study labor relations with particular emphasis. To perform its functions, Congress allowed it one year of existence, beginning on September 22, 1922.[3]

[2] Borah is quoted as favoring government operation in the *Christian Science Monitor*, Feb. 16, 1922. For Borah's criticism of the administration, see Borah to Hoover, June 7 and Aug. 16, 1922, Borah Papers, Box 213. For the proposals of progressives, see Heber Blankenhorn to Borah, Feb. 17, and J. A. H. Hopkins to Borah, June 5, 29, and July 25, 26, and 28, 1922, Borah Papers, Box 213. For the senator's communication with Harding, see his letter to the president, July 27, 1922, Borah Papers Box 213.

[3] The text of the enactment is contained in U.S., Coal Commission,

Although Lewis and some mine operators wanted the body to be composed of labor officials and representatives of management, Harding's appointees were all public representatives. To head the group, the president chose John Hays Hammond, a wealthy Republican former mining engineer who in the 1890s had been an associate of Cecil Rhodes in South Africa. Joining him were Clark Howell, founder of the Associated Press and editor-in-chief of the Atlanta *Constitution*; Edward T. Devine, social worker and editor; Thomas R. Marshall, former vice president; George Neill, former commissioner of labor; Samuel Altschuler, federal judge;[4] and George Otis Smith, who resigned as head of the United States Geological Survey to take this post. The commission's secretary, who served as the administrative coordinator, was Edward Eyre Hunt, Hoover's most trusted aide in the Department of Commerce.[5]

The membership of the commission insured that it would propose no drastic solutions. Despite the wishes of the miners and operators, who were anxious to have it justify their respective viewpoints, and of progressives who made the

---

Report of the United States Coal Commission, 5 parts (Washington, D. C., 1925), pt. 1, pp. 283-85.

[4] Judge Altschuler served only in an advisory capacity because as a federal judge he could not formally join the body. Legislation passed on March 4, 1923, amended the act, allowing him to sit, but by this time he had already severed his connection.

[5] For Lewis' desire to have union officials appointed, see Lewis to James J. Davis, Oct. 5, 1922, USCSR, File 165/411, while an estimate of Hoover's and Secretary of the Treasury Mellon's influence over appointments is contained in Sen. George Wharton Pepper to Sen. David Reed, Sept. 30, 1922, George Wharton Pepper Papers (Van Pelt Library, University of Pennsylvania), Box 69; hereafter cited as Pepper Papers. Hammond, who usually spoke for the commission in labor matters, was a prominent member of the National Civic Federation. As such, he was a cautious supporter of the AFL and other conservative trade unions. For his labor views, see Hammond's letter that was read at the NCF luncheon, April 15, 1921, John Hays Hammond Papers (Yale University Library), Box 20; hereafter cited as Hammond Papers; and William Leavitt, "Strikes—How to Avoid Them: An Interview with John Hays Hammond," *Industrial Engineering*, LXI (Feb. 1, 1921), reprint in Hammond Papers, Box 20.

original proposal to Borah in hopes of focusing attention upon the need for public ownership, Hammond and his colleagues were determined that the commission would not be radical or openly partisan. The chairman recalled that two assumptions governed the body's work and shaped its outlook. One was that coal, although of great importance to the public, was susceptible only to minimal governmental regulation, and not under any circumstances to price or wage fixing. The second assumption, a corollary of the first, was that the key to success in the efforts to revitalize the industry lay in self-management, not in legislation. Compulsory laws, the chairman asserted, would reduce efficiency, while "private development, if carried on honestly and as a quasi-public utility, ought to be encouraged." Hammond and the others were unalterably opposed to government ownership and to tight federal regulation. Even the middle ground of a government-sponsored code for the industry was characterized by Joseph Willits, the director of the Commission's Labor Relations Study, as "nearly one hundred years ahead of the times."[6]

The commission faced a formidable task. Many of the industry's problems had developed from long-established mining methods and labor relations machinery. Others sprang from technological change, such as the replacement of coal by fuel oil in home heating. Still others were traceable to outside factors, such as the shortage of coal-carrying freight cars and controversial Interstate Commerce Commission freight rate differentials between the various coal-producing regions. Adding to the commission's burdens was the sense of apathy and anticlimax with which the administration and the public soon came to regard its efforts. Harding viewed its establishment as an obligation incurred during the strike negotiations in 1922. The public and the press characteris-

[6] John Hays Hammond, *The Autobiography of John Hays Hammond* (New York, 1935), 684; Willits to Thomas R. Marshall, June 25, 1923, USCCR, Drawer 380.

tically ignored coal problems as soon as an immediate crisis had passed. Indeed, halfway through the commission's existence Congress almost halted its work entirely by threatening to deny it the funds necessary to complete its studies.[7]

The new agency labored under built-in limitations as well. Chief among these was the failure of Harding or Congress to define its precise function. Although it was often referred to as a factfinding body, Borah noted that "the fundamental propositions are understood" in the coal situation. For at least fifty years governmental committees and commissions had been probing into the industry. Most recently, there had been major Senate investigations of the 1913 Colorado coal strike and in 1921 of the unrest in West Virginia mining regions. Regular surveys, reports, and studies from the Departments of Labor, Commerce, and the Interior added to this fund of information. Was the main task of the commission to increase this mountain of data? George Otis Smith, the most knowledgeable of the commissioners, thought not: "We already have more facts about coal than are accepted," he contended. He saw the commission's function as that of synthesizing the data for public use. Hammond's remarks did little to clarify its role. Nothing that the coal situation was "exceedingly complicated," he stated simply, "The function of the commission was to discover what could be done to cure the almost continuous crisis."[8]

Adding to this confusion was the inability of the administration, the public, and the commission itself to separate the long-range aspects of the coal problem from immediate strike threats. Although it was created as part of a strike settlement,

[7] "Minutes of Staff Meetings," entry for Feb. 6, 1923, USCCR, Drawer 365; Marie L. Obenauer, chief of Investigation of Living Conditions, to Theresa S. Haley, Feb. 28, 1923, USCCR, Drawer 238; *Congressional Record*, 67th Cong., 4th sess., 1923, 64:4703, 5164-65.
[8] Borah to Heber Blankenhorn, Feb. 18, 1922, Borah Papers, Box 213; George Otis Smith to Borah, Nov. 4, 1922, Borah Papers, Box 213; Hammond, *Autobiography*, 682.

Congress gave it no formal mediation or negotiation directives. Still, journalists and public figures often looked to the commission for vigorous action in strike situations, and Hammond and the Harding and Coolidge administrations contributed to this identification by involving the body on two occasions in sensitive negotiations between the UMW and the coal operators. Early in 1923 it helped to conduct conferences between soft coal miners and operators, and later in the year the body unsuccessfully sought an anthracite settlement. In both cases the commission stepped out of its apparently prescribed role, reinforcing the public view of it as a sort of labor board, whose effectiveness and value depended upon its ability to stop strikes. Hoover shared responsibility for this difficulty, for he declared that "The Coal Commission has an independent responsibility to Congress and the public for peace in the coal industry," and was instrumental in injecting it into the 1923 hard coal negotiations. Curiously, it was Edward Eyre Hunt, whom Hoover had recommended as the USCC's secretary, who most articulately objected to this view of the commission's purpose. As the body began efforts in December 1922 to prevent a soft coal strike, Hunt warned of public confusion about the commission's purpose. Many people wrongly attributed extraordinary powers to the USCC, and he feared that the public would judge its usefulness and recommendations primarily on the basis of its success or failure in labor negotiations, a role that Congress had not given it. Although the secretary urged the commissioners to make a public statement disavowing primary responsibility for day-to-day labor peace, the group soon became deeply involved in strike prevention.[9]

Both operators and miners sought to influence its findings and recommendations, and both groups claimed that the

[9] For Hoover's remark, see his letter to Harding, Dec. 12, 1922, Hoover Papers, Box 243, while Hunt's views are expressed in his memorandum to George Otis Smith, Dec. 13, 1922, USCCR, Drawer 18.

USCC unfairly favored its opponent. The UMW made many presentations to the commission and to its subsidiary investigatory bodies. Some unionists claimed that the USCC field representatives spent too much time being lavishly entertained by mineowners and not enough time talking to miners and touring the pits and the workers' shacks. But the miners "appreciated the spirit of fairness, etc." shown them by the fieldworkers for the commission's Living Conditions Study. These young ladies, many of whom were teachers and social workers with degrees from such colleges as Radcliffe, Smith, and Mt. Holyoke, diligently toured the mining slums and the company towns, talking earnestly with miners and unionists, and sending back vivid reports of the poverty and helplessness that was often the miner's lot.[10]

Operators also presented their side to the commission and its staff members. Some, especially in the nonunion areas, resented the alleged snooping and prying of the investigators, and many felt that the federal body's primary function was to serve as a sounding board for antilabor propaganda. A number of soft coal companies retained former Secretary of War Henry L. Stimson to survey the coal industry and to present their case against the UMW to the commission. Stimson soon became convinced that the union and the government were the main agents of soft coal's instability and labor difficulties. He termed the UMW "an arrogant minority—challenging the American Republic by its attempts to fasten a monopoly of coal labor upon American industry." The union, he charged, had frequently resorted to intimidation and murder. So convinced became the New Yorker that in addition to submitting a lengthy report for the bituminous coal operators, who in turn passed it on to the USCC, he

---

[10] The reports and declarations that the UMW sent to the commission are listed in the commission's *Report*, pt. 1, pp. 311-14. The complaints of union officials in West Virginia—as well as their appreciation—are reflected in a letter from Clare Butler, a USCC field investigator, to Marie L. Obenauer, May 22, 1923, USCCR, Drawer 238.

communicated his findings to prominent Republicans, alerting them to the menace of Lewis' organization.[11]

Caught in this labor-management crossfire, sidetracked into direct labor relations functions, hobbled by its own limitations, and faced with congressional distaste for its expense, the commission nonetheless finished its work and reported in September 1923. The five-part study, not published by the government until 1925, added much specific data to the huge quantity of information already available, and even hostile critics attested to the value of some of its statistical reports. Its recommendations regarding bituminous coal, however, were vague, platitudinous, and occasionally even meaningless. "Common interest," it asserted, "should lead both operators and miners . . . to . . . seek to stabilize the industry . . . and to perfect the machinery for settling disputes." The report urged the operators to pay more attention to labor relations and to choose "men of the highest type, who can work out a national labor policy." As for the most vexing problem of the Central Competitive Field—the insistence of the miners upon traditional regional negotiations and of the operators upon state and local bargaining—the report urged "that the two parties . . . work out a system of national negotiation, with district agreements," thus effectively straddling the issues that lay at the heart of the 1922 strike. It dealt similarly with another crucial question, that of whether it was desirable fo the UMW to organize the nonunion areas. "The history of the past 30 years," declared the commissioners, "affords conclusive evidence that the United Mine Workers of America has been

[11] For an example of the hostility of West Virginia operators, see the letter from William Ord, in behalf of several West Virginia coal operators, to the commission, reprinted on Feb. 6, 1923, in *Congressional Record*, 67th Cong., 4th sess., 1923, 64:3160-63. Stimson's report is quoted in Elting E. Morison, *Turmoil and Tradition: A Study of the Life and Times of Henry L. Stimson* (New York, 1960), 262. See also Stimson to Gifford Pinchot, March 31 and April 4, 1923, Gifford Pinchot Papers, Box 254; Stimson to Sen. George Wharton Pepper, April 14, 1923, Pepper Papers, Box 69; and Stimson to Russell R. Whitman, June 4, 1923, Henry L. Stimson Papers (Yale University Library), Box 218.

a potent agency in the betterment of the miners' working and living conditions." The report added that the union was necessary for the maintenance of the gains that had been won. But lest this appear an endorsement of UMW expansion, the commissioners warned UMW leaders that "unless the union accepts in practice the principle that the public interest is superior to that of any monopolistic group" and becomes more amenable to "fair and orderly adjustment of controversies . . . the public will not view with sympathy the efforts of the union to extend itself over the whole field of the industry." Thus, a statement that at first seemed to support further unionization closed with criticisms that called for the UMW first to prove its good intentions.[12]

The USCC's one concrete proposal was to recommend the the creation of a permanent federal factfinding agency that would draw together the various reports and studies from established federal bodies that dealt in one way or another with coal. This agency would also be empowered to conduct special compulsory investigations under presidential authority whenever a strike threatened. The commissioners hoped that continuous publicity would "focus upon the negotiators the irresistible moral pressure . . . to furnish the public with coal."[13]

The report satisfied almost no one. John Brophy, the anti-Lewis UMW organizer, termed it "timid, platitudinous, and empty." "The Mountain," aphorized the Cincinnati *Commercial-Tribune*, "labored and brought forth a mouse." As early as the previous November Heber Blankenhorn, a reform-minded journalist who had often sent coal reform suggestions to Borah, had anticipated the criticism that many observers later leveled at the USCC. While some of the studies were worthwhile, he reported to Borah that "the vital questions . . . they keep referring to as 'controversial' and 'ticklish' rather than resolutely planning how to meet the

[12] USCC, *Report*, pt. 1, pp. 271-76.
[13] *Ibid.*, 271.

problem." Unionists, mineowners, and supporters of public ownership differed regarding solutions to the coal problems, but almost all were disappointed by the commission's report.[14]

Borah and Coolidge were no happier. The Idaho Senator felt that the Coal Commission should have drafted legislation to submit to Congress. Early in 1924 he asked Hammond to prepare such specific bills, but the chairman demurred. Coolidge urged the commissioners "to recommend some positive and constructive plan by which peaceful employment relations may be soundly established and maintained," but they did not respond even to the president's request for draft legislation along these lines. Coolidge included the general recommendations in subsequent annual messages to Congress, but he exerted little pressure for their adoption. Within four months of the completion of its work, one interested publicist concluded that the USCC's failure to make its findings available to interested laymen had contributed to the massive public apathy that once again enveloped the coal problem. Paul U. Kellogg, editor of the *Graphic Survey*, contended early in 1924 that the commission's work would be wasted and that the coal problems would be as far as ever from resolution.[15]

The commission's disappointing report and its failure to submit and press for specific legislation spelled an end to the first major effort of the Republican party to cope with the problems of the coal industry. Its expenditures of more than $500,000, its impressive studies, its lengthy reports, and its numerous press releases did nothing to improve labor relations. This failure was driven home even as it finished its work and issued its report, for late in 1923 threats of a major soft coal

[14] Brophy, *A Miner's Life*, 207; Cincinnati *Commercial-Tribune*, Nov. 25, 1923, clipping in USCCR, Drawer 19; Blankenhorn to Borah, Nov. 22, 1922, Borah Papers, Box 213.

[15] Borah to Paul U. Kellogg, Jan. 26, 1924; Borah to Hammond, Jan. 14, and Hammond reply, Jan. 15, 1924, Borah Papers, Box 237; Coolidge to the members of the USCC, Sept. 11, 1923, Coolidge Papers, File 175 B; Paul U. Kellogg to George Otis Smith, Jan. 25, 1924, with enclosed editorial from the Feb. 1924 issue of the *Graphic Survey*, USCCR, Drawer 19.

strike once again distressed the nation and dismayed the Coolidge administration.

Early in 1923 the miners and operators had reached an agreement in the Central Competitive Field, extending the settlement made as a result of the 1922 strike until March 31, 1924. The two parties also agreed to conduct negotiations in February 1924 in Jacksonville, Florida, and to revise and further extend the existing agreement. The strike threat arose from the same circumstances that had led to disruption in 1922; particularly at issue late in 1923 and early in 1924 was whether important mining interests in Illinois and western Pennsylvania would attend the Jacksonville meeting and thus continue the Central Competitive Field bargaining unit that they sought to dismantle.[16]

Republicans recoiled at the possibility of still another coal strike. The 1922 disputes had damaged the party, and a presidential election faced them in 1924. Labor unrest could not help the party, and Republicans were keenly aware that coal shortages and violence would diminish their chances for electoral success. Still, there seemed little that the government could do. In November 1923 Hoover informed the president that there was little prospect of averting a strike. The secretary of commerce reminded Coolidge that the government possessed no adequate machinery with which to help settle the dispute or protect the public from shortages and profiteering.[17]

To Hoover, the impending strike was particularly unfortunate. In addition to his general repugnance for labor disputes, he feared that a strike would postpone a final resolution of the soft coal industry's problems. Strikes, he maintained, created artificially high demand which encouraged high cost,

[16] Edmond Beame, "The Jacksonville Agreement," *Industrial and Labor Relations Review*, VIII (Jan. 1955), 195-203; testimony of John L. Lewis in U.S., Congress, Senate, Committee on Interstate Commerce, 70th Cong., 1st sess., *Conditions in the Coal Fields of Pennsylvania, West Virginia, and Ohio: Hearings* . . . , 2 vols. (Washington, D. C., 1928), I, 379-80.

[17] Hoover to Coolidge, Nov. 17, 1923, Hoover Papers, Box 354.

low efficiency mines to open in hopes of exploiting the temporary need. These boom periods caused too many men to seek employment in the mines, for, he noted, while yearly average wages for miners were low, the daily wage, especially in the union fields, was relatively high. The result of this chaotic situation was that "There are more than 30 per cent too many mines" which "are giving only part-time employment to 30 per cent too many employees." Drastic fluctuations in demand and prices caused cycles of drastic coal shortages and huge oversupplies. The result of all this was that in the soft coal areas "we have a constant center of discontent, the main reason for [which] . . . is that we have for many years had periodic strikes and lockouts."[18]

According to Hoover's analysis, the only way through which the soft coal industry could regain its health was for it to function without labor stoppage for a period long enough to drive the high cost, inefficient mines out of business. He declared that "Continuous smooth operation . . . over a period of years . . . would result in a concentration of labor in more continuous employment in the more economically worked mines." The nation simply had put an end to the chronic strikes. Failure to achieve a period of labor peace, Hoover felt, would cause not only a long and costly strike, but more importantly it would increase instability and uneconomic practices and would quicken the unfortunate "demand of the public for regulation of the industry and of employment relations by law." In short, a coal strike in 1924 would produce the very opposite of Hoover's desires for the economy in general: renewed labor-management bitterness, turmoil, coercive legislation, and inefficiency.[19]

[18] Hoover to C. J. Goodyear, Jan. 26, 1924, Hoover Papers, Box 347. This important letter was printed in the UMW Journal, Feb. 15, 1924. See also U.S., Department of Commerce, Twelfth Annual Report of the Secretary of Commerce (Washington, D. C., 1924), 12-14.
[19] Hoover to Goodyear, Jan. 26, 1924, Hoover Papers, Box 347. See also Hoover's statement in U.S., Congress, House, 69th Cong., 1st sess., Hearings on Coal Legislation, pt. 3 (Washington, D. C., 1926), 525-39.

So, despite his warnings to Coolidge of the impotence of the government, he sought to insure the holding of the Jacksonville conference. In the last months of 1923 he discussed the problem with Lewis and various mine operators. Lewis informed him that the major threat of a strike arose from the reluctance of Illinois and powerful western Pennsylvania mining interests to participate in the forthcoming meeting. Actually, the Mellon-controlled Pittsburgh Coal Company was the key to settlement, for the dissident Illinois companies and the other Pennsylvania concerns would do as it did. If the Pennsylvania interests boycotted the conference, Lewis stated flatly, there could be no settlement, for others would follow its lead and the UMW would not bargain unless the Central Competitive Field remained intact. But, the union chieftain asserted, if the Pittsburgh operators participated and sincerely sought a reasonable settlement, the other dissident operators would fall into line.[20] Clearly, then, it was in the interest of both Lewis and Hoover to persuade the mine operators to honor their commitment to meet in Jacksonville.

Throughout late 1923 and into the new year Hoover worked to bring about the meetings. During the critical period he kept closely in touch with Lewis and the important mine-owners. Perhaps his most important effort in behalf of the conference was a letter that he sent on January 26 to C. J. Goodyear of the Pittsburgh Coal Association that received wide circulation, being reprinted, for example, in the UMW *Journal*. In it Hoover outlined his analysis of the bituminous coal problem and reiterated strongly his plea for continuous mining as the key to general stability and order. He concluded with a strong plea urging the western Pennsylvania coal producers to "attend the conference and make every endeavor to set up a wage contract fair to both sides." This public appeal made it difficult for the operators to refuse to negotiate, especially in view of the Pittsburgh Coal Company's unique

---

[20] Lewis to Hoover, Jan. 5, 1924, Hoover Papers, Box 349.

relationship to the Coolidge administration through Secretary of the Treasury Andrew Mellon. Later a number of operators charged that administration pressure had induced them to negotiate against their wills. Hoover did not seem inclined to disagree, for when the holding of the conference became certain he remarked, "I believe that the development of this situation up to date has been largely due to these efforts which have been carried on without any notoriety."[21]

As the operators and miners gathered in Jacksonville, vague rumors started, indicating that the administration had suddenly reconsidered its endorsement of the conference. To scotch these rumors, Hoover on February 6 issued a press release vigorously restating the administration's support for the conference.[22] Within a year the precise role of the administration and particularly of Hoover would become a source of hot controversy, with the secretary of commerce and the president presenting a sharply limited view of their roles. Yet early in 1924 Hoover's various statements made it clear that his efforts were decisive in persuading the parties to confer in Jacksonville.

Having insured the holding of the meeting, Hoover kept in close touch with the deliberations. He received frequent reports from Lewis and from Francis R. Wadleigh, former chief of the coal division of the Department of Commerce and now associated with a coal company. With the Pennsylvania interests in line, the conference proceeded smoothly. On February 12 Wadleigh reported that although a few operators spoke of wage reductions, most were willing to retain the existing scale. Lewis' telegrams were similarly optimistic, and on February 15 he told Hoover that the only remaining issue was the duration of the contract.[23] Soon even this obstacle

21 Hoover to Julius Barnes, Jan. 28, 1924; Hoover to C. J. Goodyear, Jan. 26, 1924, Hoover Papers, Box 347.
22 Hoover press release draft, Feb. 6, 1924, Coolidge Papers, File 175.
23 Wadleigh to Hoover, Feb. 12, 1924; Lewis to Hoover, Feb. 12 and 15, 1924, Hoover Papers, Box 349.

fell, and on February 19 Lewis and Michael Gallagher, head
of the coal operators' scale committee, announced a settlement
that provided for maintenance of the existing pay scale for
a three-year period and the continuation of the Central
Competitive Field bargaining unit.[24]

While some operators signed with misgivings, most appeared
content. Newspapers too expressed satisfaction with a settlement that seemingly insured labor peace for at least three
years. But it was Hoover and Lewis who had reason to be most
jubilant. The agreement contained precisely what each wanted
for the industry: for Hoover, it meant continuous operation,
an end to the threat of legislation, and a major step toward
efficiency; to Lewis, it meant maintenance of the regionwide
bargaining area, apparent vindication for his "no backward
step" wage policy, and prestige that was even further enhanced
by his close cooperation with Hoover. Labor and government,
it seemed, had joined together to prod reluctant management
into a mutually beneficial agreement. Soon, however, cracks
began to appear in the Hoover-Lewis association and in the
agreement. In less than a year it became clear that Lewis and
Hoover, while following the same policy, had different ends
in mind. To Lewis, preservation of the union and its pay
scale was crucial; to Hoover, the insurance of industrial peace
was essential to creating more efficient operation. Early in
1924 neither man showed any understanding that the agreement might well encourage wage cuts in nonunion areas and
hence undermine further the competitive position of the
Central Competitive Field and the strength of the UMW.[25]

[24] UMW *Journal*, March 1, 1924.
[25] Lewis' "no backward step" wage policy is discussed in his book *The
Miners' Fight for American Standards* (Indianapolis, Ind., 1925). The
cooperation between Lewis and Hoover is revealed in numerous communications between the two men in Jan. and Feb. 1924, which are
contained in the Hoover Papers, esp. Box 349. See also *Hearings on Coal
Legislation*, 1926, pt. 2, pp. 218-19, for a prominent UMW official's view of
this cooperation, and *ibid.*, pt. 3, p. 529, for Hoover's. A third view is that
of UMW organizer John Brophy, who later claimed that "Lewis, during
this period was cultivating Herbert Hoover." When Hoover sought sup-

But in February 1924 the Jacksonville Agreement seemed a spectacular success. If operators gave it only grudging approval, Lewis and Hoover greeted it with enthusiasm that bordered on euphoria. The UMW *Journal* declared that February 19, 1924 (the date of the signing), "will go down in history as one of the [union's] red letter days." The union editorialist characterized the pact as the best agreement the union had ever obtained in the union fields. A front-page cartoon showed Lewis bringing home the "bacon," to the delight of his miners and to the satisfaction of the public.[26]

Hoover discarded his usual reserve and issued unrestrained congratulations. Upon hearing news of the settlement, he telegraphed Lewis, expressing "appreciation of your success in carrying through the program which we discussed in December." The secretary characterized the agreement as "one of the most statesmanlike labor settlements in many years." He called the settlement to Coolidge's attention and asked the president to express to Lewis and Gallagher the administration's "satisfaction that they were able to carry through the undertakings that each of them made with me in December." Indeed, in the Department of Commerce's *Annual Report*, Hoover made sweeping claims for the agreement. "Through cooperation by the department with the unionized operators and with the leaders of the United Mine Workers," he wrote triumphantly, "a long term agreement has been entered upon, which insures industrial peace in the [soft coal] industry."[27]

The jubilation of Hoover and Lewis did not last long. Almost as soon as the agreement took effect, reports of violations began to circulate. Mine operators in the partially

---

port for his bituminous coal program, "He found his man in John L. Lewis, whose economic and political thinking was, if anything, to the right of Hoover's." *A Miner's Life*, 207.

[26] UMW *Journal*, March 1, 1924.

[27] Hoover to Lewis, Feb. 20, 1924, Hoover Papers, Box 349; Hoover to Coolidge, Feb. 20, 1924, and Coolidge to Lewis and to Gallagher, Feb. 29, 1924, Coolidge Papers, File 175; Department of Commerce, *Twelfth Annual Report*, p. 13.

unionized areas of western Kentucky and West Virginia refused
to agree to the settlement that their northern colleagues had
signed, claiming that nearby nonunion production would
quickly drive them out of business. In August one labor
publicist reported that the mining districts in the unionized
fields were "practically paralyzed," due to nonunion
competition. "Hundreds of thousands of miners are in
idleness and imminent disaster threatens," he claimed. In the
fall operators sought unsuccessfully to persuade the UMW of
the necessity for a wage reduction to enable them to compete
with the nonunion fields.[28]

Initially neither the administration nor the UMW expressed
concern about these reports. Coolidge's aides shunted all
inquiries off to Hoover, who in turn generally replied with
noncommittal expressions of optimism. The secretary of
commerce admitted that the agreement would expose the
overdevelopment of the industry and that some locales might
suffer temporary hardship, but he felt this necessary to allow
"the shaking out" that bituminous coal mining needed.[29]

For their part, the mineworkers' leaders regarded these early
problems and the complaints of the union field operators as
temporary irritants. Operators always sought lower wages, but,
the *Journal* argued, if union wages dropped, nonunion
operators would simply lower their wages still further. The
mineworkers' organ cited Hoover's advice to the operators
to abide by the agreement and repeated its pledge to support
what it described as the "Hoover plan of coal stabilization."[30]

[28] Beame, "Jacksonville Agreement," 198-99; report dated April 28,
1924, from F. M. Shore, acting head of the Department of Commerce
coal division, to Richard Emmet, Hoover's secretary, Hoover Papers, Box
347. The dire words are those of J. H. Vitchestian, editor of the conservative *Labor National Tribune*, Aug. 14, 1924, Coolidge Papers, File 175.

[29] Hoover to Eugene McAuliffe, May 28, 1924, Hoover Papers, Box
347. Late in September, Hoover declared that he took "a rather more
optimistic view of the future in the unionized bituminous industry" than
those who were predicting disaster. Hoover to W. K. Kavanaugh, Sept. 25,
1924, Hoover Papers, Box 347.

[30] UMW *Journal*, Jan. 1 and 15, 1925.

In 1925, however, no room for optimism remained. In January one Ohio informant told Hoover that even the operators most sympathetic to the UMW were pressing for a downward wage revision. In March Secretary of Labor Davis warned Coolidge that the unionized operators were abandoning the Jacksonville Agreement, in the face of competition from Kentucky and West Virginia coal. Davis reminded the president that the anthracite contract expired on August 31. The failure of soft coal operators to abide by the agreement and the reluctance of the administration to intervene might lead Lewis to ask for a strike in the hard coal region in order to protest noncompliance in the bituminous coal region. The coal operators' refusal to abide by the Jacksonville Agreement, he advised, might bring about "another of our disastrous coal strikes this fall." Reports from another administration observer, C. P. White, chief of the Department of Commerce coal division, corroborated Davis' statements. White described to Hoover the unemployment and restiveness infecting the unionized areas, and noted that businessmen were giving their coal orders to nonunion fields as a means of protesting the Jacksonville Agreement and gaining price advantages. Unemployed union men, he reported in April 1925, were growing increasingly resentful, but the Department of Commerce official doubted whether the UMW leadership "takes this present attitude into proper account."[31]

By the summer of 1925 a massive coal crisis was developing.[32] The effect of the Jacksonville Agreement was to penalize

[31] Richard Campbell to Hoover, Jan. 26, 1925, Hoover Papers, Box 347, describes the plight of the unionized operators, while Davis' warning is contained in his letter to Coolidge, March 9, 1925, Coolidge Papers, File 175. For White's revealing reports, see his memoranda to Hoover, April 3 and 7, 1925, Hoover Papers, Boxes 347 and 349 respectively. The words quoted are in the April 3 memorandum.

[32] In addition to the breakdown of the Jacksonville Agreement, still another anthracite strike (the third since 1922) threatened throughout the summer and broke out in Sept. 1925. Once again operators and miners quarreled over wages, duration of contract, the checkoff, and other issues, while anthracite steadily declined in importance as a domestic fuel.

the unionized operators, for they faced increased competition as more and more mines opened up or shifted to nonunion production. The maintenance of the high wage rate in the union field, coupled with the refusal of many weakly organized mines in Kentucky and West Virginia to adhere to it, gave impetus to nonunion production. As southern coal encroached upon middle western markets, prices dropped, mines suspended operations, and miners were laid off. A favorite device of hitherto unionized operators was to close down, wait a few weeks or months, and then reopen, with nonunion scales posted. Through this method they hoped to rid themselves of the unionized miners, many of whom moved away during the suspension, and hoped to employ more tractable workers who by the time of resumption were desperate for any job. The Mellon-controlled Pittsburgh Coal Company followed this path, closing down in the early summer and reopening on a nonunion basis in August.[33]

These developments shattered Lewis' hopes. He had admitted tacitly that there were too many miners and that the stabilization of the industry required that some workers leave the mines. However, he thought that the Jacksonville Agreement, by insuring labor peace and continuous production, would force closing of high cost, newly opened mines to the south, restoring the Central Competitive Field and the UMW to their former health. No doubt the UMW leader expected some temporary dislocation and bitterness in the union areas, for the high percentage of wages in total production costs insured that the operation would not be performed with surgical precision. But as more and more union mines closed

---

This strike lasted until Feb. 1926. See Robert H. Zieger, "The Republicans and Labor: Politics and Policies, 1919-1929" (unpublished Ph.D. dissertation, University of Maryland, 1965), 265-72.

[33] Beame, "Jacksonville Agreement." For the Pittsburgh Coal Company's activities, see also *Conditions in the Coal Fields . . . : Hearings,* 1928, I, 387-88 (for Lewis' view) and 1351-67 (for the view of R. B. Mellon, the secretary of the treasury's brother and chairman of the board of directors of the Pittsburgh Coal Company during 1923-1925).

or reverted to the lower 1917 pay scale, miner dissatisfaction grew. As early as April 1925 a Department of Commerce observer reported that "individual miners and even local groups are very unhappy and in some instances restless." At the time the union leaders did not appear to recognize the gravity of the situation, but, the informant declared, "the union organization is under severe strain."[34] The high hopes of 1924 soured and the Jacksonville Agreement, rather than being a means of restoring the UMW, was operating to help cripple the union and discredit its leadership.

Confronted with defections from the heralded agreement and with the mounting antagonism of many rank-and-file miners, UMW leaders grew uneasy about their own positions and the future of their union. Since they attributed to the government a major role in the signing of the agreement, some UMW officials began publicly to criticize the administration for its silence and its apparent unwillingness to act against violators. On July 21 Van A. Bittner, head of UMW operations in northern West Virginia, sent a telegram to Hoover and Davis, describing several specific examples of noncompliance and charging the government with the responsibility for obtaining adherence. Ominously, in view of anthracite negotiations that were then taking place in Atlantic City, the message contained the warning that the UMW might resort to a general strike if violations were not halted.[35] Lewis did not endorse Bittner's threat, and as late as September one Department of Labor source described his attitude as being "anxious to avoid any action which will reflect upon the administration." Still, as autumn brought no relief he began to exert pressure upon Hoover and Coolidge to act in support

[34] Reports of Lewis' tacit acknowledgment that some miners would suffer and of the unhappiness of many UMW men are contained in the memorandum from White to Hoover, April 3, 1925, Hoover Papers, Box 347.

[35] Bittner to Hoover, July 21, 1925, Hoover Papers, Box 347; New York *Times*, July 22, 1925.

of the agreement. The anthracite coal strike did start on September 1 and, although Lewis did not explicitly relate it to the soft coal crisis, he indicated that he would cooperate with no federal mediation efforts until the government demonstrated its good faith with regard to the bituminous coal situation. Throughout the summer he had been asserting that the federal government bore a heavy responsibility for the success of the agreement and in the fall the tempo and strength of his public statements increased. On several occasions he urged the government to acknowledge its role in the agreement, to admit its responsibility for keeping it operating, and to condemn publicly those operators who violated it. Particularly, reported Edward Eyre Hunt, Hoover's aide, Lewis wanted the administration to act against the Pittsburgh Coal Company, which was so important because of its control by the Mellons and its influential position in the western Pennsylvania fields. Hunt quoted the UMW chieftain as declaring that "the industry has a right to expect that the moral influence and power of those . . . Government officials [who helped to arrange the settlement] will be utilized to preserve [its] . . . integrity." The mineworkers' leader expected vigorous administration support and since it was not forthcoming, Hunt informed Hoover, "Mr. Lewis' personal attitude toward you is not cordial."[36]

In this effort to secure federal action to maintain the agreement, Lewis received some indirect verbal support within

[36] Still, the UMW *Journal* did not openly criticize Hoover. Indeed, as late as July 1, 1926, it described him as "a brilliant man and a gifted economist." For Lewis' desire not to embarrass the administration, see "Article on the Possibility of Suspension of Operators in Bituminous Coal Fields; Re Jacksonville Agreement," author unidentified, Sept. 8, 1925, Davis Papers, Box 41. This memorandum also notes Lewis' repeated efforts to prod the government into action and his refusal to cooperate with federal mediators in the anthracite situation. For other reports of Lewis' attitude toward the administration, see memoranda from C. P. White and Edward Eyre Hunt, both to Hoover, and dated Sept. 28, 1925, Hoover Papers, Boxes 347 and 356 respectively. The words quoted are in Hunt's memorandum.

the administration. In August, memoranda from Robe Carl White, acting secretary of labor, objectively stated Lewis' case to the president, pointing out the seriousness of the situation. Upon his return from England, Davis also cautioned Coolidge about the attitude of the unionists. Indeed, in November 1925 he told the president of his disappointment in the noncomplying operators. He reminded his chief that on several occasions he had warned unionists, including the mineworkers, of the need to adhere to signed contracts. The 1924 agreement, in which he had been deeply interested and which was signed partly as a result of his and Hoover's efforts to persuade the parties to negotiate, was a valid, legitimate contract, arrived at through procedures first established in 1898. "You can see," he told Coolidge, "that it was somewhat embarrassing when I took to task certain local unions [which had conducted short unauthorized strikes] to have officials of the miners later call to my attention alleged violations of a signed agreement by certain leading coal companies," an obvious reference to the Pittsburgh Coal Company. Davis indicated that he was hard put to defend the government's failure to condemn violators.[37]

Davis' misgivings seemed justified. The influence of the administration had been a major factor in the holding of the conference. It was Hoover who had persuaded the western Pennsylvania operators to attend,[38] and one Ohio operator

[37] Robe Carl White to Everett Sanders, July 25, August 1, 11, 1925, Coolidge Papers, File 175; Davis to Coolidge, Sept. 14 and Nov. 25, 1925, Coolidge Papers, File 175. The words quoted are in the Nov. 25 letter.

[38] Throughout 1925 and 1926 Hoover stoutly denied responsibility for the Jacksonville Agreement. "It is of course not true that I suggested the terms of the Jacksonville agreement," he declared. His role was simply to urge the parties to negotiate. "The terms of the contract later signed were agreed to by the parties themselves without direction or pressure of any kind from the Administration," he asserted. Hoover to F. R. Wadleigh, March 2, 1925, Hoover Papers, Box 349. Strictly speaking, Hoover was correct, for apparently no one in the administration directly specified the *terms* of the agreement. However, these terms were largely implicit in the very fact of holding a meeting. The western Pennsylvania operators objected to the Jacksonville conference precisely because they

claimed that pressure from the administration had caused many of his colleagues to agree to a contract that they considered suicidal. Moreover, Hoover had acknowledged his role in glowing public and private statements, and as late as January 1925 he stated that the violations of the agreement were unthinkable.[39] The Jacksonville Agreement was far more than simply another labor contract negotiated with the friendly offices of government; it represented Hoover's program of action for the troubled industry, and unionists had a right to expect the Coolidge administration to stand firmly and publicly behind it and to exert the influence that had been used to arrange the agreement to maintain it.

But Hoover, having in 1924 claimed credit for his role in the agreement, now demurred. In March 1925 he declared that while he and other members of the administration had, of course, encouraged a long-term agreement, no one in the government had exerted unusual pressure, nor had the government provided the terms of the contract. In April he described the Jacksonville Agreement as a matter solely between the miners and the operators. While he had considered the problem carefully and wished that he could suggest a solution, he did not feel that he could properly intervene. He asserted that the administration had no legal authority under existing statutes to enforce the agreement and hence it was powerless.

---

realized that the mere holding of the meeting would virtually insure maintenance of the 1920 wage scale and the regionwide bargaining unit for several years. Thus, the administration's pressure upon them to negotiate was in effect pressure upon them to accept the UMW's terms. See the testimony of Philip Murray, UMW vice president, in *Hearings on Coal Legislation*, 1926, pt. 2, pp. 218-19. Murray acknowledged that federal officials were not involved in the actual conferences, but he added, "Mr. Hoover expressed to the conferees or at least to the mineworkers—I do not know what he said to the operators—that it was his desire, the desire of the Government, that the Jacksonville contract be continued for a period of three years." Murray also asserted that it was Hoover's direct communication with W. H. Field, president of the Pittsburgh Coal Company, that persuaded the firm to negotiate.

[39] John S. Jones to Coolidge, Nov. 27, 1925, Coolidge Papers, File 175; Hoover to Richard Campbell, Jan. 26, 1925, Hoover Papers, Box 347.

He contended that the mounting turbulence in the bituminous coal areas was simply unavoidable, that it was the result of the reorganization which the industry had to undergo. He was aware of the deplorable conditions, and proclaimed that he would be glad to do anything in his power to stabilize affairs, but that he felt powerless to act in the private dispute between coal miners and coal operators.[40]

Late in 1925 the debate between Lewis and Hoover over the administration's responsibility for the agreement (and hence for maintenance of it) reached a climax. On November 21 Lewis, deeply disturbed by the chaos and restiveness in the union fields, released to the press a letter to Coolidge in which the mineworkers' chieftain sought to fix responsibility upon the administration. Lewis contended that an agreement in 1924 would have been impossible without the aid of the federal Departments of Justice, Commerce, and Labor. He cited at length Hoover's *Annual Report* for 1924, in which the secretary had hailed the fruits of federal-union-operator cooperation. "Without question," continued Lewis, Hoover's "declaration of accomplishment by the Federal Government in the public interest was heartily approved by every thoughtful citizen." But since 1924 major coal companies had violated the solemn agreement and had been seeking to break the union through "coercive and oppressive methods." Federal reports bore witness to their dishonorable actions. Having established a connection between the government and the agreement, and having vividly described violations of the agreement, the unionist went on to remind Coolidge that the government often had intervened in the coal industry. Miners and operators had felt the government's influence, and the mineworkers "now inquire whether the Federal Government desires to intervene to maintain the morality and integrity of

40 Hoover to Wadleigh, March 2, 1925, Hoover Papers, Box 349; Hoover to Merchants' Division, Board of Trade, Martin's Ferry, Ohio, April 23, 1925, and to Congressman Frank Murphy, May 28, 1925, Hoover Papers, Box 347.

the existing agreement." If the government did not act to uphold the agreement, he concluded, "might the mine workers believe that their own efforts in that direction may be considered as being justified?" Thus, Lewis attempted to put the president in the position of either coming to the union's aid or sanctioning a coal strike.[41]

Lewis' letter received wide publicity and created concern and some disagreement within the administration. Hoover responded immediately, drafting a letter of reply and sending it to the president and Davis for their comments. In it, the secretary of commerce strongly disassociated the administration from responsibility for the agreement. Although he and Davis had indeed encouraged the holding of the meeting, he stated that the government had taken no further part in the meeting. Thus the administration could not be considered a party to the contract. It had lent its aid in the negotiation of many other labor agreements, and Hoover saw no reason why its responsibility should be different in regard to this one. He deplored contract violations, of course, but he reminded Lewis that the "arm of Government provided for the enforcement of contracts is the courts." He further reminded the UMW president that over 90 percent of the operators still adhered to the agreement. "Obviously," he went on, suddenly carrying the assault to Lewis, "for the United Mine Workers to break their agreement . . . would be a fatal blow." Quickly the adroit secretary had shifted the issue from the government's condemnation of operators' actual violations to Lewis' responsibility for possible future union actions.[42]

Having disclaimed the administration's responsibility, having suggested appeals through the courts, and having cautioned Lewis against rashness, Hoover went on to discuss

[41] Lewis' letter is printed in *Conditions in the Coal Fields* . . . : *Hearings*, 1928, I, 378-79. See also New York *Times*, Nov. 25, 1925.
[42] Draft of letter by Hoover (for Coolidge's signature) to Lewis, dated Nov. 25, 1925, Hoover Papers, Box 241.

the roots of the labor problems in the soft coal industry. He sought to enlist Lewis' support for stimulating the industry to undertake the creation of adjustment boards. Diverting the discussion entirely from the Jacksonville Agreement, Hoover suggested that Lewis lead in the creation of labor relations machinery in both the bituminous coal and anthracite coal regions. In a neat conclusion, Hoover related this proposal to the government's unwillingness to intervene in the present difficulty, declaring, "It is far better that the industry shall develop its own processes . . . than that the government should be driven to legislate methods."[43]

Hoover's bold letter at once denied responsibility and urged Lewis to assume constructive leadership. Davis, however, objected to the last paragraphs, arguing that mention of the anthracite industry could only jeopardize the delicate negotiations then in progress to end the hard coal strike. Davis also felt that broadening the issue to include peace-keeping machinery in general would only give the mineworkers broader grounds upon which to embarrass the administration and to keep the controversy alive in the press. Hoover defended his approach, declaring that he had tried to frame the letter in such a way as to enlist Lewis' support for a wise and enlightened future policy. Hoover implied that in turning the attention of Lewis and the public from the Jacksonville Agreement itself to the general problem of keeping labor peace, he was enabling the administration to fix attention upon the relevant problem of the industry's ability to forge adequate labor relations methods while avoiding the fruitless (and embarrassing) problem of the Jacksonville Agreement.[44]

For once Coolidge found Davis' advice more appealing than Hoover's. On December 5 he issued a reply to Lewis that duplicated Hoover's letter except for the sections to which Davis objected. It repeated Hoover's denials and

[43] *Ibid.*
[44] Hoover to Coolidge, Nov. 27, 1925, Hoover Papers, Box 356.

regrets, although Coolidge did acknowledge the government's role in bringing about the meeting. The final letter too called upon the union to bring violators to court, an action which "would perform a distinct public service by getting an authoritative court decision on this subject." In a shrewd ending, Coolidge reminded Lewis that most companies were not in violation of the agreement, and, refusing to understand the implications of Lewis' conclusion, the president declared himself "very glad to hear that the United Mine Workers have no intention to call a strike . . . because of these grievances."[45]

So far as Hoover, Coolidge, and Davis were concerned, this reply to Lewis ended the matter. Lewis would have to confront the problems of unemployment, declining membership, and decimation of his union by himself. Throughout 1926, while violations of the agreement continued, a brief boom in the industry drove prices up and alleviated some of the effects of the ruthless price competition. The UMW continued to lose members and the southern operators, aided by ICC freight rate rulings favorable to them, continued to encroach upon traditionally northern markets.[46]

Members of the administration consistently opposed efforts to expand the federal government's responsibility in the soft coal industry. As the end of the Jacksonville Agreement drew near, Lewis and other UMW officials proclaimed the likelihood of a strike. A number of measures were introduced in Congress that would have provided the government with broad powers to compel arbitration, fix prices, or even seize the mines. But

[45] New York Times, Dec. 6, 1925. The final version dated Dec. 5, 1925, is in Conditions in the Coal Fields . . . : Hearings, 1928, I, 380-81.

[46] For a thorough discussion of the freight rate factor, see Harvey C. Mansfield, The Lake Cargo Coal Rate Controversy: A Study in Governmental Adjustment of a Sectional Dispute, Columbia University Studies in History, Economics and Public Law, Number 373 (New York, 1932). For a statement of the view of northern operators, unionists, and public officials, see George Wharton Pepper, speech before the Uniontown, Pa., Chamber of Commerce, Jan. 29, 1926, Pepper Papers, Box 27. See also UMW Journal, Dec. 15, 1925, March 15, Sept. 1, 1926.

Davis and Hoover, with Coolidge's full support, disavowed most of these proposals. In May 1926 Hoover outlined his and the administration's position in testimony before the House Committee on Interstate and Foreign Commerce, which was holding hearings on various coal measures. The secretary of commerce acknowledged that unemployment, profiteering, and the threat of strikes still plagued the industry, but he counseled that "Congress would be well justified in suspending any legislative action." If legislation proved necessary, he declared, it should be in the form of providing the government with additional factfinding and coal distribution powers in the event of a labor suspension. Basically, though, the secretary said, "My own feeling is that it might be quite well to give these folks an opportunity to see whether they can set up some sort of [labor relations] machinery on their own." Even if a strike occurred without Congress' having supplied the government with emergency powers, Hoover thought that the situation would be manageable. The production of the non-union mines, he stated, would be adequate to supply the country's needs in an emergency. No broad or extraordinary federal powers would be necessary.[47]

Hoover's response to Lewis in 1925 and these remarks a few months later revealed his basic attitude toward the problems of the soft coal industry. They made it clear that his aim from the start had been to subject the industry to a ruthless reorganization through untrammeled competition, which would eventually allow a relatively few large concerns or pools to dominate the industry. Since labor disputes encouraged inefficient mining operations, a substantial period of labor peace was essential to achieve his goal. Thus, in 1923 and 1924, as the Coal Commission's failure became apparent, he worked

---

[47] *Hearings on Coal Legislation,* 1926, pt. 3, pp. 526-39. See also Hoover to Sen. Simeon D. Fess, Aug. 3, 1926, Hoover Papers, Box 347. Despite the crisis in the union and the failure of the Jacksonville Agreement, the UMW *Journal* heartily endorsed Hoover's opposition to legislative proposals (July 1, 1926).

with Lewis and coal operators to secure the Jacksonville meeting. Although he later sought to minimize the government's
responsibility for the resulting agreement, he more than anyone else was responsible for the decision of the key western
Pennsylvania operators to attend, and his enthusiastic statements at the time of the agreement were more accurate
indications of his part than his later denials of responsibility.
While Hoover eagerly cooperated with Lewis to insure labor
settlement, he did not consider the UMW basic to the health
and stability of the bituminous coal industry. He worked
vigorously throughout the winter of 1923-1924, conferring with
Lewis, cajoling recalcitrant operators, and linking the administration unofficially, but strongly, to the resulting agreement,
but he did nothing to see that it was maintained. Legally, of
course, he and the administration were correct: the government
technically had no more responsibility to enforce this particular
agreement than it had regarding other labor agreements that
it encouraged. But Lewis had based his efforts at reinvigorating
the Central Competitive Field and the UMW upon the
assumption of strong federal support for the Jacksonville
Agreement. He assumed that the secretary of commerce
considered the union an essential ingredient for the stability
he sought. Hoover's actions and statements in 1923 and 1924
certainly did nothing to disabuse the mineworkers' chief of
this assumption, and Lewis had cause to expect the administration, which had acted so quickly and so vigorously to
achieve an agreement and which so openly proclaimed that
agreement, to lend its support to its maintenance.[48] But with

[48] At the time of its signing, both the UMW *Journal*, in public statements, and Lewis, in private communications, took every opportunity to
emphasize that the Jacksonville Agreement was a cooperative UMW-adminis-
tration achievement. The administration issued no denials until the controversy over violations began to boil. See UMW *Journal*, Feb. 15, March 1,
1924, and Lewis to Coolidge, March 7, 1924, Coolidge Papers, File 175.
In this letter, the UMW leader remarked, "I recall with pleasure our several
conservations upon this subject matter [negotiating an agreement] and it
may be pleasant for you to know that I consider your own official influence,

his membership slipping away and with the Mellon-controlled Pittsburgh Coal Company and other concerns openly violating the Jacksonville Agreement, Lewis found in the administration not support or broad sympathy, but rather narrow legalism and even encouragement for the nonunion operators.[49]

By early 1927 the soft coal industry was settling down. Competition was either forcing the unionized operators out of business or encouraging them to reopen on nonunion bases. The more efficient mines—those paying low wages—captured more and more of the soft coal market, and the UMW, once a powerful force of 500,000 miners, dwindled to a corporal's guard of less than 80,000.[50] Some unionists, such as Brophy, blamed the fiasco on Lewis, who, they argued, had based his hopes upon maintaining high wages in the unionized areas while abandoning the effort to organize the southern fields.[51] A more justified charge against Lewis would have been that he had trusted and cooperated with Herbert Hoover without being clear as to the terms of cooperation. Both men wanted stability, but Lewis failed to realize that the secretary of commerce did not include the UMW in his definition of stability. For the Jacksonville Agreement to have been successful, Lewis would have had to secure either federal support for eliminating favorable southern freight rate differentials, massive public endorsement of his efforts to organize the nonunion

as directed through your several Cabinet representatives, . . . a most important factor [in] arriving at the settlement." Increasingly, this was not "pleasant" for Coolidge to know.

[49] Yet Lewis supported Hoover for the presidency in 1928.

[50] Morton S. Baratz, *The Union and the Coal Industry* (New Haven, Conn., 1955), 60-61; Brophy, *A Miner's Life*, 206.

[51] *Ibid.*, 207-13; McAllister Coleman, *Men and Coal* (New York, 1943), 125-30. Brophy, Coleman, and other critics charged that Lewis neglected the southern organizing drives, hoping unrealistically to keep the UMW entrenched in the Central Competitive Field. Commentators more sympathetic to Lewis point out the massive resistance to unionization, the absence of guarantees for organizers of even the most basic civil liberties, and the repeated failure of earlier UMW efforts in the upper south fields. See Philip A. Taft, *Organized Labor in American History* (New York, 1964), 399.

fields, or both. But, despite warnings by unionists and observers from the unionized soft coal regions, neither architect of the Jacksonville Agreement appeared to give these related factors any consideration. Lewis, faced with hard alternatives, gambled the future of his union on the good intentions of the administration, while Hoover felt no qualms about using the UMW for his own purposes.

11 The Late Twenties

REPUBLICAN LABOR POLICY reached maturity in the late 1920s. In an apparently healthy economy, strikes and open labor unrest declined sharply. Labor unionists became ever more concerned with proving the economic and social benefits of unions to the public and to businessmen than with voicing protest and extending organizational efforts. As Herbert Hoover captured his party's nomination, two significant labor issues, the problems of the soft coal industry and the labor injunction, still claimed public attention. But the party's response, coupled with good fortune, insured that neither would play an important role in the election. The lack of labor issues and of vigorous laborite opposition to the GOP in 1928 stood in sharp contrast to the hard-fought elections of 1920, 1922, and 1924, and allowed Herbert Hoover and other Republicans to announce the end of the labor problem as they swept to victory.

In August 1928 Herbert Hoover, formally accepting his party's nomination for the presidency, advanced the GOP's claim to credit for virtually eliminating labor. problems. A paean to his party's (and hence to his own) economic policies, his speech painted in glowing words the picture of a prosperous, contented people whose economic and social achievements were stimulated by a wise and vigorous government. Indeed, Hoover declared, "given a chance to go forward with the policies of the last eight years, we shall soon with the help of God be in sight of the day when poverty will be banished from the nation."[1] Republican policies, especially during the Coolidge years, had finally confronted the question of the role of the wageworker in America, and the industrial peace, social improvement, and economic gains of the past five years attested to the success of these policies. Thus, as the former secretary of commerce began his campaign for the presidency, he could expect the American people to recognize that the labor problem, which only a decade before had seemed as dangerous and frustrating as ever, had yielded to his and his party's determined efforts and enlightened programs.

Indeed, the Coolidge years were peaceful and comparatively prosperous for American workers. Wages rose and unemployment declined from postwar levels. Corporation welfare programs gathered momentum and the hostile rhetoric of previous years was heard less often. Of all the facts and statistics that government officials and economists used to describe America's affluence and well-being, none were more impressive than those reflecting the decline of strikes. In 1919, one worker of every five had left his job in an industrial dispute; in 1925, one in every fifty. And between 1925 and 1928 even that figure diminished. Labor and capital, argued economist Thomas Nixon Carver in 1925, had finally grasped the fact of their mutual dependence. This recognition, he predicted, would soon bring about harmony between them.[2]

In reality, the prosperity of the late 1920s was neither so extensive nor so firmly rooted as Hoover and Carver believed. While many industrial workers enjoyed a high standard of living, their share of affluence was disproportionately small, and less fortunate wage earners in some major industries experienced hard times. Although Hoover declared in 1928 that "the primary purpose of the economic policies we advocate" was "a job for every man," unemployment affected

[1] Hoover's speech was published in the New York *Times*, Aug. 12, 1928.

[2] The strike figures are in U.S., Bureau of the Census, *Historical Statistics of the United States, 1789-1945* (Washington, D. C., 1949), 73. Carver's statement is in his book *The Present Economic Revolution in the United States* (Boston, 1925), 14.

at least 5 percent of American workers even during the height of the boom. Hoover's claim in 1928 that "Unemployment in the sense of distress is widely disappearing," was simply not true, although the continuing lack of adequate statistics helped to obscure the problem. Nor could the worker turn to an aggressive and articulate labor movement to give voice to his grievances. Union membership declined from a postwar peak of 5,034,000 to 3,625,000 in 1929. Moreover, never had labor's main bodies been so conservative and so willing to cooperate with the business community. Virtually abandoning its feeble efforts to organize the unskilled workers who comprised the majority of the work force, the AFL sought diligently to ingratiate itself with the nation's industrialists. Unsupported by a vigorous labor movement, America's workers had to accept the benefits of affluence that businessmen deemed appropriate to dole out, rather than demanding a greater share. Indeed, far from being solved, the labor problem rumbled beneath the complacent surface of American life, ready to explode when the jerry-built structure of Coolidge prosperity received its first jolts.[3]

[3] Hoover's statements are in his speech published in the New York Times, Aug. 12, 1928. The problems of continuing unemployment and general economic imbalance are succinctly stated in Irving Bernstein, The Lean Years: A History of the American Worker, 1920-1933 (Boston, 1960), 58-66, while the decline in union membership is indicated in Historical Statistics, 72. See also George Soule, Prosperity Decade: From War to Depression, 1917-1929, Economic History of the United States, Vol. IX (New York, 1947), 130-31. Labor's efforts to justify unionization and to seek harmonious relationships with industrial leaders, basically a change in emphasis and not in goals, are discussed in Milton J. Nadworny, Scientific Management and the Unions, 1900-1932: A Historical Analysis (Cambridge, Mass., 1955), 148; Ronald Radosh, "The Corporate Ideology of American Labor Leaders from Gompers to Hillman," Studies on the Left, VI (Nov.-Dec. 1966), 66-72; and Milton Derber, "The Idea of Industrial Democracy in America, 1915-1933," Labor History, VIII (Winter 1967), 8-9. In addition to the bituminous coal industry, the textile industry showed signs of restiveness. Major strikes broke out in 1926 in Passaic, N.J., and in 1929 in the southern piedmont mills. See Robert H. Zieger, "The Republicans and Labor: Politics and Policies, 1919-1929" (unpublished Ph.D. dissertation, University of Maryland, 1965), 288-91, for the Passaic strike, and Bernstein, The Lean Years, 1-43, for the southern strikes.

Republicans did acknowledge and were concerned about some labor problems, even during the calm days of the late 1920s. In 1927 Coolidge allowed that there was "some unemployment in certain lines," and Hoover's acceptance speech admitted that "the agricultural, coal, and textile industries still lag in their recovery." In 1927 Davis reported that Department of Labor employment figures showed a slight downward trend and cautioned the president that the situation was potentially dangerous. But the administration's public recognition of unemployment and other economic problems was limited to a few general statements tucked inconspicuously into the reports of affluence that came from the government departments and party spokesmen.[4]

Even in these tranquil years, however, there were labor issues significant and dramatic enough to command national attention. Particularly, the continuing soft coal difficulties and the endless debate over the labor injunction, occupied much public attention and challenged the GOP to formulate specific policies. It was around these two issues that most of relatively small amount of public discussion regarding labor in the late 1920s revolved. The Republican party's ability to soften the impact of even these unresolved problems gave further proof of its successful political handling of the labor problem in general and helped its candidates to support the party's claims that the labor issue no longer troubled the nation.

The collapse of the Jacksonville Agreement during 1925-1926 encouraged the operators in the Central Competitive Field in their fight to eliminate the regional bargaining system. By March 31, 1927, the terminal date of the discredited agreement, the UMW had become decimated. When the operators refused to yield in their insistence upon district and

---

[4] Coolidge's remarks were made in a press conference on Aug. 12, 1927, in Howard Quint and Robert Ferrell, eds., *The Talkative President: The Off-the-Record Press Conferences of Calvin Coolidge* (Amherst, Mass., 1964), 135, while Davis' comment is in a letter to Coolidge, Nov. 9, 1927, Coolidge Papers, File 358. Hoover's speech of Aug. 11, New York *Times*, Aug. 12, 1928, contains his statement.

local contracts, Lewis led the miners out on strike in protest, but the umw leader now commanded only a shattered batallion, without hope of victory.[5]

This was the most forlorn and piteous of the coal strikes of the 1920s. With umw membership greatly diminished, coal companies easily filled the strikers' jobs with nonunion men. Harsh conditions prevailed among strikers and other unemployed miners throughout the mining regions, festering with particular ugliness in western Pennsylvania. Local judges issued far-reaching injunctions, one of which banned the union from feeding strikers and prohibited union members from talking to strangers. Unhindered by a powerful union, the coal companies resorted to every antiunion device extant. They employed private armies or controlled the local constabulary. They evicted from company homes miners who engaged in union activities. They hired Negro strikebreakers, thus adding racial animosity to an already explosive situation. With the Mellon and Rockefeller interests leading the way, the operators completed the deunionization of the western Pennsylvania bituminous coalfields, often revealing shocking lack of concern about the welfare of their miners. When asked in a Senate investigation about starvation among the miners in the Pittsburgh Coal Company fields, Richard B. Mellon replied, "I do not go out feeding them or anything." In reply to a question concerning the use of machineguns by detectives employed by the coal company, Andrew Mellon's brother declared, "It is necessary [because] you cannot run the mines without them."[6]

For the first time in a decade, a soft coal strike failed to

[5] New York *Times*, April 1 and 2, 1927, and *Times* editorial "The Coal Strike," April 1.

[6] The best view of the situation in the coal areas is in U.S., Congress, Senate, Committee on Interstate Commerce, 70th Cong., 1st sess., *Conditions in the Coal Fields of Pennsylvania, West Virginia, and Ohio: Hearings*, 2 vols. (Washington, D. C., 1928). Mellon's testimony is in I, 1351-67. See also McAllister Coleman, *Men and Coal* (New York, 1943), 131-35.

rouse the government into vigorous action. In 1919, 1922, and 1924 the unionized areas produced a significant portion of the nation's bituminous coal, but the growth of nonunion production and the weakness of the UMW insured that this strike would have no major impact upon the economy. For the first seven months of the dispute, the administration remained inactive. Hoover's remarks in 1926, wherein he declared that nonunion production could supply the nation even in the event of a strike, and Coolidge's unwillingness to press for even mild coal legislation in 1926 and early 1927 foreshadowed this response.[7]

In November 1927 Lewis and William Green, president of the AFL since Gompers' death in 1924, led a delegation of unionists which called upon Coolidge, asking him to intervene, at least to the extent of helping to prevent violations of civil liberties. Coolidge felt that the soft coal industry was simply going through a reorganization and that the government could do little in the situation. Eventually he agreed to refer to Davis the union leaders' suggestion for a miner-operator conference, but he had no enthusiasm for the idea. Davis issued a call for a conference to be held in mid-December, but only a handful of operators responded, despite his personal appeals. The conference quickly collapsed, for with the miners in retreat and the president and Hoover obviously unwilling to press the issue, coal operators felt no necessity to attend. In 1922 and 1924, when the unionized soft coal tonnage was significant, the Harding and Coolidge administrations had attempted to persuade reluctant operators to confer, and in the latter year even managed to get them to agree to terms that they otherwise would have rejected. But this time, except

[7] See Hoover's testimony in U.S., Congress, House, 69th Cong., 1st sess., *Hearings on Coal Legislation*, 3 parts (Washington, D. C., 1926), pt. 3, pp. 526-39. Coolidge's attitude toward coal legislation is revealed in the New York *Times*, Jan. 14, 1927, and in a letter from his secretary, Everett Sanders, to Sen. Royal Copeland of New York, Jan. 18, 1927, Coolidge Papers, File 175.

for the most routine efforts at settlement, the Coolidge administration stood aloof.[8]

The length and misery of the strike, however, led others to initiate action. In Congress, liberal Republicans, together with urban Democrats, became concerned. In January 1928 California's Hiram Johnson demanded that Davis reveal the Department of Labor's strategy for coping with the strike. When the secretary replied that he and the administration ·were powerless and were planning no further action, Johnson and others in Congress began to consider the possibility of congressional action. New York Republican Congressman Fiorello La Guardia provided added impetus for this course. Early in February he toured strike-torn western Pennsylvania and issued vivid reports of the deprivation of the strikers and the brutality of the company police. He returned to Washington to urge a congressoinal investigation.[9]

Meanwhile, the strike continued, with the union growing ever weaker. At last, in July 1928, over fifteen months after the beginning of the strike, Lewis capitulated. Faced with the possibility of complete destruction of the union, the UMW International Policy Committee agreed to the dismantling of the Central Competitive Field bargaining unit and authorized union districts to negotiate their own wage contracts. In this

[8] Coolidge's conference with the unionists, his attitude toward the coal problem, and his reluctant endorsement of a miner-operator conference under government auspices are indicated in his press conference of March 20, 1928, Quint and Ferrell, *The Talkative President*, 140-41, and in the New York *Times* reports throughout Nov. and Dec. 1927, particularly those of Nov. 22, 23, and Dec. 4, 7, and 10. Davis' call for a conference is indicated in Davis to bituminous coal operators in Pennsylvania, West Virginia, and Ohio, Dec. 9, 1927, and in a Department of Labor press release, Dec. 10, both in Davis Papers, Box 43. An example of Davis' appeal for operator cooperation is his telegram to S. M. Robbins, president of the Youghiogheny and Ohio Coal Company, Dec. 12, 1927, Davis Papers, Box 43.

[9] Letter of Davis, in reply to a phone call from Johnson, Jan. 31, 1928, USCSR, File 170/3918-7; Howard Zinn, *La Guardia in Congress* (Ithaca, N.Y., 1959), 147-48; George Kaplan, "The Labor Views of Fiorello La Guardia" (unpublished Ph.D. dissertation, New York University, 1962), 118-23; New York *Times*, Feb. 4 and 9, 1928.

desperate effort to salvage the battered remnant of the union, Lewis and the Policy Committee were forced to abandon a bargaining arrangement that had lasted for over a quarter of a century and one for which they had fought repeatedly during the past decade. The UMW *Journal* declared that the decision reflected the miners' "loyalty to the public welfare," but John Brophy had harsher words: "The end product of Lewis's booming talk about 'no backward step' was the disintegration of the whole collective bargaining position of the miners, won by a generation of struggles." James J. Davis, on the other hand, seemed not to realize the implications of the UMW decision to negotiate on subregional levels, declaring, "I am very glad that they [the UMW] have reached this understanding," which, he felt certain, would undoubtedly end the strike.[10]

From the administration's viewpoint, the decision to allow subregional conferences terminated not only the strike but also the need for deep concern with the labor problems of the bituminous coal industry. However, Lewis was unwilling to accept permanent defeat. Even before he agreed to local settlements, he had begun to weigh the prospects of federal legislation in behalf of the mineworkers. In 1927 W. Jett Lauck, an economic consultant to the union, had suggested that the UMW abandon its traditional hostility to legislative solutions for labor problems and "stage a demand before Congress with the object of securing the right to collective bargaining" in the coal industry. Lauck admitted that Congress would not act, but he contended that "the interjection of the matter at this Congress might be so embarrassing in the face of the approaching presidential election that you might be able to force a successful settlement." At the time, Lewis,

---

[10] For the decision to seek state and local agreements and for the UMW's claim that it was motivated by public interest considerations, see UMW *Journal*, Aug. 1, 1928. For Brophy's bitter comments, see *A Miner's Life*, ed. John O. P. Hall (Madison, Wis., 1964), 231, and for Davis' sanguine ones, see his letter to Coolidge, July 18, 1928, Coolidge Papers, File 15.

the epitome of "pure and simple" unionism, did not follow Lauck's advice to seek settlement through political means, but now, with utter defeat facing him, the UMW chieftain began to change his mind.[11]

While Lewis reconsidered his opposition to legislation, congressional action was taking shape. Within a month of La Guardia's trip to the coal regions, the Senate Committee on Interstate Commerce began extensive hearings, which uncovered the unhappy details of the miners' plight. Miners, clergymen, social workers, and even a novelist, Fanny Hurst, testified before the committee, describing the ruthlessness and callousness of the coal companies. The remarks most injurious to the coal interests, however, were those of Richard B. Mellon, the brother of the secretary of the treasury and former chairman of the board of Pittsburgh Coal Company. Under vigorous questioning he revealed a damaging combination of arrogance and careless unconcern about the condition of the miners which drew censure from several senators.[12]

As the testimony proceeded, Senator James E. Watson, Republican of Indiana and chairman of the committee, began to draft coal legislation. Supported ardently by Lewis, now convinced of the necessity of legislative action, the resulting bill represented the final GOP proposal for a permanent solution to the soft coal industry's labor difficulties and other economic problems. By the fall of 1928 Watson's bill was ready and he began to hold hearings on it, assuring UMW leaders that it would undoubtedly become law shortly after the election.[13]

[11] Lauck to Lewis, Dec. 3, 1927, W. Jett Lauck Papers (Alderman Library, University of Virginia), Correspondence File Cabinets; UMW Journal, April 1, Sept. 15, and Oct. 1, 1928.

[12] Conditions in the Coal Fields . . . : Hearings; New York Times, March 21, 1928; Coleman, Men and Coal, 131-35.

[13] For the text of the Watson bill and the hearings on it, see U.S., Congress, Senate, Committee on Interstate Commerce, Hearings on S. 4490, A Bill to Regulate Bituminous Coal . . . , 70th Cong., 2d sess., 1928. A good discussion of the origins and provisions of the bill is in Glen Lawhorn Parker, The Coal Industry: A Study in Social Control (Wash-

The Watson bill departed drastically from previous legislative efforts to deal with the coal industry. Earlier bills, which appeared during and after each strike, had been consumer-oriented. Their sponsors were eastern urban congressmen whose major concern was the health, comfort, and votes of their constituents. Typically, these earlier bills called for emergency federal powers for fuel distribution and price fixing; some even provided for federal seizure of the mines in emergencies. None attacked the bituminous coal problem as such, for none attempted to deal with overproduction, wage and freight rate differentials, or disorganization in the industry.[14]

The new proposal envisioned the creation of a federal bituminous coal commission. The law would establish a code for the industry which would guarantee the right of collective bargaining and would regulate wages, prices, and profits. To enforce the code, the new commission would issue licenses to all companies desiring entry into the soft coal business. Old companies could operate without licenses, but as an inducement for them to apply and to come under the authority of the commission, the proposed legislation set aside the antimonopoly provisions of the Sherman Act for license holders, thereby permitting extensive pooling and cooperative marketing arrangements. Thus, in return for regulation and acceptance of the union as a permanent force in the industry, coal operators could presumably more efficiently gear production to demand and more surely claim a share of the market and the profits.

Aside from Senator William Kenyon's coal code proposal in 1922, which had received little attention, this was the first congressional attempt to regulate the entire soft coal industry, as opposed to its purely retail aspects. In conception it was

ington, D. C., 1940), 97-101, while Watson's prediction of enactment is noted in an editorial in UMW *Journal*, Oct. 1, 1928.

[14] Earlier attempts to legislate for regulation of the coal industry are indicated in *Hearings on Coal Legislation*, 1926.

much akin to federal regulation of the railroads under the ICC and the railroad labor statutes. Probably it would have been beneficial to the UMW, enabling the union to organize hitherto unorganized workers, and, through its pooling features, it may have encouraged greater efficiency of mining and mine-related transportation.[15]

In the 1928 campaign, both parties endorsed the principle of stabilization of the coal mines, with its implied endorsement of collective bargaining. Despite Watson's assurances, however, nothing came of the bill. It received little recognition from the Coolidge administration, and Hoover paid no attention to it in his campaign speeches. After the election, Davis did endorse it in principle, but by 1929 the issue was dead and the UMW had insufficient influence to revive it.[16] As the last of the Republican efforts to deal with the labor problems of the soft coal industry in the 1920s, the Watson bill did foreshadow the industrial codes later to be established in the National Industrial Recovery Act in 1933. Its chief function in 1928, however, was to offer a specious hope to Lewis and to obscure the disaster suffered by organized labor in this major industry.

Thus, Republicans neatly avoided damage from the labor troubles in the coal industry. The other prominent labor issue of the late 1920s—the role of the courts in labor affairs—proved more troublesome. As criticism against the courts mounted and especially as the drive to curb the issuance of injunctions in labor disputes gained force, Republicans faced the task of placating labor while upholding the integrity of the courts. Fortunate circumstances and timely utterances enabled Republicans to avoid labor antagonism on this issue as well. While the passage in 1932 of the Norris-La Guardia Act was primarily due to the pressure of organized labor, the support of Democrats, the work of academic opponents of

[15] Parker, *The Coal Industry*, 98-101.
[16] Davis' statement of Dec. 14, 1928, appears in *Hearings on S. 4490*, pp. 4-23.

injunctions, and the contributions of Senator George W. Norris and other progressive Republicans, regular and conservative Republicans eventually accommodated themselves to this legislation, and, in one important instance, even helped to clear the way for legal relief for labor.

Despite organized labor's conservatism in the 1920s, its bitterness toward the courts remained constant. Eventually unionists adjusted themselves to most aspects of the New Era and they attempted to justify their union activities by proving the efficiency and helpfulness of organized labor; but regarding the activities of the courts, and particularly their frequent resort to injunctions, laborites were united in a belligerent attitude.

In the 1920s labor's legislative demands were few, reflecting the feeling on the part of most leaders that labor's future lay in voluntarism, economic activity, and general adjustment to the existing order. In 1923, for example, Andrew Furuseth, the president of the seamen's union, congratulated Supreme Court Associate Justice George Sutherland on his majority opinion in the Adkins v. Children's Hospital case, wherein the court struck down a District of Columbia minimum wage law. Said Furuseth, "If the legislative body has the power to determine a minimum wage it seems to me to follow -that it may determine a maximum wage." While many unionists regarded Furuseth's view in this instance extreme, the leaders of America's major labor unions agreed with the general principle that since in the past the coercive powers of government had been used against labor, workers ought to be very skeptical about extension of governmental authority in labor matters.[17]

17 Furuseth's comment is contained in a letter to Sutherland, May 5, 1923, Sutherland Papers, Box 5. Declared John Philip Frey, president of the Molders' International Union, "Where the wage earners' main faith is placed upon political activity, his disappointments will be much greater, and his reverses more serious than where he places his reliance upon the economic strength acquired through trades unionism." Frey to W. A. Appleton, May 29, 1922, Frey Papers, Box 1. Gompers shared this view-

Indeed, it was this attitude that animated laborite criticism of the courts. It was through the judicial branch of government, argued unionists, that the powers of government had most often been directed against labor's activities. Thus, efforts to curb the courts and to limit injunctions were consistent with labor's goals, for the anti-injunction fight represented an effort to curtail the influence of government and to enable unions to employ their economic weapons without odious official restraints.[18]

The 1920s marked the climax of antilabor judicial activities. In a series of decisions mostly in the early 1920s the Supreme Court stripped labor of its presumed protection under the Clayton Act, extended the application of the Sherman Act, invalidated a national child labor law, struck down a minimum wage statute in the District of Columbia, and strengthened prohibitions or restrictions on boycotts, picketing, and other union activities. Moreover, the courts reaffirmed their acquiescence in the yellow-dog contract, while a key circuit-court ruling in the 1927 Red Jacket case rendered the UMW virtually powerless to undertake organization of nonunion miners in West Virginia.[19] Added to previous court decisions inimical to labor and to the long history of federal injunctions in labor disputes, these rulings angered even conservative labor leaders and led them to seek political and legislative redress.

---

point but he often became embroiled in political controversy. After the accession of William Green in 1924 to the presidency of the AFL, however, there was a sharp decline in the amount of political comment in the pages of the *American Federationist*. A good general account of this attitude toward legislation in the 1920s is Milton Lewis Farber, "Changing Attitudes of the American Federation of Labor Toward Business and Government, 1929-1933" (unpublished Ph.D. dissertation, Ohio State University, 1959), chapt. 1.

[18] Hyman Weintraub, *Andrew Furuseth: Emancipator of the Seamen* (Berkeley and Los Angeles, 1959), 186-89.

[19] Stanley Ira Kutler, "The Judicial Philosophy of Chief Justice Taft and Organized Labor, 1921-1930" (unpublished Ph.D. dissertation, Ohio State University, 1960), *passim*.; Kutler, "Labor, the Clayton Act, and the Supreme Court," *Labor History*, III (Winter 1962), 19-38; Bernstein, *The Lean Years*, 190-237.

Adding to the laborites' sense of outrage were the statements made by members of the judiciary. Most of the labor decisions of the 1920s rested on a solid body of precedent; the Taft court broke no new ground but largely applied and extended previous decisions to new cases in the 1920s, which appeared in great number.[20] But members of the court, and particularly Chief Justice William Howard Taft, were not content with rendering decisions; they also made public and private comments that revealed an active hostility toward organized labor and its goals. Of labor, Taft wrote in 1922, "That faction we have to hit every little while." In 1921 Taft published a book entitled *Representative Government* in which he declared that recent events had revealed attempts by organized labor "to choke the country and Congress into a compliance with the economic demands of this particular class." He termed such laborite activities as the pressure in 1916 for the Adamson Act and the strikes of 1919 a "selfish and Bolshevistic use of a combination of a minority to compel a majority to yield to its demands." Indeed, toward the end of his life Taft told his brother Horace that his main objective on the court had been "to prevent the Bolsheviki from getting control."[21]

Stung by such criticism, angered by the trend of court decisions, and outraged by the Daugherty-Wilkerson injunction, through the early 1920s laborites leveled broad criticism at the courts. Organized labor had so many grievances against the courts that it participated in an attack upon the whole legal

[20] Kutler, "The Judicial Philosophy of Chief Justice Taft," chapt. 8. But see Bernstein's comment on the *Adkins* case in *The Lean Years*, 227-32. Organized labor found several important decisions advantageous, particularly those striking down the Kansas Court of Industrial Relations (*Charles Wolff Packing Co.* v. *Kansas Court of Industrial Relations*, 262 U.S. 522 [1923] and denying enforcement power to the Railroad Labor Board (*Pennsylvania Railroad* v. *Railroad Labor Board*, 261 U.S. 72 [1923]), although enthusiasm over the latter decision was tempered by the procarrier effect of the specific case.

[21] The first and fourth of Taft's remarks in this paragraph are quoted in Bernstein, *The Lean Years*, 191 and 242, respectively. The two in the middle are quoted in Alpheus T. Mason, *William Howard Taft: Chief Justice* (New York, 1964), 140.

and judiciary establishment of the Harding and Coolidge administrations. In addition to its usual demand for anti-injunction legislation, it joined in 1922 in opposition to Harding's appointment of Pierce Butler to the Supreme Court, supported Congressman Oscar Keller's impeachment proceedings against Daugherty, and approved the successful senatorial effort in 1925 to reject Coolidge's appointment of Charles B. Warren, a prominent corporation lawyer, to the attorney generalship.[22]

Indeed, much of labor's political hostility to the GOP between 1922 and 1924 derived from its antagonism to the judicial and legal activities of the party's appointees to court and legal posts. In June 1922 La Follette addressed the AFL convention and received a tremendous response when he lashed out at the courts and called for the curtailment of their powers. And the provisions in the 1924 Progressive and CPPA platforms that called for congressional review of Supreme Court rulings met with labor's strong approval.[23]

Labor's vocal hostility alarmed and dismayed many Republicans. Progressives generally sympathized with labor's grievances and voiced their alarm in terms of criticizing the president, his appointees, and their actions. In 1921, for example, Hiram Johnson, upon learning of Harding's appointment of Taft, declared, "When I think of the industrial disputes that are coming . . . my heart grows sick." In 1922

[22] Kenneth Campbell MacKay, *The Progressive Movement of 1924*, Columbia University Studies in History, Economics and Public Law, no. 527 (New York, 1947), 151; John D. Hicks, *Republican Ascendancy, 1921-1933* (New York, 1960), 72-73; David J. Danielski, *A Supreme Court Justice Is Appointed* (paperback ed.; New York, 1964), 77, 115.

[23] La Follette's speech is reprinted in *Congressional Record*, 67th Cong., 2d sess., 1922, 62:9076-82, while an account describing the enthusiastic response appears in the New York *Times*, June 15, 1922. For the La Follette Progressive and CPPA planks, see Kirk H. Porter and Donald B. Johnson, comps., *National Party Platforms*, 3d ed. (Urbana, Ill., 1966), 252-53, 256. See also MacKay, *The Progressive Movement of 1924*, p. 151, and editorial entitled "Labor's Political Demands," *American Federationist*, XXXI (July 1924), 554-55.

after the Daugherty-Wilkerson injunction Senator Borah expressed fear that the courts were forfeiting the allegiance of workers and their supporters. Throughout the decade progressives in and out of Congress maintained a steady barrage of criticism of the courts' treatment of labor. Indeed, recalls Dean Acheson, one's stand on the injunction issue served as a basic test of one's liberalism in the 1920s.[24]

Conservatives became aroused also, but their concern was directed at the labor-progressive attacks upon the courts. In June 1922 Republican Senator Frank B. Kellogg of Minnesota, referring to the anticourt remarks made by La Follette at the 1922 AFL convention, described the Wisconsinite's speech as "one of the most vicious and dangerous I have ever read." To the Minnesotan, "the most sinister part of it is that it was cheered uproariously" by the unionists. Taft was equally concerned, although more sanguine. In 1922 he predicted that "From the attacks made on the Court by the labor unions and by La Follette . . . I see before us an active agitation against the Court . . . [which] will probably last a decade." But in 1924 the chief justice was confident that labor's foolish effort to draw class lines on this issue would lead the American people to defend the courts "and deal a body blow to La Follettism, labor union tyranny and socialism."[25]

In the 1924 campaign the labor-progressive hostility toward the courts reached a climax. La Follette's platform and the Wisconsinite's frequent and often sweeping attacks upon the courts, while popular with laborites, provided GOP orators with an excellent opportunity to attack both La Follette and his

[24] Hiram Johnson to Raymond Robins, July 1, 1921, Robins Papers, Box 17; Borah to Ray N. Castle, Sept. 14, 1922, Borah Papers, Box 214; Zinn, La Guardia in Congress, 227; George W. Norris, Fighting Liberal: The Autobiography of George W. Norris (New York, 1945), 308-10; Dean Acheson, Morning and Noon (Boston, 1965), 104.

[25] Kellogg to C. A. Severance, June 22, 1922, Frank B. Kellogg Papers (Minnesota Historical Society), Box 7; William Howard Taft to Charles P. Taft, Sept. 10, 1922, and to Coolidge, Sept. 16, 1924, Taft Papers, Boxes 523 and 565 respectively.

laborite allies. Although most Republicans realized that direct attacks upon organized labor, whatever its announced support for La Follette, were unwise, they could depict their party as the staunch defender of the courts and of the constitutional system, thus taking a slap at the Wisconsin senator and by implication those laborites who agreed with him on this issue. Davis, for example, was particularly vocal, but he was always careful to draw a sharp line between organized labor, which he supported, and the anticourt assaults of some of its misguided leaders.[26]

After La Follette's defeat, laborite hostility toward the courts in general lost momentum. Not only had their candidate been beaten, but after 1925 there were no further appointments to the Supreme Court and, in contrast to the early 1920s, fewer major labor decisions. But if the Supreme Court was proving impregnable and if laborites became less aroused over its membership and decisions, the issue of the labor injunction remained lively, and labor's antagonism toward this type of judicial intervention in labor disputes continued unappeased. From 1925 until 1932, when Congress passed the anti-injunction Norris-La Guardia Act, labor devoted most of its legislative energies to the fight against the injunction.

Laborites found this concentration upon the injunction far more practical and effective than it did the earlier broad attack upon the courts. · In the 1920s there were an unusually large number of injunctions, a circumstance that constantly reminded the public and its elected representatives of the problem. Moreover, the 1922 railroad injunction, perpetrated as it was by the soon-discredited Daugherty, was so extreme and one-sided that even conservatives and ardent defenders of the courts opposed it. Hoover and Charles Evans Hughes criticized it in a cabinet meeting, while Senator George Wharton Pepper, formerly a leading corporation lawyer,

<hr />

[26] Davis, "Statement Re: La Follette Socialist Party," Aug. 31, 1924, Davis Papers, Box 40.

indirectly but firmly, attacked it publicly. Indeed, even Taft, who regarded the strike as a test of the public will against labor arrogance, told his brother Horace, "confidentially . . . I don't think Harding has been well advised in instituting his injunction suit . . . and in securing an injunction apparently so wide in its effect."[27]

This injunction and the outcry against it had two important effects upon labor's campaign to eliminate or restrict injunctions. Not only did it provide labor with a clear-cut and obvious national example of the dangers and abuses of injunctions, but the uproar following its issuance persuaded some conservatives that the courts had to be removed from the frontlines of industrial warfare. Of course, even after the 1922 edict many businessmen, lawyers, and defenders of the courts held to their opposition to efforts to curb injunctions, and even some of those who grew concerned about the exposure of the courts to public criticism did not necessarily sanction a legislative solution. Still, once the issue of injunctions became somewhat separated from the progressive-labor attacks upon the courts as such, ardent and influential defenders of the courts could and did criticize injunctions also.[28]

The Republican party bore the main weight of the debate over injunctions. Not only did it control Congress and the presidency, but Harding and Coolidge had had the opportunity to appoint an unusually large number of Supreme Court justices in a short time. Most important, though, it was a Republican attorney general and a Republican appointee to the district judgeship of Northern Illinois, James H. Wilkerson, who had collaborated to issue the notorious 1922 restraining order and the subsequent injunction. Democrats had for many

[27] Edwin E. Witte, *The Government in Labor Disputes* (New York, 1932), 84. Taft's comment is contained in his letter to Horace Taft, Sept. 7, 1922, Taft Papers, Box 523.

[28] For a discussion of conservative anti-injunction sentiment, see Robert H. Zieger, "Senator George Wharton Pepper and Labor Issues in the 1920s," *Labor History*, IX (Spring 1968), 177-82.

years included anti-injunction planks in their platforms, and being out of power in the 1920s they escaped the sort of criticism that had descended upon Republicans.

Thus, in the late 1920s, with the presidential election approaching and the drive against injunctions gaining force, Republicans had to confront the injunction issue. The problem was a hard one, because the GOP for political reasons could not entirely repudiate its legal policies regarding labor and because many Republicans were convinced that, whatever the abuses that labor had suffered, the party had to uphold the integrity of the courts and to stand against efforts to rob them of their power to act in emergencies.

In the injunction issue, as in so many labor issues during the 1920s, the GOP proved both fortunate and resourceful. Happily, a number of prominent Republicans such as Davis, Hoover, Hughes, Borah, and Pepper had spoken out against the Daugherty-Wilkerson injunction, and, though often in general language, some had voiced general criticism of injunctions. The party was no more wedded in principle to the use of the injunction than were the Democrats because of the notorious injunctions authored by Richard Olney in 1894 and A. Mitchell Palmer in 1919.

Even more happily, there was a way to criticize the injunction while upholding the integrity of the courts and opposing the sweeping criticism of the courts offered by progressives and laborites. For example, Senator George Wharton Pepper of Pennsylvania, a highly conservative lawyer, legal scholar, and defender of the courts, argued that industrial disputes were too emotional and too bitter to be dumped upon the courts for decisions. Even though the country had for the past fifty years been experiencing explosive and often violent strikes, he noted, Americans had constructed no effective machinery for their peaceful settlement. The legislative and executive branches of government had proved unable or unwilling to deal with the problem, so it was thrust upon the courts. No doubt, at first this was unavoidable and even necessary, but in 1924 Pepper began "to raise the question whether the Federal Court is the proper agency to take up the shock of our industrial warfare."[29]

Pepper soon answered his own question. In general, he argued, the courts had served the nation well in industrial disputes. But judges often had to react quickly without sufficient information. Sometimes judges made mistakes— even, in the case of the 1922 injunction, costly and damaging ones. In a very influential speech in 1924 the Pennsylvanian warned against the tendency toward "more and more comprehensive and far-reaching injunctions," and he coupled this theme with pleas (and even tentative proposals) for the establishment of other means of coping with labor strife. In Pepper's view, the removal of the courts from the battlefield of labor disputes would in no way constitute a criticism of the courts or undermine their crucial function in American government. The effect of such a policy, he predicted, would be to allay criticism of the courts and to thwart dangerous proposals to limit or destroy the general powers of the courts.[30]

Pepper's approach received considerable support among Republicans, and his 1924 speech on injunctions before the combined meeting of the American and Philadelphia Bar Associations became something of a classic statement of conservative anti-injunction opinion. Influential Republican editor Arthur Vandenberg, a thorough conservative both as editor of the Grand Rapids *Herald* and later as United States senator from Michigan, agreed with the Pennsylvanian "that the constantly expanding use of the injunction . . . in labor disputes is gradually breaking down mass loyalty to the Courts." Later, as significant anti-injunction legislation began

[29] George Wharton Pepper, *Injunctions in Labor Disputes*, speech delivered on July 8, 1924, pamphlet in Pepper Papers, Box 24; Pepper to J. W. Turnbull, July 11, 1924, Pepper Papers, Box 24.

[30] *Injunctions in Labor Disputes*; New York *Times*, Sept. 29, 1922; Pepper to S. P. Hutchinson, Sept. 23, 1924, Pepper Papers, Box 24.

to make its way through the first stages of the lawmaking process, Pepper received many messages of congratulation from foes of injunctions who remembered his earlier stand. In 1929, for example, economist Sumner H. Slichter told the former senator that his 1924 speech was "one of the most illuminating and penetrating examinations of the injunction problem."[31]

In addition to its good fortune in having articulate and influential spokesmen who were critical of injunctions yet cautious in their approaches to the problem, the GOP also benefited from the inability of organized labor and its friends to agree upon specific anti-injunction legislation. For many years, the approach of most unionists to the problem had been to urge legislation that would greatly restrict the courts' power to issue equity decrees in labor disputes.[32] This approach had been followed in previous legislative efforts and was the view of John Philip Frey, president of the International Molders' Union in his recent book *The Labor Injunction: An Exposition of Government by Judicial Conscience and Its Menace*. Thus, in December 1927 when Furuseth, as strong a foe of injunctions

[31] Vandenberg to Pepper, July 11, 1924; Slichter to Pepper, Feb. 27, 1929, Pepper Papers, Box 24. In this box in the Pepper Papers there are many communications to Pepper from students of the labor injunction such as Felix Frankfurter, Edwin E. Witte, and others remarking on the perceptiveness and importance of his 1924 speech. Pepper did not necessarily support legislation designed to limit the courts' injunctive powers, and people who congratulated him on his 1924 stand did not always realize that his main concern was the safety of the courts, not the rights of labor. See Pepper to William Green, Feb. 16, 1928, Pepper Papers, Box 6, Book 15.

[32] Courts frequently issued injunctions in labor disputes to protect intangible property, particularly expected profits that would be jeopardized by a strike. Unionists claimed that in the common law, equity jurisdiction had traditionally applied only to tangible property, and they sought legislative action to limit labor injunctions to protection of this form of property. Critics of this effort, including many who were opposed to the labor injunction, however, declared that the judicial expansion of the definition of property was irreversible, making labor's antiequity approach unfeasible. See Witte, *The Government in Labor Disputes*, 105-106, and Alpheus T. Mason, *Organized Labor and the Law: With Especial Reference to the Sherman and Clayton Acts* (Durham, N. C., 1925), 102, 114-16.

as he was of welfare legislation, introduced an anti-injunction bill through Farmer-Labor Senator Henrik Shipstead of Minnesota, it relied upon curtailment of the courts' equity powers.[33]

Had the bill commanded widespread and immediate enthusiasm among anti-injunction groups, it would have posed a political problem for the GOP in 1928. But when a subcommittee of the Senate Judiciary Committee, consisting of progressive Republicans Norris and John Blaine of Wisconsin and Democrat Thomas Walsh of Montana, considered it in the spring of 1928, the senators determined that the Shipstead bill was inadequate. It rested its case upon the assumption that by restricting equity jurisdiction in labor disputes to protection only of "tangible and transferable property" and by reference to the Thirteenth Amendment to the Constitution, the courts would effectively be denied the justification for issuing injunctions. Experts, such as Felix Frankfurter and Francis B. Sayre of the Harvard Law School, and Edwin E. Witte of the Wisconsin Legislative Reference Library, testified before the subcommittee and argued that Furuseth's approach was essentially the same as that attempted in the Pearre bill of 1908 and the Clayton Act of 1914, neither of which had been effective. Contending that the courts' broad definition of property was firmly entrenched and probably even proper, these men at first despaired of finding a solution to the injunction problem. Witte, probably the most knowledgeable student of injunctions in the country, admitted that he was "stumped to know what ought to be done." He was sure, however, that the Shipstead bill simply would not suffice. Eventually, after frequent testimony before the Norris subcommittee and much consultation, Witte and the other academicians hit upon the device of placing procedural restraints upon the courts' injunctive powers and

[33] Weintraub, *Andrew Furuseth*, 186-89; Philip A. Taft, *The A.F. of L. from the Death of Gompers to the Merger* (New York, 1959), 23-24.

of simply exempting from injunctions certain labor tactics, such as picketing and propaganda activities.[34]

Furuseth, however, was wedded to his approach, whatever the arguments of politicians and academicians. He induced both the 1927 and 1928 AFL conventions to endorse the Shipstead bill, in spite of the efforts of Norris and others to dissuade him. Meanwhile, it was difficult for opponents of injunctions to wage a unified campaign in behalf of legislation, for the disagreement of the AFL and its congressional, academic, and reform-minded friends prevented the issue from emerging in clear focus. The 1928 election occurred in the middle of this internal debate among friends of anti-injunction legislation, insuring that platforms, parties, and candidates could avoid a specific stand and shroud their hesitancy in generalities. Thus, the Republican platform's vague declaration that "We believe that injunctions . . . have in some instances been abused and have given rise to a serious question for legislation," adequately covered the party during the campaign.[35]

By the summer of 1928, the Republican party was in the

[34] Taft, *The A.F. of L. from the Death of Gompers*, 23-24; Felix Frankfurter to Roger Baldwin, Dec. 9, 1931, copy in George W. Norris Papers (Manuscript Division, Library of Congress), Tray 79, Box 7; hereafter cited as Norris Papers. Witte's remark is contained in a letter to Sen. John J. Blaine, Mar. 6, 1928, Edwin E. Witte Papers (State Historical Society of Wisconsin), Box 1. There are many other communications from such critics of injunctions as Donald Richberg, Witte, Francis B. Sayre, and Frankfurter criticizing Furuseth's proposal and urging the procedural approach in Norris Papers, Tray 79, Box 7, and Tray 42, Box 8. See also Norris, *Fighting Liberal*, 303-309.

[35] Weintraub, *Andrew Furuseth*, 189; Andrew Furuseth, *Injunction Legislation: Is It an Anti-Injunction Bill or a Pro-Injunction Code?* pamphlet (Washington, D.C., 1931), copy in Norris Papers, Tray 79, Box 7. The Republican platform statement is contained in Porter and Johnson, *National Party Platforms*, 286. Soon the AFL joined the academicians and Norris in repudiating Furuseth's approach and in urging anti-injunction legislation along procedural lines. The Norris-La Guardia Act, signed by Hoover on March 23, 1932, embraced this concept and was a major legislative victory for organized labor. See Taft, *The A.F. of L. from the Death of Gompers*, 24, and Norris, *Fighting Liberal*, 308-17.

process of effectively coping politically with the only two major controversial labor issues remaining in public view. Added to the sharp decline in strikes, the heady prosperity, and the passage of the Railway Labor Act in 1926, the temporary shelving of the soft coal and injunction issues enabled the party to conduct a national campaign for the first time since 1912 in which it faced no significant and specific challenge from organized labor. The labor issue seemed to have all but vanished, eliminated, the GOP platform asserted, by an administration that had "lifted [the country] from the depths of a great depression to a level of prosperity" and had successfully fostered "increasingly harmonious relations between employers and employees."[36]

Herbert Hoover's place at the head of the Republican ticket further diminished controversy over labor issues. As secretary of commerce, he had been the single most important and articulate shaper of most GOP economic policies; their apparent success vindicated his efforts. In strictly labor matters, he also had an impressive record. Not only had he scrupulously avoided commitment to antilabor views, but he maintained close and cordial relations with prominent labor leaders. In addition, he had been the administration's key figure in the unemployment conference in 1921 and 1922 and in the ending of the twelve-hour day in the steel industry in 1923. Moreover, his encouragement of employer-employee harmony had often led him to defend the activities of the major labor unions and at times to criticize the actions of unyielding capitalists. True, there were flaws in his labor record. In the early 1920s he had voiced open shop sentiments; his soft coal policy was not helping the UMW in its desperate struggle for survival; and he had made no general stand against injunctions. But even on these issues, laborites could find some comfort. His open shop sentiments had been vague and had been coupled with defense of unions such as the AFL;

[36] Porter and Johnson, *National Party Platforms*, 280-81.

whatever the situation in the soft coal areas, he had in 1924 supported the UMW insistence upon regionwide bargaining; and even if he had uttered no general indictment of labor injunctions, in 1922 he had helped to arrange a fair settlement for many railroad workers through the Baltimore Agreement and had opposed the Daugherty-Wilkerson injunction.

Not only had Hoover's efforts helped to deal with important specific labor issues in a manner agreeable to unionists, but his general approach to industrial relations also appeared to be working well. In the postwar years the country had faced strikes, unemployment, industrial unrest, and renewed radical activity. The outright suppression that A. Mitchell Palmer and Daugherty had initiated, and the virulent open shop movement had imposed a certain constraint, but the price of such actions was continued confrontation between labor and capital. Antilabor elements called for antistrike laws and political support for the open shop, while even some conservative unionists coupled militant rhetoric with vigorous involvement in insurgent politics.

Hoover had resisted extremism. Sometimes his counsel had been ignored, as in the handling of the railroad strike. But his appeals to business and labor, his leadership in federal concern with unemployment, his use of engineering studies and experts to accomplish desirable social ends, and his general program of seeking scientific and noncoercive solutions to labor problems began to have effect even in the tumultuous Harding years. With the accession of Coolidge, the departure of Daugherty, and the fading of the more emotional aspects of the postwar controversies, Hoover's approach came increasingly to characterize the labor policies of the GOP. By the time of the 1928 campaign the labor problem, the subject of decades of acrimony and violence, seemed to have been settled. In the view of Hoover and his party the tranquility of the late 1920s was no mere accident or temporary lull. Rather it was an indication that the labor problem had yielded to a rational and modern method of solution, a method that used legislation to help the economy in general, but largely avoided it in specifically labor matters, relying in this area upon governmental leadership to stimulate voluntary cooperation between labor and capital.

That the Hoover approach had severe limitations and that the country's economic stability and prosperity rested upon shaky foundations was not apparent to most of America's workers and labor leaders in 1928. Organized labor took little part in the campaign. President William Green of the AFL confined his political stand to a declaration that "By no stretch of the imagination could any statement I have made be construed as an endorsement of any candidate." Frank Morrison, the secretary-treasurer of the AFL and leader of the organization's previous political drives, asserted that "today party spirit has disappeared as far as the great mass of workers is concerned."[37]

Most of labor's organized political action was conducted on the state and local levels. State federations generally refrained from endorsing either Democrat Alfred E. Smith or Hoover, but those that took this step favored the Democratic candidate. The Progressive League for Smith sought to arouse labor opposition to Hoover by circulating open shop statements that the GOP candidate had made in 1921, but neither the endorsements nor this campaign appeared to have much impact. Individual union leaders made endorsements, generally for Smith, but Hoover and the Republicans captured some of this support as well. In June, Raymond Robins reported much pro-Hoover labor sentiment at the GOP convention in Kansas City. William Doak, legislative representative of the Brotherhood of Railway Trainmen, served as director of the Republican party's labor bureau during the

[37] Vaughn Davis Bornet, *Labor Politics in a Democratic Republic: Moderation, Division, and Disruption in the Presidential Election of 1928* (Washington, D.C., 1964), chapt. 11. Green and Morrison are quoted on p. 232.

campaign, declaring, "I hope all employees will now be convinced that Herbert Hoover is the friend of the working people." John L. Lewis, despite his former attacks upon the Coolidge administration regarding the Jacksonville Agreement, came out for Hoover also, describing him as "the foremost industrial statesman of modern times."[38]

Headed by Doak, the GOP labor bureau largely confined its activities to counteracting anti-Hoover material. The party, secure in its candidate and untroubled by specific labor issues, hard times, or concentrated labor opposition, pursued the labor vote with less vigor than it had in 1920 and 1924. Aside from the vague statement on injunctions, the platform's labor planks simply extolled the economic policies and achievements of the past eight years. Republican campaign literature dwelt upon the themes of prosperity and industrial peace, attributing labor's well-being to Republican policies such as the conference on unemployment, the protective tariff, and immigration restriction. Summing up the Republican appeal to workers with more enthusiasm than syntax, one writer in the *Republican Campaign Textbook* declared, "Labor in the United States has, on the whole, a good job."[39]

Hoover made only one campaign speech dealing specifically with labor. On September 18, before an audience of 10,000 people, the Republican nominee spoke at the state armory in Newark, New Jersey. He appealed for the support of workers, asserting that the GOP had engineered the unparalleled prosperity that they enjoyed. Hoover recalled the party's assault on unemployment, its job-protecting high tariff stand, and its commitment to restrictive immigration. New Jersey's

[38] *Ibid.*, 240-41. The charges of the Progressive League are described in the New York *Times*, Oct. 31, 1928. Robins noted the pro-Hoover labor sentiment in a letter to Borah, June 16, 1928, Borah Papers, Box 295, while the comments of Doak and Lewis are in the New York *Times*, Sept. 19 and Oct. 18, 1928, respectively. In 1930, Hoover appointed Doak as secretary of labor.

[39] Porter and Johnson, *National Party Platforms*, 280-86; *Republican Campaign Textbook* (n.p., 1928), 326-39, 350-54.

workers, he warned, would face insecurity and lower wages without the Republican tariff. Restriction of immigration, which the nominee described as a policy undertaken primarily to protect the American worker, "is the necessary and natural companion piece of a protective tariff"; these twin policies joined to keep wages high, jobs secure, and prosperity constant.[40] With good times apparently justifying these claims and with no vital labor issues such as those of the 1919-1925 period facing the country, in 1928 there was little talk of a labor vote and even less indication of its impact at the polls.[41]

The eclipse of the labor issue in 1928 represented a remarkable political achievement of the Republican party. In the elections of 1920, 1922, and 1924 organized labor had opposed the party either through nonpartisan support for Democrats and insurgents or through independent political action. Sharp controversies involving labor had characterized these years; inevitably issues such as the open shop, injunctions, the coal and railroad strikes, and railroad labor legislation became involved in politics, often presenting the GOP with difficult choices and political dilemmas. But with the accession of Calvin Coolidge and especially after the election of 1924 the party was able to settle, mute, or avoid these controversies. Although general economic prosperity and organized labor's growing conservatism were major factors in reducing the level of tension, the Republican party actively contributed as well. It acquiesced in and supported the Railway Labor Act of 1926, temporarily eliminating the troublesome railroad labor issue. Under Hoover it minimized the impact of labor difficulties in bituminous coal industry while keeping the support of the UMW leadership. It avoided intimate identification with labor groups, which pleased conservatives, while

[40] New York *Times*, Sept. 18, 1928; Herbert Hoover, *The New Day: Campaign Speeches of Herbert Hoover, 1928* (Stanford, Calif., 1928), 63-71.
[41] Bornet, *Labor Politics*, chapt. 11.

rejecting the programs of antilabor extremists in the party, which soothed laborites. During the Coolidge administration the GOP showed itself quite receptive to the legislative aims of the AFL, the railroad brotherhoods, and other conservative unions, for during this period of Republican control Congress enacted the Watson-Parker measure and in 1929 the Hawes-Cooper Act, which placed restrictions upon the interstate transportation of the products of convict labor. Moreover, Republicans authored and endorsed the Watson coal bill and at least acknowledged the injunction problem. While these activities did not induce organized labor to embrace the party, they did help to diminish labor's pro-Democratic efforts, and they did remove the controversies of the early 1920s and allow the GOP to claim plausibly in 1928 that the labor problem was no more.

While many Republicans were satisfied with this political achievement, Hoover's ambitions had been larger. Always the engineer, as early as 1909 in a book about mine management, he had described the engineer as "a buffer between labor and capital."[42] During his membership in the cabinet he had claimed this function for government, which, he asserted, should employ the ideas, data, and services of engineers to uncover the technological problems that gave rise to social unrest. Throughout the 1920s one of his most important aims had been to bring about an economic and social solution to the labor problem through this method. Of course, as an astute public man he recognized that political factors sometimes presented obstacles, and he was keenly aware of the need to compromise to promote party ends, but this larger effort had been his most cherished goal.

Yet it was in this area that his and his party's labor policies ultimately failed, although the failure did not become generally apparent until the depression. The weaknesses in the

[42] Hoover's remarks are in his book *Principles of Mining: Valuation, Organization, and Administration* (New York, 1909), 167.

economy, which even in the most prosperous months were revealed in statistics regarding unemployment and real wages, would soon be ruthlessly exposed, as would the inadequacy of much of the GOP's economic program of the 1920s. Had the party been as diligent in weighing the effects of the economics of the 1920s upon the worker as it was in seeking to soften his political voice, and had Hoover's plans for industrial peace contained a commitment to strong unions through which workers could express their grievances and make known their wishes, the results might have been different. Given the country's economic conditions, the great popularity and influence of businessmen, and the unimaginative and timorous behavior of the major unions in the late 1920s, however, Republicans received neither encouragement to be more astute in their policies nor warnings to be more restrained in their claims. In all, in the 1920s, the GOP dealt with the labor issue as American political parties deal with most controversial issues, that is, through a combination of compromise, avoidance, and obfuscation, not through specific and comprehensive programs. While Herbert Hoover had worked diligently for this latter approach, it remained for Americans in the next decade to enact modern America's fundamental labor legislation and to define with more clarity public labor policy and the government's responsibility to underwrite general economic health.

Bibliographical Note

FROM ABOUT 1840 onward, journalists, clergymen, academicians, business-men, politicians, and reformers frequently spoke of "the labor problem" (or "the labor issue," "the labor question," or other variations) as if the term required no further elaboration. Implicit in this lack of definition, of course, was the assumption that the labor problem was so obvious, so immediate, and so general that it needed no explanation. While the labor problem and reactions to it varied from period to period, several themes run through the literature. First, by the term most commentators meant or implied two conditions: some specific labor crisis, such as a strike or a wave of unemployment; and the more general and pervasive issue of the status of the worker and his relationship to society. Another common theme, closely associated with the first, was the feeling that the crucial test of a democratic, capitalistic society's ability to function and to survive lay in its ability to deal with labor conditions and industrial relations. For reformers, it was expressed in urgent appeals for social justice; for businessmen and their defenders, it arose from concern over radicalism, inefficiency, and violence. Another common theme was the sense of urgency with which many writers and orators over a long span of years confronted the labor problem. Men and women during each decade felt called upon to solve the problem or face disaster; each generation saw itself on trial. It is in this broad, emotional, and even apocalyptical sense that the phrase "the labor problem" is used in this study.

In my footnotes I have tried to provide a running bibliographical commentary in the main text. This additional note is meant to indicate those materials that I found to be most useful and stimulating and is not intended to be a thorough bibliography.

General Materials

General accounts of the postwar decade, such as John D. Hicks, *Republican Ascendancy, 1921-1933* (1960), Arthur M. Schlesinger, Jr., *The Age of Roosevelt. I: The Crisis of the Old Order, 1919-1933* (1957), William E. Leuchtenberg, *The Perils of Prosperity, 1914-1932* (1958), and David A. Shannon, *Between the Wars: America, 1919-1941* (1965) contain relatively little on labor matters during the 1920s, but they are indispensable for establishing the context of the times. Frederick Lewis Allen's influential *Only Yesterday* (1931) contributes in this regard as well but is even less useful for labor matters. Henry F. May, "Shifting Perspectives on the 1920's," *Mississippi Valley Historical Review* (Dec. 1956), offers penetrating insight into the decade as a whole and into social scientific and historiographical treatments of it, while an article by Burl Noggle, "The Twenties: A New Historiographical Frontier," *Journal of American History* (Sept. 1966), summarizes trends in more recent scholarship and offers suggestions for additional efforts. Valuable overviews of economic and social changes during the 1920s appear in the President's Conference on Unemployment, *Recent Economic Changes in the United States*, 2 vols. (1929) and George Soule, *Prosperity Decade: From War to Depression, 1917-1929* (1947).

For the Republican party, the best and most recent general history is George H. Mayer, *The Republican Party, 1854-1964* (1964). See also Wilfred E. Binkley, *President and Congress*, 3d rev. ed. (1962) and Wesley M. Bagby, *The Road to Normalcy: The Campaign and Election of 1920* (1962). Frequently cited older works, Samuel Hopkins Adams, *Incredible Era: The Life and Times of Warren Gamaliel Harding* (1939) and Karl Shriftgiesser, *This Was Normalcy: An Account of Party Politics During Twelve Republican Years, 1920-1932* (1948), contribute little.

Several political biographies are useful, although in common with the books cited above they deal but little with labor affairs. Andrew Sinclair, *The Available Man: The Life Behind the Masks of Warren Gamaliel Harding* (1965) is sketchy and at times inaccurate in its treatment of labor problems. Books in progress on Harding and his era by Dean Albertson and Robert K. Murray should help considerably. Coolidge has been fortunate in his biographers. Older works by William Allen White, *A Puritan in Babylon: The Story of Calvin Coolidge* (1938) and Claude M. Fuess, *Calvin Coolidge: The Man From Vermont* (1940) are still extremely useful on their subject and the GOP. Donald R. McCoy, *Calvin Coolidge: The Quiet President* (1967) adds some information but by no means replaces these venerable works. Coolidge's *Autobiography* (1929) is useless. Howard Quint and Robert Ferrell, eds., *The Talkative President: The Off-the-Record Press Conferences of Calvin Coolidge* (1964) fills some gaps, although there is little in this otherwise useful book on labor matters.

Hoover has not received adequate biographical treatment. The most useful of the works now available are William Appleman Williams, *Contours of American History* (1961); Carl N. Degler, "The Ordeal of Herbert Hoover," *Yale Review* (Summer 1963); and Richard Hofstadter, "Herbert Hoover and the Crisis of American Individualism," in *The American Political Tradition and the Men Who Made It* (1948). Suggestive but based on inadequate materials is Kent Michael Schofield, "The Figure of Herbert Hoover in the 1928 Campaign" (unpublished dissertation, 1966). Eugene Lyons, *Herbert Hoover: A Biography* (1964) is completely uncritical of Hoover. Hoover's various roles as engineer, social thinker, and politician, as well as his political and economic principles are revealed in his books *Principles of Mining: Valuation, Organization, and Administration* (1909), *American Individualism* (1922), and *The New Day: Campaign Speeches of Herbert Hoover, 1928* (1928). His *Memoirs* (vol. II, 1952) are useful, but often fail to establish a context for Hoover's activities and must be used with care.

There are several very useful doctoral dissertations dealing with the

GOP. In addition to Schofield's, cited above, I profited from Howard Allen, "Miles Poindexter: A Political Biography" (1959); William R. Hingston, "Gifford Pinchot, 1922-1927" (1962); Albert Heisey Pike, Jr., "Jonathan Bourne, Jr., Progressive" (1957); and Ralph Mills Sayre, "Albert Baird Cummins and the Progressive Movement in Iowa" (1958). Helpful far beyond its subject is Darrell Le Roy Ashby, "Senator William E. Borah and Progressivism in the 1920's" (1966).

Several autobiographical works and collections of contemporary speeches help to form a picture of the GOP. See Nicholas Murray Butler, *Across the Busy Years: Recollections and Reflections* (1939), I; Butler, *The Faith of a Liberal: Essays and Addresses on Political Principles and Public Policies* (1924); George W. Norris, *Fighting Liberal: The Autobiography of George W. Norris* (1945); George Wharton Pepper, *In the Senate* (1930); Pepper, *Philadelphia Lawyer: An Autobiography* (1944); James Eli Watson, *As I Knew Them: Memoirs of [Senator] James E. Watson* (1936); and William Allen White, *The Autobiography of William Allen White* (1946).

The *Congressional Record*, the *Annual Messages* of Harding and Coolidge, the various *Republican Campaign Textbooks*, and Kirk H. Porter and Donald Johnson, comps., *National Party Platforms*, 3d ed. (1966) are also essential for an understanding of the GOP, as are the New York *Times* and the *Literary Digest*.

Aside from the *Times*, I made relatively little use of newspapers, except in discussing the election of 1920 and the anthracite strike of 1923. Of those I did consult, the reports of Mark Sullivan in the New York *Tribune* most frequently illuminated the political situation at any given time. The Washington *Post* was close to the Harding administration through the friendship of its proprietor Edward McLean with the president and several of his aides, but I see no particular evidence of its influence upon Harding's labor policies. Together with the *Post*, the *Wall Street Journal* and the Chicago *Tribune* supplied conservative Republican viewpoints, while the Baltimore *Sun* supplied opposition newspaper commentary. H. L. Mencken wrote for the *Sun*; his articles on politics, collected in Malcolm Moos, ed., *H. L. Mencken on Politics: A Carnival of Buncombe* (1956), are delightful to read and often most perceptive. Other journalists who provided sound insights on labor and political matters were William Hard, whose pieces frequently appeared in *The Nation* and *The New Republic*, and William L. Chenery, who wrote on labor affairs for the New York *Times* and other publications.

There are many works on the labor movement in the 1920s which are usfeul to the student. Irving Bernstein, *The Lean Years: A History of the American Worker, 1920-1933* (1960) provides an excellent account of the tribulations of American workers, both organized and unorganized, from a distinctly progressive point of view. Also useful are three books by Philip Taft, *The A. F. of L. in the Time of Gompers* (1957), *The A. F. of L. from the Death of Gompers to the Merger* (1959), and *Organized Labor in American History* (1964), all of which focus upon the inner workings of the AFL and other major unions. Selig Perlman and Philip Taft, *Labor Movements, 1896-1932*, vol. IV of *History of Labor in the United States*, ed. John R. Commons and others, 4 vols. (1918-

1935) offers a wealth of useful information, despite its age. Perlman's *A History of Trade Unionism in the United States* (1922) and *A Theory of the Labor Movement* (1928), together with Taft's books and their joint effort, provide a basic statement of the American labor movement's conservativism and lack of political consciousness which is still persuasive, even if one does not necessarily share Perlman's enthusiasm for these traits. In the 1920s organized labor was unusually willing to embrace the American business system and to cooperate with corporate leaders, a circumstance related to labor's attraction to the scientific management and engineering movements. Milton Lewis Farber, "Changing Attitudes of the American Federation of Labor Toward Business and Government, 1929-1933" (unpublished dissertation, 1959), chapt. I, and James O. Morris, *Conflict Within the AFL: A Study of Craft Versus Industrial Unionism, 1901-1938* (1958) accurately depict labor's conservatism and lack of militancy during the late 1920s, while Milton J. Nadworny, *Scientific Management and the Unions, 1900-1932: A Historical Analysis* (1955) deals perceptively with the influence of scientific management concepts upon the unions.

Many important unions, such as the United Mine Workers and most of the railroad brotherhoods, have not received extensive scholarly treatment. Accounts of other unions and unionists were generally of little use to me. But two books by David Brody, *Steelworkers in America: The Nonunion Era* (1960), and *Labor In Crisis: The Steel Strike of 1919* (1965) are careful and scholarly, and contribute much toward a general understanding of the troubled postwar period as well as illuminating the labor problems peculiar to the steel industry.

Suggestive of a broad reinterpretation of organized labor's relationship to the political and economic structure of American society in the 1920s are the brief but provocative comments regarding labor's place in the corporate economy in Williams, *Contours of American History*. A slightly more extensive discussion along these lines is Ronald Radosh, "The Corporate Ideology of American Labor Leaders from Gompers to Hillman," *Studies on the Left* (Nov.-Dec. 1966). Philip Foner's comments on Radosh's article in *ibid.* are reflective of a more traditional leftist criticism of American labor and contain some harsh judgments of Hoover's labor record as president.

Primary Materials

Manuscript and archival materials provided the great bulk of the information for this book. The most generally useful collections were the papers of Warren G. Harding (the Ohio State Museum); Calvin Coolidge (Library of Congress; hereafter cited as LC); Herbert Hoover (Hoover Presidential Library); William E. Borah (LC); Edward T. Clark (LC); James J. Davis (LC); John Philip Frey (LC); Samuel Gompers (Letterbooks; AFL-CIO Library); Samuel McCune Lindsay (Butler Library, Columbia University); Ogden L. Mills (LC); George Wharton Pepper (Van Pelt Library, University of Pennsylvania); Gifford Pinchot (LC); George Sutherland (LC); William Howard Taft (LC); William Allen White (LC); and the Gompers-AFL Collection (State Historical Society of Wisconsin). Some other collections from which I anticipated valuable information were disappointing, including the Charles Evans Hughes Papers (LC); the League of Women Voters Papers (LC); the George W. Norris Papers (LC); the Donald Richberg Papers (LC); and the James Wadsworth Papers (LC).

Fortunately, the papers of the three presidents are rich in material, although each offers its unique rewards and has its peculiar limitations. The Harding Papers are refreshing, for they contain much candid information about the twenty-seventh president. They are extremely useful for the student of labor affairs, for they yield many letters and memoranda that reveal the crosscurrents of opinion in the party and the pressures working upon Harding both as candidate and as president. It is often difficult to determine Harding's own position on a given issue, not because of lack of response on his part, but rather because he responded so frequently and so lengthily to such a wide variety of viewpoints. The contradictions and inconsistencies in Harding's utterances and actions were, I think, more often due to genuine perplexity and inability to decide than to deviousness or conscious intent to mislead.

If the Harding Papers give a shifting and uncertain view of the Ohioan, the Coolidge Papers present opposite problems. While Harding responded frequently, personally, and even hastily to comments and suggestions, his successor rarely committed himself, at least in labor matters. While Quint and Ferrell's *The Talkative President* balances the image of Silent Cal somewhat, the material presented therein deals only sketchily and marginally with labor. The papers, true to Coolidge's reputation, reveal very little about the president's own views, except in the most formal and guarded statements. Still, this large body of material is most valuable, for it contains party and governmental reports, memoranda, and correspondence relating to politics and administration in general and to coal and railroad labor matters in particular. Thus, if one learns relatively little about Coolidge's own views, he nonetheless has an opportunity to discover the views and programs of party, administration, labor, and business leaders through the vast quantity of incoming material. The papers of two of his private secretaries, Everett Sanders and Edward T. Clark, both located in the Library of Congress, help to round out the picture, with the latter being particularly useful for political affairs.

The voluminous Herbert Hoover Papers at West Branch, Iowa, give a pretty complete record of the secretary of commerce's manifold activities. The correspondence and other material regarding unemployment, the twelve-hour day, the coal problem, the railroad labor issue, and many other labor matters is extensive and invaluable in understanding not only these specific issues but also Hoover's overall approach and his tremendous influence. The biggest disappointment is the dearth of political materials. The United States Department of Commerce Records (Record Group 40, National Archives; hereinafter cited as RG . . . , NA) are thin and seem to have been denuded of the most useful materials. The *Annual Reports* of the Department of Commerce contain easily available policy statements which sometimes are quite candid and revealing. These Hoover materials are supplemented by Hoover's books, cited above, particularly his *Memoirs*.

The papers of Hoover's colleague in the cabinet, James J. Davis, are quite useful. While the secretary of labor often played a secondary role, his letters and speeches provide a record of events in regard to both administrative programs and political concerns. Supplemented by the United States Department of Labor Records (RG 174, NA) and especially by the very informative United States Conciliation Service Records (RG 280, NA), the Davis Papers reward careful scrutiny, for buried in masses of honorific and patriotic speeches and press releases are important letters and memoranda that reveal much about particular controversies and intergovernmental and interparty disagreements. Davis' *Annual Reports* do not add much, while his autobiography, *The Iron Puddler: My Life in the Rolling Mills and What Came of It* (1922), is useful only in its revelation of Davis' limited horizons and quaint views.

Other collections of general use include the Ogden L. Mills Papers, particularly helpful on the 1920 presidential campaign, the George Wharton Pepper Papers, which contain a surprisingly large amount of revealing correspondence on labor matters, and Samuel McCune Lindsay Papers, which are extraordinarily useful, containing, for example, GOP campaign questionnaires and replies as well as much party and general information on the open shop, injunctions, the twelve-hour day, and unemployment. Helpful for a running commentary on labor and other issues from a Republican progressive standpoint are the papers of William Allen White, William E. Borah, and Gifford Pinchot, while more conservative views are reflected in the papers of Charles D. Hilles (Yale University Library); Albert J. Beveridge (LC); Charles G. Dawes (Deering Library, Northwestern University); George Sutherland; and William Howard Taft, all of which have fairly extensive material on labor affairs. Sutherland's and Taft's papers, of course, contain much valuable commentary regarding legal issues involving labor as well.

Some collections, while generally meager in their yields, contain significant information on one or two topics. These include the W. Jett Lauck Papers (Alderman Library, University of Virginia) on the United Mine Workers of America; the Stanley Washburn Papers (LC) and the Miles Poindexter Papers (Alderman Library) on Republican antiradicalism and the labor issue in 1919 and 1920; the Joseph Frelinghuysen Papers (Rutgers University Library) on the early 1920s; the Oscar Straus Papers (LC) on Harding, the 1920 campaign, and the appointment of a secretary of labor; the National Civic Federation Papers (New York Public Library) on railroad labor matters; the George W. Norris Papers on injunction legislation; the James R. Garfield Diaries (LC) on the 1920 election; and the Records of the United States Senate (RG 46, NA) and of the United States House of Representatives (RG 233, NA) for occasional illustrative materials.

Labor Materials

I have made no attempt to exhaust the labor sources available for the 1920s. Since I have focused upon the largest and most active unions, I worked basically with materials relating to the AFL, the UMW, and the railroad unions. Much correspondence emanating from these organizations is available in such general collections as the Coolidge, Hoover, Davis, Borah, Amos R. E. Pinchot (LC), and National Civic Federation Papers. Also rich in laborite comment are the Conciliation Service and Department of Labor Records. The AFL-CIO Library in Washington houses the Letterbooks of Samuel Gompers and William Green and the Nonpartisan Political Campaign Letterbooks of AFL secretary-treasurer Frank Morrison. While generally unrevealing, the Gompers and Morrison material provides some useful information about the AFL's political activities in the early 1920s, but the Green Letterbooks are flat, dull, and routine. More interesting are the John Philip Frey Papers, which at times yield candid statements by this conservative unionist. The Gompers-AFL materials at the State Historical Society of Wisconsin contain much material unavailable in the holdings at the AFL-CIO Library. The AFL manuscript materials are supplemented by the *American Federationist*, particularly useful during Gomper's presidency, and the *Proceedings of Annual Conventions of the AFL*.

The Lewis Papers are not yet available, but Files 175 and 175B of the Coolidge Papers and various files in the Hoover papers contain many of his letters, as do the unorganized Lauck Papers. Also useful is the United Mine Workers *Journal*, for it often includes correspondence from government figures and coal operators, as well as the views of UMW leaders. Lewis' own position is stated in *The Miners' Fight for American Standards* (1925), while the comments of John Brophy, *A Miner's Life*, edited and supplemented by John O. P. Hall (1964), provide penetrating criticisms of the UMW chief's policies as well as of Republicans such as Harding and Hoover.

There is no single body of railroad labor materials. Again, certain files, such as 58 and 3393, in the Coolidge Papers and various containers in the Borah, Hoover, Davis, National Civic Federation, Harding, and John Gutzon Borglum Papers (LC) have important communications from railroad labor leaders. The railroad unions' publication *Labor* was well edited and provides much valuable information indicative of the postwar militancy of the railroad unions and their involvement in insurgent politics. See also the autobiographical works of its editor, Edward Keating, *The Story of "Labor": Thirty-Three Years on the Rail Workers' Fighting Front* (1953), and *The Gentleman from Colorado: A Memoir* (1964), as well as Donald Richberg, *My Hero: The Indiscreet Memoirs of an Eventful but Unheroic Life* (1954), for the remarks of the unions' chief legal counsel and legislative adviser.

Special Topics

COAL: Essential to an understanding of the vast coal crisis of the 1920s are the Records of the United States Coal Commission (RG 68, NA). These files contain a wealth of information about every aspect of the coal problem and are rich and rewarding on labor and even political matters. The student of this subject owes a debt to George Otis Smith, director of the United States Geological Survey and a member of the commission, for keeping such careful minutes, compiling clipping books, and preserving correspondence and reports. The John Hays Hammond Papers (Yale

University Library) contain little of interest. These unpublished materials can be supplemented by the commission's *Report*, 5 parts (1925); Edward Eyre Hunt and others, eds., *What the Coal Commission Found* (1925); and John Hays Hammond, *The Autobiography of John Hays Hammond* (1935). Other important primary materials, in addition to those items on the UMW cited above, include U.S., Congress, House, Committee on Interstate and Foreign Commerce, *Hearings on Coal Legislation*, 3 parts, 69th Cong., 1st sess., 1926, which contain revealing comments by Herbert Hoover; and U.S., Congress, Senate, Committee on Interstate Commerce, *Conditions in the Coal Fields of Pennsylvania, West Virginia, and Ohio: Hearings*, 2 vols., 70th Cong., 1st sess., 1928, which are a basic reference source for the soft coal industry and its problems, containing the attitudes of a wide variety of commentators and yielding testimony and documents essential for an understanding of the background, failure, and disagreement over the Jacksonville Agreement.

Secondary sources of particular note regarding coal include Glen Lawhorn Parker, *The Coal Industry: A Study in Social Control* (1940); McAlister Coleman, *Men and Coal* (1943); and Edmond Beame, "The Jacksonville Agreement," *Industrial and Labor Relations Review* (Jan. 1955). See the notes in chaps. 6, 7, and 10 for fuller bibliographical statements. Robert F. Munn, comp., *The Coal Industry in America: A Bibliography and Guide to Studies* (1965) is a very valuable research tool.

RAILROAD LABOR: Much has been written on railroad labor. I hazard to add to the accumulation because I think that other accounts have not sufficiently emphasized the political aspects of the story, and, of course, because this issue was a very important one in the 1920s. My article "From Antagonism to Accord: Railroad Labor Policy in the 1920s," *Labor History* (Winter 1968) summarizes my conclusions.

The manuscript materials on railroad labor matters contained in the Coolidge, Harding, Hoover, and National Civic Federation Papers provided the bulk of my information. The Records of the United States Railroad Labor Board (RG 13, NA) were most disappointing, but its successor, the United States Board of Mediation (RG 13, NA), provided much useful material on the functioning of that more successful board. The U.S. Conciliation Service Records are also rich in railroad labor data. I did not visit the University of Tennessee Library to use the Ben W. Hooper Papers, but his many letters to prominent Republicans available in other collections and the use of his autobiography, *Unwanted Boy*, ed. Everett Robert Boyce (1963) I hope compensate.

Documentary materials regarding railroad labor legislation, in addition to the appropriate numbers of the *Congressional Record*, include U.S., Congress, House, Committee on Interstate and Foreign Commerce, *Railroad Labor Disputes; Hearings*, 69th Cong., 1st sess., 1926; and U.S., Congress, Senate, Committee on Interstate Commerce, *Hearings on S. 2306; Railroad Labor Act 1926*, 69th Cong., 1st sess., 1926. Another set of hearings, U.S., Congress, Senate, Subcommittee of Committee on Interstate Commerce, *Hearings on S. 2646; Arbitration Between Carriers and Employees* . . . , 68th Cong., 1st sess., 1924, was unavailable to me, but the New York *Times* carried excellent reports of these and other hearings and congressional debates.

The general railroad labor policy of the GOP can be traced through the *Congressional Record*, the *Annual Reports* of Davis and Hoover, and the *Annual Messages* of Harding and Coolidge, as well as in the manuscripts noted above. Reflective of Attorney General Daugherty's views, especially on the 1922 strikes, are U.S., Department of Justice *Appendix to the Annual Report of the Attorney General* . . . *for the Fiscal Year 1922* ("Lawless Disorders and Their Suppression, 1922"; 1924), and Daugherty's book (in collaboration with Thomas Dixon), *The Inside Story of the Harding Tragedy* (1932).

The most consistently useful secondary source on railroad labor was Elwin W. Sigmund, "Federal Laws Concerning Railroad Labor Disputes: A Legislative and Legal History, 1877-1934" (1961), an excellent dissertation. H. D. Wolf, *The Railroad Labor Board* (1927) is a sound study of that controversial body, while Leonard A. Lecht, *Experience Under Railroad Labor Legislation* (1955), and Leo Troy, "Labor Representation on American Railways," *Labor History* (Fall 1961) provide additional material.

PROGRESSIVISM: Progressivism in the 1920s had many adherents, and fortunately some of those most active have left large and interesting collections. In addition to the Borah, Pinchot, and White Papers cited above, I found the Borglum Papers, the Mercer Green Johnston Papers (LC), the Raymond Robins Papers (State Historical Society of Wisconsin), and the Amos Pinchot Papers vital to my understanding of the relationship between labor and progressivism. The papers of such erstwhile progressives as Miles Poindexter, James R. Garfield, and Albert J. Beveridge helped to define this subject as well. The Norris Papers, unfortunately, were disappointing, and I am very much aware of the gap that the inaccessibility of the Robert M. La Follette Papers creates.

Several books, articles, and dissertations were particularly important on this subject. Kenneth Campbell MacKay, *The Progressive Movement of 1924* (1947) is an excellent monograph and contains important documentary material as well. Also useful are Nathan Fine's contemporary and highly interesting *Labor and Farmer Parties in the United States, 1828-1928* (1928), and Russel Blaine Nye, *Midwestern Progressive Politics: A Historical Study of its Origins and Development, 1870-1950* (1951). Two indispensable articles are Arthur S. Link, "What Happened to the Progressive Movement in the 1920's?" *American Historical Review* (July 1959) and Paul W. Glad, "Progressives and the Business Culture of the 1920's," *Journal of American History* (June 1966). James Weinstein, "Radicalism in the Midst of Normalcy," *Journal of American History* (March 1966) criticizes the unions and La Follette for failing to support a permanent third party, while James H. Shideler, "The Disintegration of the Progressive Party Movement of 1924," *The Historian* (Spring 1951) directed my attention to the useful Mercer Green Johnston Papers. Ashby, "Senator William E. Borah and Progressivism in the 1920's," is a thorough exploration of the dilemmas of progressives in the decade. See the notes in chapter 8 for more complete bibliographical data.

Some books that fall into none of the above categories still merit special mention. For example, I found Edward Berman, *Labor Disputes and the President of the United States* (1924) very useful in untangling the strands of the 1922 strikes. Samuel Haber, *Efficiency and Uplift: Scientific Management in the Progressive Era, 1890-1920* (1964) was most helpful in dealing with the engineering movement, while the Federated American Engineering Societies Committee on Elimination of Waste in Industry, *Waste in Industry* (1921) provides a superb statement of the engineers' social concern and their efforts to analyze social problems with technological insights. Robert K. Murray, *Red Scare: A Study in National Hysteria 1919-1920* (1955), Stanley Coben, *A. Mitchell Palmer: Politician* (1963), and William Preston, Jr., *Aliens and Dissenters: Federal Suppression of Radicalism, 1903-1933* (1963), soundly describe the postwar reaction, while James R. Mock and Evangeline Thurber, *Report on Demobilization* (1944) and John D. Hicks, *Rehearsal for Disaster: The Boom and Collapse of 1919-1920* (1961) are admirable on the postwar economic scene. At the other end of the decade, Vaughn Davis Bornet, *Labor Politics in a Democratic Republic: Moderation, Division, and Disruption in the Presidential Election of 1928* (1964) provided needed material.

Index

Acheson, Dean: views on labor problems, 158, 263
Adamson Act: described, 18; Republicans trace labor unrest to, 23, 24, 38; mentioned, 125, 166, 167-68, 190, 198, 200, 215, 261
Adkins v. *Children's Hospital*, 259
Allen, Henry J.: supports Kansas Court of Industrial Relations, 32, 33
Alpine, John R., 184
Altschuler, Samuel, 219, 219n
Amalgamated Association of Iron, Steel, and Tin Workers of America, 19, 58
American Federation of Labor (AFL): 1920 convention endorses Plumb plan, 9; relations with Wilson administration, 17, 27; relationship with Republican party in 1920s, 22, 29, 54-55, 65-66, 167, 184, 271-72; opposes Esch-Cummins Act's labor provisions, 25; political activities in 1920s, 36-37, 46, 49, 174, 179; supports immigration restriction, 43, 83, 86; feels threatened after 1920 election, 68, 72; supports prison labor legislation, 180; railroad unions in, 205-206, 210; seeks accommodation with business in 1920s, 250, 276; supports anticourt and anti-injunction legislation, 262, 270; mentioned, 35, 47, 55, 67, 69, 85, 149, 170, 172, 193, 263. *See also* Gompers, Samuel; Green, William; labor vote; organized labor; railroad unions

American Founders' Association, 72, 73
American Iron and Steel Association, 20
American Iron and Steel Institute, 101, 104
American Legion, 85
American plan. *See* open shop
American Tobacco Company, 80
anthracite coal industry: background of labor relations, 110n; 1922 strike, 137n, 147; 1923 strike, 145-56, 222; 1902 strike, 146, 147; 1925-1926 strike, 234, 234n, 236, 237. *See also* Lewis, John L.; United Mine Workers of America; United States Coal Commission
antipicketing proposal, 71
antistrike legislation, 71, 73
arbitration: supported by Harding and Hoover in 1922 strikes, 125, 134
Association of Railway Executives: role in 1922 railroad strike, 130, 132-34; mentioned, 212
Atchison, Topeka, and Santa Fe Railroad Company, 199
Atlantic City, New Jersey, 29, 236
Atterbury, W. W.: views on railroad labor legislation, 195
Augusta, Maine, 185

Baer, George, 5
Baker, Ray Stannard: views on labor, 21-22, 164
Baltimore Agreement, 139, 140n, 143, 272
Baltimore Sun, 155

Davies, Hywell, 211
Davis, James J.: appointed secretary of labor, 57; background and general views of, 57-59; role in labor policies in 1920s, 60, 69; quoted on importance of labor issues in early 1920s, 70; opposition to open shop, 74-75, 77; on immigration restriction, 83-85; on unemployment, 89-90, 91, 95, 251; quoted on 1922 coal and railroad strikes, 109; role in bituminous coal labor matters, 110, 114-15, 117, 124, 128, 137, 234, 236, 238, 241, 242, 243, 253-55, 258; role in 1922 railroad strike, 120, 129-30, 131, 133, 140, 143; role in 1924 election, 180-81, 182, 184, 264; role in railroad labor legislation, 191, 194, 199, 207; criticizes injunctions, 266; mentioned, 121, 138. *See also* immigration restriction; Labor, United States Department of
Davis, John W., 182, 186
Dawes, Charles G.: antilabor views and activities described, 13, 74-79, 86, 183; role in 1924 election, 177, 184, 185, 186. *See also* Minute Men of the Constitution
Debs, Eugene V., 42
Democratic party: Republicans attack labor policies of, 26, 162, 180; 1920 platform is silent on injunctions, 40; criticized by organized labor, 47, 179; coal industry under Wilson administration, 113; supports revised railroad labor legislation, 176, 200, 208; mentioned, 53-54, 184, 265-66. *See also* Wilson, Woodrow; Wilson administration
Democratic National Committee: support for Palmer among members in 1920, 36-37
depression of 1890s, 3
Detroit: success of open shop drive in, 73
Devine, Edward T., 219

Dillingham, William, 81
Doak, William: quoted on labor support for Hoover in 1928, 273-74; mentioned, 65
Donlin, John: appointed to President's Conference on Unemployment, 92-93; supports Coolidge in 1924, 182-83
Drury, Horace, 102-103
Duncan, James (AFL vice president), 56
Duncan, James (Seattle labor leader), 22

Easley, Ralph M.: role in railroad labor legislation, 195, 202, 203-204, 206n; mentioned, 53, 68. *See also* National Civic Federation
Edge, Walter E.: quoted on 1923 anthracite strike, 149
Elwood, Indiana, 58
Ely, Richard T.: quoted on reform, 5
Emporia, Kansas, 75
engineering movement: interest in labor affairs, 9-10, 67, 88; importance of, 62, 87; role in unemployment issue, 90-92, 96; role in fight against twelve-hour day in steel industry, 97, 99, 102-103. *See also* Federated American Engineering Societies; Taylor Society
Erdman Act, 197
Esch-Cummins Act: antistrike provisions in original draft, 25, 32, 43; Harding supports, 31, 43-44; organized labor opposes, 38, 173; Borah's view of, 168; 1924 Progressive platform opposes, 178-79; Coolidge supports revision of, 181, 186, 207; supported by railroad executives, 195, 203; mentioned, 190, 191. *See also* Railroad Labor Board
Evanston, Illinois, 76

Farmer-Labor party, 42, 47
farm groups: relationship to orga-

farm groups (*continued*):
nized labor, 175, 176-77; oppose
Railway Labor Act, 208-10
farm problems, 163, 186
Farrington, Frank: challenges
Lewis' leadership of United Mine
Workers, 123
Federated American Engineering
Societies: role in unemployment
issue, 90, 91; role in twelve-hour
day controversy, 103; mentioned,
87. *See also* engineering move-
ment; Taylor Society
Felton, Samuel: quoted on 1922
railroad strike, 133
Fidler, Harry: memorandum on
Republicans and labor quoted,
53-54; appointed to Board of
Vocational Education, 54n
Frankfurter, Felix, 269
Frelinghuysen, Joseph: views on
labor, 13, 17-18, 55, 74; defeated
for reelection in 1922, 171
Frey, John Philip: quoted on results of 1920 election, 47; leading critic of injunctions, 268-69
"Friend of Mankind" [*pseud.*], 5
Furuseth, Andrew: opposes most
labor legislation, 259; role in
anti-injunction legislation, 268-
70. *See also* injunctions

Galion, Ohio, 43
Gallagher, Michael, 231, 232
Gardner, Gilson, 170
Garfield, James R.: quoted on Republican victory in 1920, 162;
criticizes organized labor, 166-67;
attacks La Follette, 1924, 182
garment industry, 88
Gary, Elbert: opposes organized
labor in steel strike of 1919, 26;
opposes ending of twelve-hour
day in steel industry, 100, 101,
102, 104, 105, 106; mentioned,
74, 99. *See also* steel industry
Gillett, Frederick: opposes Howell-
Barkley Bill, 200-201
Glenn, John: quoted on appointment of secretary of labor, 55;

quoted on opposition to immigration restriction, 81
Gompers, Samuel: opposes Plumb
plan, 20n; denounces Railroad
Labor Board, 25; views on labor
legislation, 33, 71, 259-60n; political activities, 39-40, 45, 53,
179, 188; protests injunction
secured by Palmer, 40; views on
labor issues during Harding administration, 55, 56, 68, 73, 78;
relationship with Hoover, 65, 67-
69; quoted on President's Conference on Unemployment, 96;
mentioned, 35, 36, 41, 44, 46,
47, 48, 52, 54, 55, 66, 74, 76,
88, 149, 150, 172, 185, 229. *See
also* American Federation of
Labor; labor vote; organized labor
Grable, E. F.: appointment to
Railroad Labor Board opposed by
unions, 118, 193
Grand Rapids *Herald*, 267
Green, William: views on labor
legislation, 259-60n; quoted on
labor in politics, 273; mentioned,
65, 253. *See also* American Federation of Labor; Gompers, Samuel; organized labor
Gregory, Thomas, 40
Groesbeck, Alexander, J., 126

Hammond, John Hays: role in
1923 anthracite strike, 150, 151,
153; activities on United States
Coal Commission, 219, 220, 222,
226; mentioned, 53, 152. *See
also* United States Coal Commission
Hanger, G. W. W., 211, 212
Harding, Mrs. Warren G., 77, 109,
129, 138
Harding, Warren G.: influences
on, regarding labor, 13, 48, 49,
51-54, 68-69, 71, 73, 77, 79;
general labor policies discussed,
14, 156-57; presidential campaign and election, 1920, 30-31,
34, 36, 38-47, 51; appoints secretary of labor, 55-57; supports

Harding, Warren G. *(continued):*
immigration restriction, 80-81;
appoints members to President's
Conference on Unemployment,
90; role in ending twelve-hour
day in steel industry, 97, 98, 100-
101, 103-106; pursues erratic
course in 1922 industrial crisis,
109, 120, 121-22, 135-36; role in
attempts to settle 1922 bituminous coal strike, 114-15, 125-29,
137; appointments to Railroad
Labor Board criticized, 118, 193;
role in attempts to settle 1922
railroad strike, 119, 129-31, 134,
137, 138, 140; death of, 144;
views on railroad labor legislation, 194, 195, 196; role in
creation of United States Coal
Commission, 218, 219, 220; appointments to Supreme Court,
262, 265; mentioned, 35, 42, 46,
55, 75, 77, 162, 172, 265. *See
also* Harding administration; Republican party
Harding administration: progressives play little part in, 12; important labor issues facing, 15,
70, 87, 97; role of Department
of Labor in, 59-60; general labor
policies discussed, 68, 70-71, 108,
144-45, 180, 186; supports immigration restriction, 79; role in
twelve-hour day controversy, 98,
107; impact of 1922 strikes upon,
109, 110, 135; role in coal labor
affairs, 114, 115, 117, 123, 127,
146, 222, 253; role in 1922 railroad strike, 120, 132, 133, 142-
43; mentioned, 67, 152, 176-77,
198. *See also* Davis, James J.;
Harding, Warren G.; Hoover,
Herbert C.
Hawes-Cooper Act, 276
Hays, Will: on possibilities of AFL-
Republican alliance, 53
Henning, Edward J., 140
Herrin, Illinois, 124, 127
Hilles, Charles D., 56, 129
Hillman, Sidney, 172

Hillquit, Morris: comments on
1920 election, 42; mentioned,
181-82
Hoch, Homer: seeks revision in
railroad labor legislation, 208
Homestead strike, 37-38
Hooper, Ben W.: critical of railroad unions, 190, 193; controversy surrounding, 194, 215;
views on railroad labor legislation, 196, 199, 201, 202, 208
Hoover, Herbert C.: success of
labor policies assessed, vii-viii, 13,
15, 108, 248, 271-72, 275-77;
election to presidency, viii, 15,
248, 249, 273, 274-75; opposes
1922 railroad strike injunction,
14, 140, 264, 266; presidential
prospects in 1920, 30-31; influence in labor affairs in 1920s
discussed, 59-60, 63, 108; background and societal views, 60-62,
64, 65, 87; gathers political support throughout 1920s, 63; views
on labor discussed, 65, 66, 86,
87-88, 157; harmonious relationships with labor leaders, 65-67,
69, 271; quoted in opposition to
open shop, 75; views and activities regarding unemployment, 90-
91, 92, 93, 96, 97, 249-50; seeks
end of twelve-hour day in steel
industry, 97-107; seeks moderate
solutions to 1922 strikes, 109,
143; seeks end to 1922 railroad
strike, 110, 120, 129-30, 132-33,
137, 138, 143; seeks solution to
1922 bituminous coal strike, 115,
116, 117, 123-24, 125, 127-28;
views of United States Coal
Commission, 150, 222; role in
railroad labor legislation, 191,
199, 202-204, 207; efforts to deal
with bituminous coal labor problems in late 1920s, 217, 227-34,
236-47, 253, 258; mentioned, ix,
60, 121, 138, 211, 219, 251. *See
also* Commerce, United States
Department of; Coolidge administration; Harding administration